ASSESSING THE VALUE OF YOUR TRAINING

ASSESSING THE VALUE OF YOUR TRAINING

The Evaluation Process from Training Needs to the Report to the Board

LESLIE RAE

GOWER

© Leslie Rae 2002

Previously published (three editions) as *How to Measure Training Effectiveness*, by the same author.

Published by
Gower Publishing Limited
Gower House
Croft Road
Aldershot
Hants GU11 3HR
England

Gower Publishing Company
131 Main Street
Burlington VT 05401-5600 USA

Leslie Rae has asserted his right under the Copyright, Designs and Patents Act 1988 to be identified as the author of this work.

British Library Cataloguing in Publication Data
Rae, Leslie
   Assessing the value of your training : the evaluation
   process from training needs to the report to the board
   1. Employees – Training of – Evaluation
   I. Title
   658.3'12404

ISBN 0 566 08535 6

Library of Congress Control Number: 2002110103

Typeset by Bournemouth Colour Press, Parkstone and printed in Great Britain by MPG Books Ltd, Bodmin, Cornwall.

Contents

Preface

'I don't know how to start', 'I don't know what to do', 'Why should I do it?', 'It's going to take a lot of time and money', 'I haven't the time.' Such are the remarks commonly heard when questions of validation and evaluation are raised. It has always surprised me, and continues to do so, that so much training and development, in whatever form, is embarked upon without any apparent thoughts of validation or evaluation, other than an ephemeral and optimistic 'It sounds just what we want.' Has *what* the potential learners need been firmly established? Is a course/open learning/e-technology training approach the most appropriate one? Is this particular event or process *known* to be the most suitable? How will we be able to find out what the result of the training will be? Will there be an effective Return on Investment (ROI) in the training? There are so many questions that need to be asked both before and after the event.

This book sets out to suggest ways – from the initial stages to long after the programme itself has finished – in which any form of training and development can be assessed for effectiveness and value, i.e. validation and evaluation. The different approaches necessary at each stage of the process are summarized and, wherever possible, practical instruments and approaches are suggested, usually based on my own experiences.

I have intended the book to be a practical guide to the subject, rather than an academic treatise, and I hope that not only trainers and training managers will find it useful, but also the growing army of others who, although perhaps not directly involved in the process of training, have a significant and substantial role to play in ensuring effective training and development in their business. These, as we shall see later, include senior and middle management and line managers in a wide range of roles. In the past their disclaimer has always been, 'We know nothing about training, that is for the trainers. We are in operations.' Those days are long past and recognition is coming slowly that *everybody* in a business is concerned in some way with training and development.

All stages from the training concept to long-term evaluation are included, although the full range of stages may not be necessary on every training occasion – some may already have been applied and the information obtained. The approaches described include those that can be applied to single events, series of courses or modules, complete training programmes, open and distance learning and e-technology training – in other words, to any provided learning situation that demands answers to the questions 'Is the whole process range effective?' and 'Is it worthwhile (i.e. does it produce an effective ROI)?'

Effectiveness in all aspects of business is essential and this has certainly been a theme at the start of the 21st century, with world economies slowing down and rationalization the order of the day. Business is becoming more and more aware of, and alert to, the need for an effective ROI in all aspects of the business – financial investment, capital investment, investment in the best personnel possible, effective recruitment and human resource practices, and certainly not least in training and development. The latter is an aspect of business, however large or small, that must take place, and with a maximum return on ROI in the area. Effective assessment of its practice, results and value is essential in order to answer the questions posed above.

This book is the successor to the popular, best-selling *How to Measure Training Effectiveness, 3rd Edition*, from which much content has been retained, albeit modified in a number of cases. The changes and different nuances of evaluation are reflected in the new pages and the new material takes into account the increasingly important ROI, the changing involvements of roles and functions, up-to-date considerations of meaning and functions, the current enhancement of the S/NVQ and competence standards system as it applies to training and development, and an essential updating of the link that evaluation has with the growing e-technology.

As in the editions of the original title, many of the changes are as a result of my contacts with friends, colleagues, fellow trainers and consultants, training managers and, more than ever before, with line managers who have staff under training.

My own detailed model of evaluation has been reinforced, particularly from the wishes of my contacts, and part of the new scene of e-technology has helped me to learn as a result of increasing contacts world-wide via e-mail and Internet Web sites.

Some evaluation and validation instruments have been modified as a result of my own learning experiences and I hope the result is an even more useful guide for you. The world, including the world of training and evaluation, has changed substantially since the first edition of my original book in 1986 and I have tried to reflect these changes in the present title to produce a more impactive and useful approach to this vital subject. Part of an old army saying is, 'If it doesn't move, paint it': this can be related to training and development and evaluation in that 'If it's training or learning, evaluate it'!

Evaluation must be inextricably involved with training and development if we are to prove our training value to our critics when they ask 'Is it worth it?' So there is little value in setting up what you or the training department think is a good and effective training programme if:

a) you have not agreed beforehand an evaluation intention, process and instrument or methods of assessment
b) ensured that everybody else who should be involved is in fact fully involved in the process (see the Evaluation Quintet described in Chapter 13)
c) ensured that all the members of the Evaluation Quintet, particularly the senior management, training management, and above all the line management, are going to fulfil completely their roles and responsibilities.

I should like to thank Malcolm Stern (now retired from Gower), Jonathan Norman, Jo Burges and all the kind people at Gower who have been so supportive to me in my writing over these years.

Leslie Rae   E-mail: wrae804414@aol.com   Web site: www.leslierae.4t.com

1 *Where do we start?*

Many statements have been made concerning the feasibility of validation and evaluation. In many areas of training it has been said that validation and evaluation are very difficult, if not impossible, to achieve. The areas usually referred to in this context are the general aspects of management training or human relations training – in other words, all forms of training in which it cannot be shown completely objectively or quantitatively that the trainee has learned to add two plus two (or its equivalent) to produce four on x number of occasions. Training of this nature usually has problems which have a right answer and the direct validation and evaluation relate to the performance of the learner in respect of the learning – if the lessons have been taught well and the trainee has learned the lessons to the satisfaction and measurement of the trainer, the effectiveness of the training has been validated. Evaluation is also straightforward, since, if learners always, as a result of the training, produce the answer four to our original question, they are always right and thus do not cost their employer as a result of expensive mistakes.

Let us look at a different form of training. A manager is attending a course which is aimed at developing counselling techniques and skills. Note the word 'developing', since few managers will attend the course with no skills whatsoever, either learned or inherited. At the end of the course a manager can perform an interview in a manner acceptable to the trainer. But another manager might interview in some way at variance to the model presented and produce results which, in the trainer's eyes, are not satisfactory but *are* in the view of the interviewer. We shall leave the interviewee out of the equation as they are just complicatory factors! Do these results validate or invalidate the training and who is to make the pronouncement? The wider aspects are even more difficult to assess. Back at work the trainees cited above will counsel members of their staff in private. We do not know whether they use the techniques presented on the course; we do not know how successful the interview really was; we do not know whether, as a result of the interview, how successful and more effective the interview might be, and so on. We can guess; we can ask both parties for their views; we can observe. But is this sufficient to qualify as absolute validation and evaluation in the strictest sense of the words? I believe not.

So let us start from the premises that validation and evaluation are:

- possible in some forms of training
- very difficult in other forms of training
- impossible in fully objective and quantitative terms in some forms of training, although possible to assess in a controlled, and active way as the only way possible – not to be dismissed because of this
- essential in training and development to ensure effectiveness of training, learning and implementation (i.e. effective ROI).

We should first ensure that we know what we mean when we use the words validation and evaluation, as well as the word assessment which is often substituted if people are uneasy with the other terms. The 'real' meanings of these words have probably been discussed in training circles more than any other training terms, and with few positive results.

Definitions

In 2000 the recently formed Institute of Training and Occupational Learning (ITOL) – an Institute formed to satisfy the needs of members of the training and development profession, rather than look on them as an amorphous part of an organization – produced a glossary of training and learning terms (ITOL 2000). This glossary has superseded the now out of print MSC 'Glossary of Training Terms' (1981) and was compiled by a consortium of ITOL professional members.

The ITOL definitions for *validation of training* are:
The measurement of whether the training achieved what it set out to achieve:

1. Internal validation – a series of tests and assessments designed to ascertain whether a training programme has achieved the behavioural objectives specified;
2. External validation – a series of tests and assessments of whether the behavioural objectives of an internally valid training programme were realistically based on an accurate initial identification of training needs in relation to the criteria of effectiveness adopted by the organization. In short, were they the right objectives and were they achieved?

I believe it is essential to add to the above definition relating to the programme objectives *that those of the learners were also achieved.*

The definition for *evaluation* is:

> The assessment of the total value of a training programme, training system or training course in both value- and cost-effective terms (i.e. an effective ROI). It differs from validation in that it is concerned with the overall benefit of the complete training programme and its implementation and not just the achievement of the laid-down learning objectives. It includes all the pre-course and post-course action and the post-course implementation of the learning by the learner at work.

Finally, the ITOL definition of *assessment* is:

> An exercise that seeks to measure a learner's skills, performance or knowledge in a subject area. This may be either prior to, during or following the learning.

Dictionary definitions are respectably vague. To validate is to 'make valid (sound, defensible, well-grounded), ratify, confirm', and to evaluate is to 'ascertain amount of, find numerical expression for, appraise, assess'.

Warr, Bird and Rackham were concerned with evaluation only and saw evaluation as being used in a wider context than in the original (and now ITOL) MSC definitions. They saw two basic aspects of evaluation – input evaluation and outcome evaluation. Input evaluation considers the question 'What procedures are most likely to bring about change?' and covers the questions which need to be asked before a training event can be organized. Such questions will relate to training aspects over which the trainer has control and choice such as:

- Which training approach?
- External or internal resources?
- Format of the event?
- Type of learner to be invited?

Outcome evaluation is described in terms which many people will see as a combination of validation and evaluation and is concerned with identifying, from evidence, changes which have occurred as a result of the training. Various levels of evaluation are described – immediate reaction, immediate outcome, intermediate and ultimate outcomes. From the point of view of the original Manpower Services Commission (and now ITOL) definitions, the immediate outcome and immediate reaction levels are approaches more inclined to the validation of training, and the intermediate and ultimate outcome levels more in terms of the wider aspects of evaluation.

Hamblin dismissed such definitions as suggesting differences between validation and evaluation which were not always meaningful. He defines evaluation as 'any attempt to obtain information (feedback) on the effects of a training programme and to assess the value of the training in the light of that information'. As with Warr, Bird and Rackham's comments, Hamblin's use of 'evaluation' is a comprehensive term to include both the evaluation and validation definitions.

Models of validation and evaluation

A number of models of validation and evaluation have been put forward. The three principal ones are those attributed to Kirkpatrick (1976), Hamblin (1974), and Warr, Bird and Rackham (1970). Although differing in a number of respects, two of the models are very similar and restrict their coverage to the actual acts of validation and evaluation rather than a complete approach to evaluation. The third (Warr et al., 1970) is much more suggestive of a wider appreciation of evaluation as a total system and relates more closely to my own view of the process, which covers the full evaluation process from the training needs analysis to the final assessment and report on the achievement of the programme. Figure 1.1 summarizes the stages of this model.

KIRKPATRICK'S MODEL

Four levels are identified in this model:

1. Reaction: the learner's reaction to the training process, their feelings about the event's structure, content and methods
2. Learning: the learning achieved within the event
3. Behavioural: any change brought about by the event in terms of job behaviour and performance

4. Results: the tangible and positive effects of that change on the organization in terms of organizational improvement.

Kirkpatrick's model is the one that has probably received the most attention since he produced it in 1976, although to some extent it has received and weathered, in many cases, significant criticism.

Level 1. Reaction: Evaluation at this level measures the reactions of the participants in the programme. This is quite different from an objective assessment of the programme in real evaluation terms. Many evaluators, myself included, cannot accept reaction assessments as part of true evaluation as learner 'reactions' are individual, subjective views, opinions and feelings that are subject to many contaminatory and personal value factors. Some trainers see the reactions as measures of customer satisfaction, but again those from an individual with possibly easily influenced personalized views can mean little. I shall return to this aspect in Chapter 8. This level asks in effect, 'What did you think of the course?';

Level 2. Learning: Kirkpatrick defines this level as the extent to which the participants change attitudes, improve knowledge and/or increase their skill levels as a result of attending the programme. Validation measures at the end of the programme provide information about this, i.e. 'What did they learn?';

Level 3. Behaviour: The 'behaviour' referred to here is not just interpersonal behaviour, but also the transfer to work of the learners' knowledge, attitudes and skills following attendance on the programme, the implementation of this learning and its eventual review for effectiveness. The principal question here is, 'What did they do with the learning?';

Level 4. Results: This level extends the changes observed and implemented in Level 3 in an attempt to rationalize the cost- and value-effectiveness of the learning.

Critics of Kirkpatrick have suggested two additional levels:

Level 0. This covers activities before the learner attends a programme, actions that in effect kick-start the full evaluation process, including the calculation of the 'at-that-time' base level of the value of the people who are to attend the training and their work level at that stage. I agree with this view as the various pre-training activities are essential to the start of the learning process and demonstrate the base, starting levels of the change referred to in Level 2 – if you don't know where the learner is coming from, how will you know whether they have arrived and where they have arrived?;

Level 5. This is to include financial assessment of the Level 4 results as they affect the business, i.e. the ROI. Most evaluators feel that Kirkpatrick covers this aspect adequately in his Level 4 and as true evaluation has £ signs only Level 4 qualifies as evaluation.

Other critics have commented that Kirkpatrick's Level 4 always ignores the importance of a pre-training baseline level (pre- and post-test scores are validation only and so do not qualify as business measures), and that he does not make a clear distinction between evaluation and validation.

Kirkpatrick's model with its four levels gives an appearance of simplicity and ease of operation, but the bare statements of the levels hide the substantial amount of activity and difficulties within each one. In his book (Kirkpatrick, 1996) he describes in greater detail his model and it can be seen there that the model contains a substantial number of stages within the levels. These are included in my own model.

HAMBLIN'S MODEL

Hamblin's initial model is very similar to that of Kirkpatrick in general terms and suggests five levels:

Level 1. Reaction: carried out during, immediately after and some time after the event; the learners' reactions to a range of factors are sought
Level 2. Learning: carried out before and after the event; an evaluation of the developmental change that has taken place in knowledge, skills and attitude
Level 3. Job behaviour: a determination of any change in job performance as a result of the event; carried out before and after the event
Level 4. Functioning: a quantification of the effect of the event on the learners' department or organization, preferably in terms of cost benefit analysis
Level 5. Ultimate value: the extent to which the event has affected the ultimate profitability and/or survival of the organization.

WARR, BIRD AND RACKHAM'S MODEL

These authors identify four categories of evaluation:

1. Context evaluation: reviewing such aspects as the current conditions of the operational context of the event, training needs identification, the performance problems to be overcome in ultimate objectives, changes in operational performance at an intermediate stage, immediate objectives and their achievement;
2. Input evaluation: evaluation of the training event itself;
3. Reaction evaluation: the reaction of the learners during and after the event;
4. Outcome evaluation: comprising four stages
   • Definition of the training objectives
   • Construction of evaluation instruments
   • Use of the instruments
   • Review of the results.

THE RAE MODEL OF EVALUATION

This model has been developed, over a number of years of experience in training and development and the practical evaluation of the programmes, as part of a more comprehensive training cycle model. It certainly takes account of the other models described here, but attempts to extend them to a logical, descriptive and practicable set of stages. Figure 1.1 summarizes the model, most of the stages of which are self-explanatory or will become clearer as this book, which is based on the model, includes guidance on the various stages.

Rae model of evaluation

1. Training needs analysis leading to training objectives
2. Design of the evaluation process
3. Establishing the business base level for post-training implementation to determine the ROI or other cost- and value-effectiveness
4. Pre-course testing or assessment of knowledge, skills and attitudes (if possible)
5. Line-manager pre-course briefing
6. Start-of-course testing or assessment of knowledge, skills and attitudes (if possible/necessary)
7. Interim assessment and validation

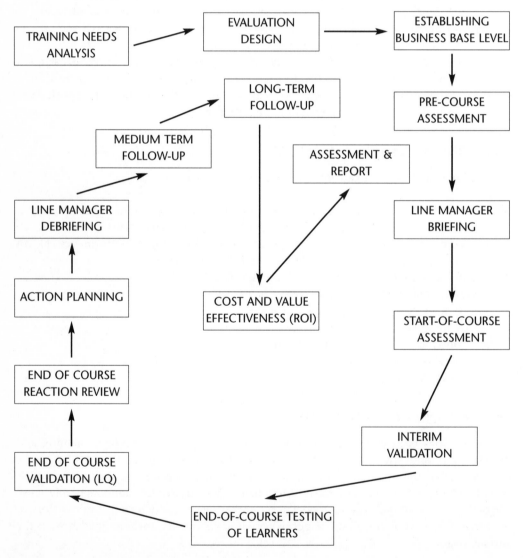

Figure 1.1   The evaluation model

8. End-of-programme testing or assessment of learners
9. End-of-programme validation of objectives – both of the training and the learners, by Learning Questionnaire
10. End-of-programme reaction review (on specific occasions for specific purposes)
11. Learner action planning at end of programme
12. Line-manager post-course debriefing and support for implementation of learning
13. Medium-term follow-up and review of implementation of learning – learner and line manager
14. Long-term follow-up and review of implementation of learning – learner and line manager
15. Cost and value effectiveness analysis by line manager (ROI – Return on Investment of the training)
16. Assessment and report on achievement of the programme.

It will be noted that, in my model, evaluation starts right at the commencement of the training planning and implementation cycle, namely with the training needs analysis. The design of the evaluation system related to a proposed programme must also be approached at a very early stage in the process – too often it is simply tagged on, almost as an afterthought. But what is so valuable, but is so often omitted, is the assessment by the line manager of the value of the potential learners' business value in an quantitative terms as possible, 'How much are they worth before training?' This base level assessment will obviously be used again at the end of the training and the implementation of the learning to re-assess the learners and the new business level value, that is the Return on Investment (ROI) of the training.

Reasons

One of the most frequent questions I am asked on learning events concerned with evaluation is, 'Why should we do it?' This is a very relevant question, for, as we shall see later in the book, validation and evaluation require a substantial input of resources – time, people, money – and, as in every area concerned with training and development, we should constantly be asking whether we should be performing any activity. The risks involved in evaluation are high and may result in the following:

- If there is an excessive use of tests, questionnaires, interviews, validation discussions and so on, the learners may feel that these are getting in the way of the learning (the trainers may have the same feelings).
- Training schedules may be so tight that there is no space available for evaluation measures, space that is essential, not only to enable the measures to be taken, but also to demonstrate that the activities are important.
- The purse-string holders who may have little or no understanding of the demands of training and development may make statements such as 'Evaluation! You should be spending your time and money on training!'

But in many cases it is the practitioner who resists evaluation as part of the training programme. Some of the common excuses are:

- 'I didn't feel it was necessary'
- 'I didn't have time to do anything like that'
- 'Evaluation. What's that?'
- 'I don't know how to do it properly'
- 'It costs too much to do it'
- 'I couldn't be bothered'
- 'Nobody asked me to do it'
- 'I didn't think the learners would do it'
- 'The organization doesn't want it done'/'I don't know whether my organization wants me to do it'
- 'You can't evaluate this type of training'.

If these types of arguments and excuses are accepted, evaluation will not commence, usually resulting in adverse consequences to the training, the learners and the organizations, including:

- Failure of the trainers to judge effectively their performance level
- Failure of the training managers to judge effectively the performance of their training staff
- The efficiency and effectiveness of the training event cannot be assessed accurately
- The views of the participants cannot be recorded
- The learners have no mechanism to help them to assess their own progress in an objective manner
- There is no way in which any change in knowledge, skill or attitude can be attributed to the training
- The trainers, line managers, or organization cannot assess the extent of the implementation of learning
- The value in learning or cost terms cannot be even approximated.

There must be strong reasons and arguments to refute these and other criticisms and attacks. What then are the reasons why we should evaluate?

REASONS FOR EVALUATING

There are several compelling reasons for carrying out the most extensive form of evaluation that is possible in your circumstances. Full evaluation may not be possible in every case owing to a lack of finance, resources, skill, support, and so on, but there is always something that can be done, and it is worth trying to extend the process in your organization by marketing, particularly with senior management, the values of using an effective evaluation system – a powerful one being a demonstration of ROI. Evaluation offers relative proof that:

- training objectives have been met
- clients' objectives/needs have been met
- learners' objectives/needs have been met
- performance has been changed.

(Or not as the case may be, and usually 'why', if not.)

It also supports:

- the transfer of learning to work
- the likelihood that any performance change is due to the training

and enables:

- the assessment of the ROI in the training.

A self-assessment activity from which you can assess the *raison d'être* behind any evaluation you might do or want to do, is to consider the questions that follow. From your responses you may draw one of the following conclusions:

1. If most of your answers are very positive this suggests that your organization and particularly your senior management are interested in the training function. Consequently they are likely to ask questions to which you must have clear and valid answers. In this case, evaluation or its active continuation is an essential part of your training activities. Examples of very positive answers might include, 'The training participants are chosen carefully according to their needs and those of the organization. A strong interest is taken and support given by staff throughout the organization, at all levels. Senior management put out a policy statement about training and development and require regular evaluative reports from the training manager. And so on.'

2. If your answers are a mixture of positive responses mixed with some decidedly negative, this suggests that there is some doubt about the value of what you are doing and how you are doing it. You should consider conducting in-depth evaluation to answer the questions that particularly have a more negative response, otherwise you could have difficulty in answering questions about whether you are approaching training in the most appropriate way.

3. If you have answered in a mainly negative way, your courses, and so on may be vulnerable, not just to questions, but to attack. You should consider conducting some evaluation in that area aimed at proving that the system works and is of value.

4. If you have answered in a negative or unhelpful manner to most of the questions, then it is probably not worth bothering with evaluation because the system deserves to be wound up anyway! Responses of this nature will include 'People are just sent on courses whether they need them or not. There is little encouragement for them back at work to implement their learning. Nobody else, outside the training department, seems to take any real interest in training. If you did no evaluation at all, nobody would ask why it is not done.' And so on!

But there is another question to ask which has considerable significance, not only for your interpretation of the responses, but for your ability to ask the questions at all – *are you able to complete this activity because you are aware of the answers?* Or can you not assess any of the views, feelings or reactions? In this latter case, perhaps not only *they* but also *you* have not considered evaluation or taken it seriously.

The positive types of responses to the questions listed above provide the reasons for evaluation and, in particular, the needs and desires to demonstrate the effectiveness of your training, its success in helping the learners to learn and to implement their learning. At the absolute minimum, *you* should want to know, for your own peace of mind, that what you

Take some time out and list the reasons why you feel you should or should not have evaluation as an integral part of your training and development programme.

- How are the participants of your training and development programmes selected? By whom? *Is there real selection or are people chosen with little regard for needs?*
- How much interest is taken, and by whom, in the learning by the participants and their implementation of their learning? *Are they encouraged or even allowed to implement the learning?*
- How much interest is taken in the actual training programmes – their format, methods, approaches, etc. – by others outside the training department? Who takes this interest?
- Do you have to justify your training expenditure? If so, to whom? To what depth do you have to account for the expenditure?
- To what extent do your learners' line managers take an interest in any evaluation you might do?
- To what extent do your senior managers take an interest in your training and development activities?
- To what extent do your senior managers take an interest in any evaluation you might do? Do they require you to evaluate and present analyses and reports from this evaluation?
- How often are you asked how effective your training and development activities are? Who asks these questions? Do they require you to prove any statements you might make?
  If asked this last question, can you provide proof?
- *If you did no evaluation at all, would anyone ask why you do none?*

are doing is worthwhile and effective. At successive levels, different areas of the organization should also have the needs and desires to be aware of this effectiveness, until the following statement can be made by the entire organization: *'This organization has an effective training and development function which enables people to learn effectively and implement the learning – and this statement can be proven to be objective and relevant.'*

Whatever definition we place on words which describe what we are doing, or should be doing, our intention must be to determine certain facts in order to gauge the success of our training. The argument will still remain as to whether we should be determining this success or measuring it, but what we want to know must attempt to answer certain questions:

1. Has the training satisfied its objectives?
2. Has the training satisfied the needs of the clients?
3. Are people operating differently at the end of, and as a result of, the training?
4. Did the training contribute directly to this different behaviour?
5. Is the learning achieved being used in the real work situation?
6. Has the learning contributed to the production of a more effective and efficient worker?

7. Has the training contributed to a more effective and efficient (hence most cost-effective) organization?

These questions fall naturally into two aspects related to the training: questions 1, 2 and 3 are concerned with the training itself more than anything else, whereas 4, 5, 6 and 7 are more concerned with the effect of the training on the work.

This approach correlates well with the basic ITOL definitions, namely in that validation is concerned with the efficiency of the training and evaluation with its effectiveness when applied to work. Such an approach may appear simplistic, but it attempts to separate two elements which can so easily become confused and hence cause confusion. This approach will form the basis of the methods recommended in this book.

If there are so many problems connected with validation and evaluation, why should we consider attempting to resolve them? The need stems from a number of sources.

Trainer interest

If we are performing a training function, and if we are at all concerned about our skill levels as trainers, and how we are able to help others to learn, we must want to know the extent of the efficiency and effectiveness of that training. This is not self-vindication but an essentially practical approach to confirm that:

- our training ideas are in step with the learning needs
- our skills are being maintained
- the opportunity is available for us to improve.

It is only logical that we should consider these factors in order to obtain information. One of the major teaching points for trainers, particularly if they are involved in human relations training, is that if an individual or an organization is to become and continue to be effective, there must be a regular supply of open feedback. Feedback in this instance is validation when it is measured against the desired objectives.

The trainers who are independent consultants are at a disadvantage in obtaining feedback compared with the in-company trainer. The in-company trainer, in addition to the formal validation measures, also has recourse to the internal grapevine and direct or indirect contact with their trainees' bosses. They also know that if things are gong wrong there is a managerial element in the company hierarchy which will ensure that they are informed. The independent trainer has, to a major extent, to rely on the formal, written validation instruments alone. However, there is also another indicator available which should at least give a warning that there are questions they should be asking about themselves and others – this is their business indicator. Are former clients returning for more of the same training or the next stages in a progressive training plan, and/or is the supply of new clients drying up more quickly than might have been predicted? A negative response is not an answer in itself since a number of factors might be contributing to declining business, such as a declining economy, none of which is directly attributable to the trainer.

Training manager interest

In the same way that trainers have an interest in their own skills and acceptability, so has the training manager an interest in the level of performance of the trainer group. The trainers can and should be observed directly in action as frequently as possible. But these observations may not always be possible and when they are, they are made from a singular position. The manager's views may not reflect those of the people who matter – the learners. The views of the training clients are given in the validation instruments and the training manager will need to balance all views. The training manager's role is in many ways more difficult than that of the trainer's; they are responsible for ensuring that the training given satisfies the needs, and they are also managers of people. The connecting lines from the manager extend up as well as down. There will be some form of senior management above who will be interested in both validation and evaluation. The validation interest will be whether the training department is operating as an efficient and effective organization. So the training manager will certainly be called upon to produce evidence towards this, evidence that will need to be as objective and as quantitative as possible.

Senior management interest

In addition to having the internal interest through the training manager on the efficiency of the training department, an organization's senior management will also have an interest in evaluation in the widest sense of this term. Once it has been satisfied that the training itself is effective, the senior level of management will want to know whether:

*   The training is being applied in the work situation
*   The training is producing sufficient change in organizational efficiency to warrant the continuation of the training expenditure.

It is in this investigatory area of evaluation that least work is done because it is very difficult and time- and resource-consuming, particularly in the case of the training of managers and in human relations training. There are also strong links between evaluation of this nature and management development in the controlling hands of line management. It is rare for these investigations to be carried out fully and effectively, although lip service is frequently paid to the principle.

Client interest

Trainees taking part in a training programme have a number of needs in both the organizational and the personal development areas. The trainer needs to know if he is satisfying these needs and only the client can give advice on this.

In many cases the client accepts the training on trust. In the case of the organization with a training department, the client accepts to a large extent that the training has been validated and evaluated by the organization. But a rather more informal system of validation and evaluation exists and cannot be ignored, although it may not necessarily be accurate. This is the internal grapevine which can produce such evaluatory statements as 'I wouldn't go on that course if I were you, it's a waste of time' or 'It was a super course, but of course I haven't done anything with what we talked about' or 'That training changed my whole outlook and I can do everything so much better now'.

The grapevine can work equally for or against the external training consultant and often it is only the word of mouth validation and evaluation which may clinch a contract. If the Managing Director who is considering a training event has a Managing Director friend with previous experience of the training consultant being considered, the friend's comments will result in either acceptance or rejection. Perhaps a less biased method of obtaining information about training organizations or individual consultants is to obtain assessments, if these are available, from an organization such as the Management Training Index which collates the (albeit subjective) views of people who attend courses run by organizations which support the Index.

Questions for validation and evaluation

Questions also arise in validation and evaluation, but particularly the former, as to what aspects of a training course should be assessed. Possible aspects will include:

CONTENT OF TRAINING

Is it relevant and in step with the training needs? Is it up to date?

METHOD OF TRAINING

Were the methods used the most appropriate ones for the subject? Were the methods used the most appropriate for the learning styles of the participants?

AMOUNT OF LEARNING

What was the material of the course? Was it new to the learner or merely the mixture as before? Was it useful, although not new to the learner, as confirmatory or revision material?

TRAINER SKILLS

Did the trainer have the necessary attitude and skill to present the material in a way which encouraged learning?

LENGTH AND PACE OF THE TRAINING

Given the material essential to learning, was the learning event of the appropriate length and pace? Were some aspects laboured and others skimped?

OBJECTIVES

Did the training satisfy its declared objectives? Was the learner given the opportunity to try to satisfy any personal objectives? Was this need welcomed? Were personal objectives actually satisfied?

OMISSIONS

Were any essential aspects omitted from the learning event? Was any material included which was not essential to the learning?

LEARNING TRANSFER

How much of the learning is likely to be put into action on return to work? If it is to be a limited amount only or none, why is this? What factors will deter or assist transfer of the learning?

ACCOMMODATION

If course accommodation is within the control of the trainer, or is relevant to the type of training event, he or she may wish to ask whether the hotel/conference centre/training centre was suitable. Was the accommodation acceptable? Were the meals satisfactory?

RELEVANCE

The final question in a validation assessment may be concerned with the relevance of the total training approach. Was this course/seminar/conference/workshop/tutorial/coaching assignment/project/etc. the most appropriate means of presenting a learning opportunity?

Questions of evaluation would, in the defined approach suggested, be concerned with subsequent matters of application of the learning. The questions asked might depend on the period of time which had elapsed between the training event and the evaluation.

APPLICATION OF LEARNING

Which aspects of your work now include elements which are a direct result of the learning event? Which new aspects of work have you introduced as a result of your learning? Which aspects of your previous work have you replaced or modified as a result of the learning? Which aspects of your learning have you not applied? Why not?

EFFICIENCY

How much more efficient and/or effective are you in your work as a result of the training? Why/Why not? This question could also be posed to the learner's boss and his or her subordinates, but, as in so many cases, it will be highly subjective evidence and the questioning will need to be extensive.

HINDSIGHT

With the passage of time and attempts to apply the learning, are there any amendments you would wish to make to your immediate outcome validation answers?

At the beginning of this chapter I suggested that we start with certain premises of possibility, difficulty and objective impossibility in attempting to evaluate and validate. The attitudes expressed so far do not change these views, but suggest that first we can attempt *some* form of validation and evaluation, however crude and sometimes necessarily subjective, and secondly, we must attempt it, otherwise there is no measure at all in any form of effectiveness in order to satisfy ourselves, our clients or others.

2 *In the beginning*

One of the most commonly heard statements uttered by a senior manager about a new training programme, or in fact any new event in the organization, is 'We must evaluate this …'. This view is very laudable and is one which I fully support. Unfortunately on so many occasions the statement is made during the event or even after its conclusion. Sometimes, however, it is made before the event starts, either the day before the event is due to commence or as a statement of intent about what should be done after the event. It is too late to consider evaluation at such times. Evaluation starts at the birth of the programme.

Let us consider the inception of a training programme. It is assumed (or hoped) that the training proposed is the result of an identified training need and not the consequence of the whim of a training officer or manager who likes the idea of presenting this form of training, or the pronouncement of someone in high authority who feels that the company should be engaged in this type of training. Effective training starts with the identification of a need and it is also at this stage that evaluation starts. A training need stems from an equation which shows that a factor is missing and the training event supplies that missing factor. The existence of a training need states that a change is necessary: a change from a situation or performance which is below that level required to at least the required level. The change agent is the training event.

Identification of training needs

What we have been considering is an existing level of achievement and an outcome level as the end result. In order to talk objectively about this approach we must have an assessment or measurement of these levels. If the level is –3 at the start of the process and the level is +3 at the end of the training, depending on the objectives, this positive change of 6 units demonstrates that the training has been effective.

The two aspects, therefore, go hand in hand – the identification of a training need means that performance is not up to the level required and this in turn means that both the existing level of achievement and that required have been measured and assessed.

Training needs can obviously be many and various depending on the nature of the job to be done and the people who have to perform the jobs. They can be expressed generally in terms of skills, attitudes and knowledge. Some needs may cover this whole spectrum while others, perhaps, may concentrate on singular aspects only. School-leavers entering an electronics manufacturing industry will probably have learning needs in all three areas – knowledge, skills and attitudes. They will need to be aware of such aspects of knowledge as the product range, the limits of the job they will be performing, the safety aspects applied to the job and so on. The processes they will need to perform will be new to them and they will need to learn the skills of operation and manipulation. At school their attitudes were possibly those of individual, scholastic achievement, whereas their new job will demand a close co-operation within a team – this may require a completely new approach to people, a change of social attitude.

On the other hand, machine operators changing companies may only need the new knowledge about the product they will be making and their new work environment, or they may only need the new skills necessary to operate a slightly different machine to which they have been accustomed. A history teacher, moving to a new school which uses more progressive teaching methods, may be fully skilled in these methods but may not have used them for a long time, certainly not in the previous school, so there may be required an adjustment of attitude to bring into use the different methods.

Some training needs are more straightforward to assess or measure than others. A manufacturing company is failing to meet its objectives by x per cent because of the lack of skill of its operatives: a meter reader is making 50 per cent errors or more because he does not know how to read the new meters: x per cent of students are reporting no progress from a training course because they are unable to understand the teacher's explanations. In the knowledge area: too many packages are going astray because there has been considerable staff movement and the porter does not know where everybody is now located. Attitude training needs are more difficult to define (and to satisfy) and in many cases must only be subjective assessments – 'Her team doesn't seem to be functioning well; probably because of a clash of personalities between y and z members.'

Too often these initial assessments are not looked at closely, either because nobody thinks there is a need to do so or the pressure (of various sorts) is such that assessment is not possible. In these cases, to look for eventual evaluation is to look for unreliable, completely subjective, or valueless results.

Who identifies needs?

Training and development are areas in which there have been considerable movements over the past few years. I would prefer to say 'advances', rather than 'movements', but so little evaluation of the new approaches has taken place or has been possible, that to do so would be dangerous. These developments have been evident in the topics of training, the use of technology as training aids, and most of all in the increasing variety of approaches used. But perhaps the major development, and here I do believe 'advance' is appropriate although I cannot prove it, is in the ownership of the training.

A few years ago, training was almost exclusively trainer-centred. The trainer determined the objectives of the course, how long it would last, its content and its format. On many occasions the training was of a pedagogic nature with the trainer in complete control of the direction of the training. The views of the trainees were rarely sought, or if they were, they were sought in a very controlled manner and almost as if the trainer was saying 'Well, I suppose I should let *them* say something.' In recent years we have seen a progressive change in this approach through an increased receptiveness to the requested views of the trainees, then receptiveness to unsolicited views, resulting in events which are completely trainee-centred and directed, such as extreme forms of T-groups or encounter groups.

Course formats have also undergone similar liberations. From a completely trainer-conceived programme construction, approaches have swung towards the trainees who may be asked in specially conceived workshops to produce a course based on their requirements, or they may attend a course which they construct from their needs as they go along, within the confines only of the original *raison d'être*.

Similar movements can be applied to the identification of training needs. Traditionally, the role of the boss included the monitoring of the skills and so on of the people for whom they were responsible, and the identification of weaknesses and shortcomings. These would be 'remedied' by unilateral nominations of the offenders for remedial training courses, irrespective of any (unsought) views of the individual. With the introduction of a more neo-paternal approach to management, the training was discussed with the individual before nomination went ahead. There is no doubt that both these approaches still exist and they surface in the comments of students at the beginning of a course when they say 'I was sent', with the implication or even direct comment on occasions 'and I didn't want to come'. The inroads of real participative management are encouraging an increasingly common approach in which the training need is identified by the individual who then comes forward to discuss both the problem and possible solutions with the boss.

A see-saw effect takes place in some organizations where management development is a living organism. The self-application by individuals is in fact reduced by the line manager fulfilling his responsibilities and being actively interested and involved in the development of his staff. As a result the individuals are no longer left in a vacuum and forced to make their own applications. However, where Managing Director and OD (organization development) work effectively in this way, the final 'nomination' for training is the result of a full discussion between the two parties, irrespective of who initiates the movement.

The Training Department may well now ask where it fits into the scheme for the identification of training needs – 'After all we are the training experts.' Much of course will depend on the identified and agreed role of the department in the organization concerned and the distribution throughout the organization of the necessary skills. There is much to recommend trainers conducting training needs surveys as they (or linked psychologists) may be the ones in the organization with the skills necessary for conducting such surveys. The trainer is the one who is more likely to have the skills to conduct Repertory Grid interviews, for example, than line managers. The psychologist has a much more extensive and intensive knowledge of the construction of diagnostic questionnaires and so on. A major role for trainers in these circumstances may be the use of their skills and expertise in helping the learners and their bosses to practise the processes. In this role the trainer can ensure maximum success but care must be taken not to usurp the rightful roles of the individual and the boss. After all, there will be considerably more commitment from the individuals if they make an important contribution to the end result. The role of the trainer will also increase in stature if guidance and help is given tactfully and professionally.

It can be argued readily that the line manager and the individual are in the best positions to identify the training needs. After all they are on the spot, know the work and should be able to identify quickly and easily any problems which may need a training solution. However, if the trainer accepts this argument completely their role will be reduced simply to a reactive agent, mounting any training demanded by the learner and their boss. A much more meaningful relationship will evolve if a partnership is produced between the three parties – learner, boss and trainer – each contributing their own special expertise. The stature of the trainers will grow as they develop the role of consultant as well as the provider of any training required. If a realistic view is taken, it must also be accepted that not every manager will be sufficiently motivated or even capable of identifying training needs. In such cases, the trainer will have a major role to play.

Whoever may identify the training needs, the process of identification is similar and can be expressed in the model shown in Figure 2.1.

Stage ① can be initiated in a variety of ways and often depends on where an organization's responsibilities lie. Unless there is a routine mechanism which surveys training needs, many training needs come to light accidentally or as the result of some unrelated activity. A common situation which can suggest the existence of training needs is when shortfalls in service or production become evident in an organization. These can suggest that the job is not being performed correctly at some stage, perhaps due to a shortfall in skills, knowledge or attitudes in the job performers. Of course the shortfall may have nothing to do with training needs at all, but once the warning signals have been given, some form of investigation is a logical step which may be taken quite naturally. Audits, whether financial or general, can also be occasions when shortfalls are discovered and usually an immediate identification of whether or not they are due to a training problem can be made.

It should not be assumed, of course, that a shortfall in skill, knowledge or attitude means that there is necessarily a training problem. This will be confirmed at Stage ②. Failure to perform effectively can be identified with one of two causes. The failure or deficiency may be due to a lack of training or ineffective training, or it may simply be due to a lack of execution – the individual has the skill or knowledge to perform the task but either fails or refuses to perform. One of the principal problems connected with training which has taken place off the job is the transfer of that learning to the job. If the individual has been trained effectively but still fails to perform effectively, further training will be useless and the problem requires a more direct line management approach.

However, training needs will arise from the identification of a deficiency in a routine inspection or survey, or result from a special survey mounted to determine whether any training needs might exist.

Stages ③ and ④ introduce the in-depth analysis of the training need related to recommendations for its fulfilment, and are characterized by two major aspects of the process of training needs identification – job analysis and data collection.

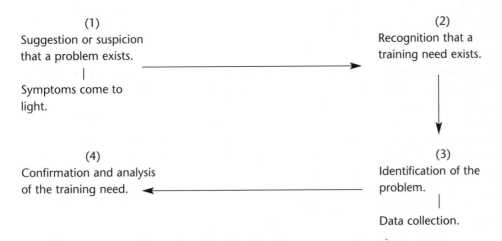

Figure 2.1   Identification of training needs

Analysis

If we are to identify what is wrong with a job or a person performing a job, before we can rectify the situation we must be fully aware of the extent and nature of the job or role. This is obtained or confirmed by an analysis of what is actually occurring. In this process there are more titles with conflicting and vague definitions than we found when considering evaluation and validation.

The three major aspects of analysis which can be considered the most useful in identifying training needs are job analysis, task analysis and skills analysis. These various aspects of analysis are arranged in descending order of describing the magnitude of extent – job relates to the full range of tasks which are required to be performed which in turn require specific skills. In an analysis of training needs there are advantages in following this order.

Job analysis

At the initial stage of the analysis we require an overall, but detailed description of the activities and requirements of the whole job, for example, that of a hotel receptionist, a wages clerk, a capstan lathe operator and so on. Obviously there should be a number of existing aids which can save a considerable amount of background knowledge build-up. The most useful of these should be what is known as the job description. I say 'should' since, in spite of the value of this document and exhortations that one should always be provided, it tends to be a rarity which has either never existed or is described as 'kept here somewhere since we wrote it fifteen years ago'.

Otherwise, the training needs analyst will have to build up his own view of the job description or rely on published descriptions of the jobs.

Job description

Job descriptions are statements of the outline of the whole job and show the duties and responsibilities involved in that job. The pattern of job descriptions varies when we go beyond this basic statement and they can include entries about lines of communication, hours of work, pay and other conditions to such an extent that they may overlap the contract of employment. For the purpose of a training needs analysis we shall be concerned principally with those parts of the description which relate to the operation of the job. However, entries which relate to lines of communication or, more significantly, the absence of these may be a first indication where the shortfall exists.

An example of a job description for a hotel receptionist is given in Figure 2.2. When the job description is being used for the purposes of training needs analysis, the duties section will be the most important part of the description as this describes what the individual worker is required to do and should be able to do. The description of duties in a job description should be complete, including an additional section showing 'occasional duties', and should be expressed in terms as simple and unambiguous as possible without going into long descriptions of each task. Probably the first step to be taken by the training needs analyst is to read the job description and observe the person performing the duties so that these duties and their relationship to each other are fully understood.

Job title:	Hotel receptionist.
Function:	To maintain the hotel's bookings, reservations and charge system and be the hotel's principal customer contact point.
Lines of communication:	Upwards – to head receptionists.
	Laterally – to other receptionists.
	Downwards – to junior receptionist and hall staff.
Responsibilities:	To – head receptionist.
	For – junior receptionist.
Hours of work:	Shift system (detailed according to practice).
Duties:	1. Dealing with room reservations made by telephone, letter, e-mail and customer contact.
	2. Allocating reservations and completing records of these reservations.
	3. Confirming reservations with customers by the relevant means.

Figure 2.2   Example of a job description

Job specification

By this stage the analyst should have a good overall knowledge of the job in which he or she is interested: the duties have been listed in a job description and these are understood. It may be at this stage that training needs have become apparent. The job description is what the job holder *should* do and *should* be capable of doing. It may be obvious that an individual does not perform a particular duty because they do not know how to do it. The training function may then be simply to train the individual from a position of not being able to perform a task to being able to do so. This could be an example for a relatively simple case of validation and evaluation.

The simple need stated is most likely to occur in an analysis of the needs of new or relatively new workers: it is necessary to delve more deeply when the needs of more experienced individuals are involved. This is where the job specification and the action leading up to it can be most valuable.

A job description details the skills, knowledge and attitudes which are required by the individual in order to carry out the duties involved in the job. For example, one duty of a painter and decorator may be paperhanging in which case the job specification would look, in part, like Figure 2.3.

In the job specification shown as an example in Figure 2.3 attitudes have not been listed. These will vary in their importance from job to job. In the case of the painter and decorator who may have to hang paper in private households the attitudes necessary will include patience, good social skills and awareness, a good attitude to hygiene both personal and in respect of the environment in which the work is being performed, and so on.

The more detailed the job specification, the easier it will be to identify where any deficiencies may lie. Obviously for some occupations the job specification will be long and detailed, whereas for others it will be relatively simple. However, the training needs analyst will certainly find that even fewer job specifications exist than job descriptions and it will often be necessary to construct them from scratch. There is no easy way to do this and the operation will include:

Job title: Painter and decorator.
Duties: 3.   Paperhanging
                                        3.1   Task: Selection of paper.
                                                Knowledge: types of
                                                    wallcovering including strengths, textures etc.
                                                Skills: ability to assess covering by manual
                                                manipulation.
                                        3.2   Task: measuring room.
                                                Knowledge: methods of estimation; unit methods
                                                of measurement.
                                                Skills: measuring in various unit methods.

Figure 2.3   Example of a job specification

- Observation of the work
- Discussion in some form with the worker.

Some of the methods used in job data collection will be discussed in the next chapter as it is in this area that the analyst has the luxury of being able to select his own approaches.

Occupational competence standards

Some years ago the British government decided that, by 1992, all major occupations to be found in industry, commerce and the professions would be subjected to a study and analysis to determine the standards of performance expected in a competent person in that occupation. These standards would be produced so that they were consistent nationally, across industries and, in some cases, across sectors. Whatever the industry there are common aspects of work in an occupation, which are transferable. The requirements placed upon a trainer in the dairy industry are the same as those required in an electrical engineering industry – the trainer has to design, construct, deliver and evaluate training even though the products are different. The job of an HGV driver has the same competence requirements whether they are driving a lorry for the transport of steel bars or the distribution of eggs.

Of course there will be some variations from one industry to another and from one company to another, but these will be minor compared with most common tasks. Many of these variations will be taken care of within the analysis, often as a separate section entitled 'Range indicators'.

There is nothing new in this approach, but for the first time the analysis of competence and standards is at a consistent national level, providing a means of a national assessment of competence. Also, many of the standards are being produced by or in close association with representatives of the occupations and the industries themselves. It is far from being a training exercise and the approach recommends that trainers do not perform the analysis, or are utilized only as supportive experts. The principal sources of information are the job itself and the job-holder.

The bodies responsible for the work involved, in association with the then Training, Enterprise and Education Directorate of the Department of Employment, are known as Lead Bodies, of which more than 150 were formed. These consisted of representatives of employers within the industries, trade unions, educationalists, consultants and relevant professional bodies. The Lead Bodies contracted consultants to produce the draft standards which were then considered by the Lead Body and eventually published for general use.

Various changes have occurred since that time, the principal one being the formation on 1 October 1997 of the Qualifications and Curriculum Authority (QCA) resulting from the merger of the body responsible for the control of standards and the provision of National Vocational Qualifications (NVQ) – the National Council for Vocational Qualifications (NCVQ) – and the School Curriculum and Assessment Authority (SCAA). National Training Organizations (NTO) were formed, taking over the roles of the original Lead Bodies – hence, for example, the EmpNTO (the Employment NTO) that among other areas is responsible for standards and NVQs in training and development. Even more recent changes proposed for 2002 are that some NTOs will start to be replaced by Skills Sector Councils.

USE OF THE STANDARDS

Because the standards of performance are being defined at consistent levels which are capable of measurement, or at least assessment, the statements are seen as having a wide and varied application.

The main use is the linkage with vocational qualifications, controlled by the SCAA. A S/NVQ (Scottish/National Vocational Qualification) is a 'can do' qualification rather than an academic one. The S/NVQ basically details a range of activities that a competent person can do in a particular role, and is able to prove to the satisfaction of a certificated Assessor that they have done or can do it. The focus is therefore on performance more than knowledge, that is to say a competency-based approach, although S/NVQs do have a knowledge requirement to underpin the practical skill application.

Apart from the S/NVQ 'official' use, the competence standards can be used more generally as the reference standards in an occupation, offering guidelines to assessors for their competent workers or highlighting a need for training to the competence level (or beyond). The competence guidelines are therefore also useful and, in the particular context of this book, form a strong thread through the evaluation process. The standards are to be accepted by the National Council for Vocational Qualifications (NCVQ) which is responsible for authorizing the award of National Vocational Qualifications (NVQs) through such bodies as City and Guilds, and so on. Accreditation towards the award of a relevant NVQ is gained by a satisfactory assessment that an individual is able to perform at the competence level in the areas of work required by the occupation.

In addition the standards will be of value to employers in a variety of ways. They will offer guidelines to the competence standards required, and consequently will be useful in recruitment, identification of job requirements, appraisal of performance, identification of training need areas, and so on.

In this way it can be seen that the applications are much wider than any analyses hitherto. Instead of being severely academic approaches based on knowledge about what is required, they define what a job-holder should actually be able to do. The standards are a marriage between the attitudes and needs of both academics and industrialists. Because we are looking at what people do *at work*, assessment will not only be in the hands of the academics. In many cases the only people who will have the ability and capability of observing and assessing a job-holder will be those who know most about the work – people, themselves highly skilled, who are in the industry or occupation: supervisors, managers, professionals. Of course, some competences may not be readily assessable, or the job-holder may not be in a position to demonstrate competence in some aspects of them in the current post. In such cases, assessment by other means may be necessary, such as academic approaches, simulations and project work.

FUNCTIONAL ANALYSIS

The principal method of identifying occupational competences and the relevant standards has been the approach known as functional analysis. The advantages of this method over other forms of task and job analysis are described by the end results. Most, but not all, task/job analyses tend to concentrate on the tasks the job includes, whereas functional analysis looks at the job in terms of outcomes. However, the borderline is at times a little hazy and the more sophisticated job analyses are not so restrictive. Perhaps the most obvious exclusion in functional analysis relates to knowledge. It is often stated that the factors relating to the requirements of a job are knowledge, skills and attitudes. Functional analysis concentrates on practical skills, with the argument that knowledge and attitude on their own do not describe an assessable aspect of performance: knowledge and attitude has to be demonstrated in an outcome to be evident. The knowledge has to be obtained in order to enable something to result – an outcome.

Acceptance of functional analysis is not universal and there are those who argue that it is too restricted itself to these practical outcomes. An occupation can be described, in these alternative approaches, as having many more attributes than outcome performances and even knowledge in its own right has a place in the job definition. The answer may be an amalgamation of several models. However, even this 'solution' has problems: it will be seen that the standards produced by functional analysis are complex and extensive without having to take a considerable amount of other information into account. If an instrument becomes too complex and unwieldy, and perhaps very difficult to understand or observe, there is less chance that it will be used. A simpler approach, even one which may not be comprehensive, may be better than nothing at all.

Competence standards and S/NVQs in training

If the standards are to be used in the achievement of an S/NVQ or used more informally as guidelines to competence, the extent of the analysis and the resulting statements of competence depend on the skill level (including the S/NVQ Level) of the occupation in question. All occupational standards and their related S/NVQs are described in progressive detail from a Key Purpose to Range Statements:

- **Key Purpose** – the overall statement of the role, occupation or sector
- **Key Roles** – describe in a general way the major functions of the role
- **Units** – are the first specific descriptions of the tasks or skills relating to the Key Roles
- **Elements** – these split the Units into more specific tasks, etc. and are the most finely detailed of the tasks and competences
- **Performance Criteria** – these list how the Elements must be carried out to be effective.

Training and development standards of competence and S/NVQs

The EmpNTO, referred to earlier, has taken on the role of providing guidance, responsibility for standards research, responsibility for S/NVQ qualifications in training and development, and generally determining the competences standards expected of people working at different levels in training and development and HR. Different levels and standards have been defined, initially by the Training and Development Lead Body in 1991, and in 2001 the EmpNTO was engaged in a consulting project to bring the standards and VQs up to date.

On 13 December 2001 the revisions for both the standards and the qualifications for Learning and Development were approved. The revised awards came into operation on 1 June 2002, until which time the old awards applied, although anyone registered for a S/NVQ prior to 31 May 2002 will have 2–3 years to complete their award under the old standards.

LEARNING AND DEVELOPMENT STANDARDS

Each S/NVQ includes several levels containing standards for different skill and knowledge levels within an occupation, sector or industry. The Learning and Development standards and qualifications are no exception and include five levels. The six levels are:

Level 5 Learning and Development (11 mandatory Units plus 1 optional from a list of 7)
Level 4 Learning and Development (8 mandatory Units plus 4 optional from a list of 12)
Level 4 Management of Learning and Development Provision (6 mandatory Units plus 2 optional from a list of 7)
Level 4 Co-ordination of Learning and Development Provision (6 mandatory Units plus 1 optional from a list of 7)
Level 3 Learning and Development (7 mandatory Units plus 4 from a list of 13)
Level 3 Direct Training and Support (6 mandatory Units plus 4 from a list of 9)

Level 5 is essentially the management of training level; level 4, in its different options, the level at which most trainers with training responsibilities and some management roles will be aiming; and level 3 the standards for the most direct training practitioners.

LEVEL 4 LEARNING AND DEVELOPMENT

The level 4 Learning and Development S/NVQ consists of demonstrating a satisfactory level in 8 mandatory Units plus 4 optional from a list of 12. As suggested earlier, such standards can be used in assessing and validating the skills of the trainer, linking this assessment with the forms of evaluation of the training to be described in this book. The full list of standards for learning and development are wide-ranging and details can be obtained through the Employment NTO (website www.empnto.co.uk). A CD-ROM giving all the up-to-date details became available from the NTO in March 2002 (*National Occupational Standards; Learning and Development, and Assessment and Verification*, Employment NTO 2002).

The Units required for the award of this level 4 Learning and Development S/NVQ demonstrate the standards used in the award and those competences that can be usefully used in the assessment mentioned above (more detailed guidance to the content of the Units is contained in the Elements and Performance Criteria of a VQ).

The eight mandatory Units are (the brief description of the standard being preceded by the new Unit number):

G2   Contribute to learning within the organization
G3   Evaluate and develop own practice
L4   Design learning programmes
L5   Agree learning programmes with learners
L8   Manage the contribution of other people to the learning process
L9   Create a climate that promotes learning
L17   Evaluate and improve learning and development programmes

and either:

L3   Identify individual learning aims and programmes

or:

L2   Identify the learning and development needs of the organization.

For the S/NVQ, in addition to the mandatory Units, a further four are required from the following list of 14 options:

L7   Prepare and develop resources to support learning
L13   Enable group learning
L14   Support learners by mentoring in the workplace
L15   Support and advise individual learners
L16   Monitor and review progress with learners
L17   Evaluate and improve learning and development programmes
L18   Respond to changes in learning and development
L19   Provide learning and development in international settings
L20   Support competence achieved in the workplace
L21   Plan how to provide basic skills in the workplace
L22   Introduce training for basic skills in the workplace
A1   Assess candidates (for S/NVQ) using a range of methods
A2   Assess candidates' performance through observation
V1   Conduct internal quality assurance of the assessment process.

As mentioned above, the Elements and Performance Criteria of a VQ offer more working detail to the Units and it is from this information that the standards can be used particularly for evaluation processes. Even though you might not be actually following a S/NVQ award, comparing the skills of the trainer with the listed Units, Elements and Performance Criteria can give you some good leads.

ELEMENTS

The Units described above are only the broad titles of the areas included in the standards and the VQs and are not sufficiently detailed to enable a realistic assessment of competence.

Each Unit is broken down into Elements which are more detailed statements of the functions.

Unit L17 is described in more detail as:

'This Unit is appropriate for you if your role involves:

- Providing quality learning and development programmes
- Evaluating learning and development programmes
- Responding to developments in learning and development
- Planning and introducing improvements in learning and development programmes.

The activities you are likely to be involved in:

- Setting evaluation objectives and criteria, including performance indicators, national standards and organizational standards
- Evaluating delivery methods and systems, assessment procedures, how resources are used, including people, finance, time, aims, objectives and outcomes
- Reviewing the possibility of greater use of technology-based learning programmes and learner support
- Collecting information from learners, practitioners, colleagues and clients through questionnaires, individual interviews, group interviews and desk research
- Analysing results
- Making proposals for improvements to programmes
- Preparing detailed plans with colleagues.'

The specific *elements* described in Unit L17 to achieve the above consist of:

L17.1   Choosing how to evaluate programmes
L17.2   Analysing information to improve learning and development programmes
L17.3   Making improvements to learning and development programmes.

PERFORMANCE CRITERIA

The Performance Criteria define in even more detail the competences included in the Units and Elements and enable an evaluator/assessor to determine whether the functions of the role are being carried out satisfactorily – the test of competence in VQ standards terms.

PERFORMANCE

Each Element has a number of associated Performance Criteria, ranging from five to ten or more criteria. If we look, for example, at Element L17.1 as described above, the eight Performance Criteria for this Element are:

'Performance Criteria: "Choosing how to evaluate programmes". You must be able to do the following:

a   Identify which of the organization's objectives the learning and development programme needs to meet and measure how far it does this

b   Identify the main objectives and outcomes of the programme against the needs of the organization and the individuals taking part in the programme
c   Identify the range, purpose and level of the evaluation
d   Choose appropriate ways of evaluating how learning is delivered
e   Specify the evaluation criteria for outcomes and delivery
f   Confirm that the resources are available to carry out the evaluation
g   Agree with the appropriate people how you will carry out the evaluation
h   Specify a plan for putting the evaluation into practice.'

KNOWLEDGE

In addition to the *Performance* Criteria described above the Units include notes giving guidance on the type of *knowledge* evidence required to satisfy the criteria. The knowledge requirements for Unit L17 are:

Unit L17: Evaluate and improve learning and development programmes. Knowledge requirements:

'You need the following knowledge to perform this Unit of Competence. You will show this through the outcome of your work activities and through evaluations of your systems and processes. You need to be able to show that you have general knowledge and understanding of the following:

The nature and role of evaluation within learning and development

1   How to identify and apply specific conditions to effectively measure:

- The quality of the learning experience
- The effectiveness of the delivery methods used
- The thoroughness of quality assurance arrangements

2   How to identify all valid sources of feedback, including learners and colleagues, and examining and inspection authorities
3   How to use information taken from evaluations to improve the quality of learning and development programmes.

Principles and concepts

4   How to analyse information and draw conclusions from it
5   How to choose methods and procedures for collecting information
6   How to identify and assess the potential of technology-based learning and e-learning when evaluating programmes
7   How to establish a representative sample
8   How to use appropriate techniques for asking questions.

External factors influencing human resource development

9   How to keep to data protection legislation
10   How to meet the requirements of awarding bodies and inspecting bodies
11   How to ensure that everyone acts in line with health, safety and environmental protection legislation and best practice

12 How to analyse and use developments in learning and new ways of delivery, including technology-based learning and e-learning.'

Although the Standards of Competence as used for the S/NVQs are not comprehensive overall, they are sufficient to demonstrate the requirements for the skills of a trainer and consequently the training programmes they produce. In this way, the standards are useful bases and supplements to the other forms of evaluation described in this book.

The use of NVQs

The use of NVQs is currently limited but is increasing slowly. The arguments against introduction range from the time and resources required on the part of the candidates and internal mentors, assessors and verifiers; through the insistence of some organizations that the candidates, although supported in many ways, should construct their portfolios in their own time; to the cost involved in registration, the necessary training and assessment and certification. Unless the organization itself has achieved the status of an accredited centre, the cost can deter many organizations (and not only small ones) in spite of the benefits accruing.

Some authorities on work analysis disagree with what they see as the narrow-bounded approach of functional analysis. As for every other model, functional analysis is not a fully comprehensive description of an occupation or function, but it is a reasonably realistic approach which makes a worthy attempt at producing a 'professional' description of the demands of an occupation. Nevertheless, it can be supplemented by other attributes demanded of a trainer. This is not the place to extend this argument which is discussed fully in *Trainer Assessment* (Rae, 2002).

If the assessment of competence standards based on functional analysis is accepted as tenable and valid, we have a soundly based, reasonably comprehensive description of many occupations. Supplementing this with other known requirements – particularly those behaviourally anchored – the next step in the identification of training and development needs becomes much clearer and easier, with fewer unanswered questions remaining.

Training specification

At the end of the job specification stage, which will include data collection in order to permit task, skill and knowledge analysis leading to a full and detailed analysis of the job, any deficiencies will be apparent. Not only will the deficiency be apparent but also the extent of the shortfall, whether total, 50 per cent or minimal. This assessment leads to the general training specification which details the existence and extent of the training need. However, before these needs can be translated into training, it is necessary to determine the training objectives – clear statements of what the training should achieve.

Training objectives

The training objectives for any form of training must result directly from the job analysis and training specification and, to have any meaning, must be stated tightly, as quantitatively as possible, and behaviourally expressed so that any changes can be observed.

Objectives of this nature not only give the lead to the actual training necessary, but also to the main theme of this book, namely validation and evaluation.

Let us return again to the case of the hotel receptionist. It has been found from feedback that she has errors in 90 per cent of any arithmetical calculations she has to do. A full job description for her showed that a part of her duties was the calculation of customers' incidental accounts and a full job specification for her showed that she needed to be able to do simple arithmetical calculations. Subsequent stages of the analysis showed that she was in fact poor at arithmetic, but a calculator was available for her use. Unfortunately nobody had ever explained the functions of the calculator to her; consequently she never used it and 'got her sums wrong'. The more this error occurred the greater became her panic and she was on the point of resigning. There was an obvious training need in this case, which, if the basic educational weakness of arithmetic was not to be tackled, when translated into training objective terms would be 'to teach the receptionist to operate a calculator in the addition mode only so that she will be able to summarize customers' incidental expense accounts to 100 per cent accuracy, even under "stress conditions"'.

This objective is the start of the validation and evaluation process. At the present time she is making 90 per cent errors. The training specification will contain a recommendation for training in the use of a calculator and the objectives will spell this out in specific terminal terms. A recommendation might also be either a training course in this subject or perhaps assistance for her to attend day release or evening classes through further education.

The training can be validated easily on its completion by examination of terminal tests which will show whether she is able to use a calculator to the required efficiency level and thus whether the objectives have been achieved. When she returns to her work and continues to perform to the required level, evaluation has also been satisfied because she will be saving her employer money. Achievement and maintenance of the objective will also allow her to remain in a job which she enjoyed and for which she was otherwise very suitable.

Aims and objectives

In training spheres, even among trainers who ought to know better, aims and objectives are often confused. It is not pedantry to comment in this way when the confusion is taken into the training and its evaluation. We considered earlier whether evaluation is only possible if the training need shortfall has been identified precisely at the start of the exercise. The aim is a statement of general intent whereas the objective states the requirement in precise terms. As an example of the differences between aims and objectives:

> *Aims* are general statements of intent which give the global approach to the problem but without exact definition – 'I shall learn to fly.' This statement is an example of a general aim which is well short of exact definition. The aim concerned with flying does not state 'what' I shall learn to fly, in what period of time, to what level of competence, and it is even so vague and imprecise that it may mean that I have grown wings and intend to learn how to use them!

> *Objectives* on the other hand are specific and precise statements of intent with

precise measures of terminal behaviour. 'I shall learn to fly a jet fighter aeroplane by the end of next month to acrobatic display standards' is a much more precise statement of my intentions which on completion can be monitored and evaluated.

Within objective setting there are general principles to be followed. For an objective to have some degree of realism it will include

- a precise statement of the complete terminal behaviour required
- a statement of conditions under which the performance is to be achieved
- a description of the standards to be attained.

Much has been written about the actual writing of objectives and the words and format to be used. One of the most useful publications on this subject is *Preparing Objectives for Programmed Instruction* by Mager (1962), later re-titled *Preparing Instructional Objectives* (1975). Mager identifies words which, because they are open to ambiguous interpretation, should not be used in objective writing, such as 'to know', 'to appreciate', 'to understand', and so on.

Advice such as that given by Mager is important and, if followed, ensures that objectives are written which are not open to misunderstanding and specify the exact nature of what is to be achieved. However, what can (and does) happen is that people become so immersed in the pedantic complexities of ensuring that the words and the construction of an objective are 'correct' that the meaning of the objective is lost. Obviously the more specific and unambiguous the terms of the objective might be, the easier it will be to validate that objective and hence the training. But we should not become slaves to the construction of objectives: it is the 'result' of the training that matters, not its description.

If the three principles cited earlier are followed, the objective will satisfy its requirements whatever the words used. Purists will shudder at this acceptance of a greater generalization, but it will certainly appeal to practising trainers who find it difficult to work to academic criteria as well as achieving the training, even though they may applaud the intent.

3 *Detailed analysis*

Some of the methods of obtaining the details for a job specification were mentioned briefly in the preceding chapter; 'briefly' not because these methods are unimportant – quite the reverse as they will involve the greater part of an investigator's time. Rather they are very wide-ranging and varied, some are simple and some are highly sophisticated techniques requiring expertise and experience.

Much will depend on the nature of the problem presented as to which type of analysis will be the most appropriate and for whom. It may be that the training needs are group- or organization-wide, or they may be confined to an individual, or an individual may be identified to take part in the analysis as a representative of the larger group.

Knowledge analysis

To determine knowledge levels and needs will require a different approach to an analysis of skills and is probably the most straightforward of the analytical approaches. Whether the approach is to an individual or a group, the analytical method consists of simple questioning to elucidate whether the required knowledge exists, observation that a set of rules or information is being followed or, in more complicated cases, a test can be set.

Although the approach will be relatively straightforward, it is necessary for the analyst to set clear objectives for the exercise. The criteria he or she will need to satisfy will include:

- What is the range of knowledge to be tested?
- What questions are to be asked? What form will they have to take?
- What answers are required?
- How detailed are the answers required to be?
- What percentage of accuracy is required?
- Who will assess the answers?
- How long can/should the questioning take?
- What should the environment be?

and so on.

The use of a knowledge analysis may, of course, come at a later stage than the initial establishment of training needs. It may be, for example, that an organizational needs analysis has identified a general need for training in Organization and Methods (O and M) techniques. Courses have been arranged, programmes produced (but on a flexible basis) and applications invited. Some time before the start of the first course the participants will have been allocated, but nothing is known about their level of knowledge of O and M techniques, except that someone has determined that they need the training. A questionnaire in the form of a test of knowledge can be sent out prior to the course to determine the level of knowledge of each participant. From the returned tests, the level of the course can be adjusted and base levels for eventual evaluation can be set.

An alternative to this approach is to retain the questionnaire until the students arrive on the course and to administer the test at an early stage, perhaps as the first activity of the course. This method ensures that all participants complete the test under identical conditions, but it also means that the tutors must be ready to modify immediately the level of their inputs and activities in the light of the information obtained.

One of the major problems of most training courses, except when completely new skills, concepts and so on are being introduced, is that those attending most courses will be heterogeneous as far as knowledge level is concerned – there will be a range of knowledge between zero or almost zero to some degree of knowledge. It is the tutor's problem to set the level of the training at an intermediate level which will satisfy all. Unfortunately, if the range of knowledge is too wide there will be some who will feel that it is far too simple for them and others who will find the material too far above their heads for them to understand. For both these groups the course will not be an effective learning event. If however the waiting list for a particular type of training is large, the test can be given to all on the list. Course membership can then be adjusted as far as possible in the light of the test results. The only problem then is to ensure that the similar level people can be released for training at the same time – something which is frequently impossible for practical reasons!

Other analyses

The analyses of skills and tasks, and particularly social skills and attitudes, are much more difficult to conduct and there must be considerable reliance on the observation and perception of others. Obviously the degree of difficulty and objectivity will depend on the skill and task being analysed. There is little doubt that management skills and attitudes, interpersonal or social skills, and attitudes generally will be the most difficult to assess.

Observational analysis

Observation of the job or task being performed, and the person performing it, is the most readily available and the most commonly used method of analysis in most cases. Even so areas will still remain which do not lend themselves readily to practical observation. Such areas will include many of the personal staff interviews including appraisal interviews and similar events. It is unfortunate that it is these areas of management operation which often have most need of training.

Preparation must be thorough so that the observer knows exactly what is required from the observation since there may be problems in being able to return to cover something omitted on the initial occasion. It is normal to use an *aide-mémoire* for most situations of this nature, but flexibility is very important and the observer must not feel that he is chained to the *aide-mémoire*.

The first stage will involve the reading of the job description and a clarification of any doubtful areas. If the job is one with which the observer is not familiar, a talk with someone who is acquainted with the job can be useful, but this discussion must be kept at the strictly factual level in order to avoid contamination of the observer's views. The observer will need to be well acquainted with the job specification as the observations may disclose significant deviations from what should be happening. The job specification will also help in any decision about whether the whole job or only some tasks should be observed.

The next, essential stage is discussion with the person or group to be observed. The observed must be fully aware of when they will be observed, what the observer will be looking at and why the observation is taking place. Naturally, disclosure of this information to the person to be observed can have the effect of producing unnatural behaviour. Operators knowing they are being observed will take notice, for example, of all the safety checks they should perform (if they are aware of them). Two consequences may result from this effect:

1. Perfect performance under observation has many similarities to training and it may be seen by the operator that the work proceeds as well or better if they do what they should be doing. This improved performance may be maintained without further training or emphasis.
2. Unnaturally perfect performance as a result of observation may continue for an initial period only. Once the individual becomes involved in the task, natural reactions are more likely to occur as the observer will be ignored. This is a common occurrence when television observation is used in training.

If the observation is not 'open', it may well result in either hostility, or suspicion and completely unnatural behaviour. It goes almost without saying that the relevant trade union(s) will have been brought in at an early stage and agreement reached. Without such co-operation the analysis could prove at best to be either abortive or an academic exercise, or, at worst, could produce adverse industrial relations.

Above all the analyst must have an objective approach. Great care must be taken in ensuring that what is noted is what the observer actually saw or heard – not what he wanted to see or hear. If it is possible, it is valuable to have the observations recorded in some way so that doubtful actions can be confirmed with objectivity. Recording is particularly useful when actions take place quickly and may possibly be missed in the observation.

As an example of observational analysis we may take one task of a hotel receptionist – the direct reception of new guests. Once the preliminaries cited above have been taken care of successfully, the analyst can take up a position where he can observe clearly, but not be too obtrusive to either the receptionist or the guest. In a situation of this kind there is only a little likelihood of observation contamination as the receptionist will be completely involved with the guest.

The work of the analyst begins when a guest enters the door and immediately predetermined questions can start to be answered. Does the receptionist see the guest at this early stage and make any signs to this effect? If so, what? The customer walks across the floor between the entry and the reception desk. Is the receptionist doing any other work? What happens? Is obvious notice being taken of the approaching guest? And so on as the interaction continues. The initial actions described all relate to non-verbal skills and attitudes and can follow a pattern which is dictated by a general interpersonal philosophy, or a specific policy laid down by the employer.

Verbal behaviour is added to the non-verbal behaviour once the guest reaches the desk. What does the receptionist do or say? How is it said? What is the response? And so the interaction progresses with functional aspects being added to the behaviours to construct a total picture of how a customer is received.

Once the analysis is complete, it can be compared with the model of what should happen in an ideal situation. Any differences may indicate, if sufficiently substantial or important, a training need or a modification of the job specification or interactive model.

Observation support interviews

It is most unlikely that an observation alone will provide a complete analysis, particularly if there are significant differences observed from the job specification or model. In such a case, the analyst will want to know why the change occurred. The only way to obtain this information is to interview the person or persons being observed and ask why the deviation has taken place.

This personal contact with the observed subject must be done with tact and skill. If subjects are asked why they took a particular action, and it is obvious that their action differed from the 'official' action, answers might not be forthcoming and they might adopt a defensive stance. The questioning will have to be more circumspect and might usefully follow along the lines of: 'In such and such a circumstance, tell me what you do.' Supplementary questions of increasingly deeper levels could then cover the variation.

Interviews of this nature require a skilled interviewer/analyst who has to be aware of the differences in the interactions involved, to be able to decide whether they are sufficiently significant to introduce, and to have interview skills sufficient to cope with any emerging problems. Considerable skill may be necessary to encourage the subject to talk freely, if only from the point of view of articulation. In the case of some subjects, for example the receptionist who is used to talking to strangers, this may not be difficult, but with other individuals whose work does not normally require them to talk about their work, bringing-out skills will be necessary. The interviewer must be a good listener and be adept at identifying 'clues' contained in the contributions made by the subject, and able to formulate questions which will develop these clues. Finally, the interviewer must be capable of assessing the information, sorting out the wheat from the chaff, and evaluating the significant information.

UNSTRUCTURED INTERVIEW

This method of approach has just been described as the follow-up to an observation analysis, but it can stand alone as an investigatory event in job analysis and training needs analysis.

The subject of the job or task is obviously the focal point of the interview, but the interviewer has no set plan for the interview. The worker is encouraged to talk about the job and by follow-up questions the necessary information is extracted. An interview of this kind can take a long time but can be pleasing to both parties as it resembles a conversation more than a stereotyped interview.

As suggested earlier, the interviewer must be acutely alive to 'clues' being given by the interviewee and be able to develop these clues with probing questions or reflective approaches. A very common and much used question in this type of interview will be 'And what else can you tell me about that part of your job?'

A modification of the unstructured approach to the analysis interview can be the use of a semi-structured method. In this instance, the significant areas which the interviewer wishes to cover form the basis of the interview, but within this structure the interviewee is given considerable scope to respond freely. The interviewer is again listening carefully for clues to follow up and makes sure that by the end of the interview all his points have been considered, whatever useful side paths may have been followed. This method can be a most effective and enjoyable interview for both persons, as the interviewee is free to talk and the interviewer has at least a basic idea of the path the interview will take.

STRUCTURED INTERVIEW

The structured interview is probably the most common of the approaches in job and task analysis and if performed well can be a very effective vehicle for investigation. In this approach the interviewer plans the interview and particularly the nature and order of his questions in advance and in a logical sequence: 'What do you do first?'; 'Then what?'; 'What do you do after you have done x?'

There are many advantages to this traditional approach to interviewing in that:

- It usually takes less time than other approaches
- It is likely to avoid traumatic or awkward situations
- Relatively unskilled interviewers find it an easier approach
- Full information is usually obtained to the predetermined questions.

There are, however, some disadvantages which are worth bearing in mind so that other approaches can be considered:

- It assumes that the interviewer knows all the questions to ask
- It is rigid and the interviewer will find difficulty in readjusting if the responses do not follow the assumed pattern
- Clues may be ignored for the sake of maintaining the structure
- The interviewee may react against the formal approach even though the appropriate method of questioning is used.

CO-COUNSELLING

The approach described as co-counselling can be very useful when a number of people are involved in the analysis. Two of the subjects are brought together and invited to interview and counsel each other about their jobs and their training needs. If the results are to be useful from a job analysis point of view, there must be a written conclusion which can be used to summarize an analysis.

Although this method is less controlled than the other types of interview, much information can be obtained as there is no longer the potential analyst/subject barrier. The two people are talking together as colleagues and, provided the organization's climate is right, will be free with each other and enjoy the interaction. The discussion may go deeper and wider than would be possible with an analyst.

The fact that this method is not analyst-centred has both advantages and disadvantages. The analyst has to be very careful when setting up the co-counselling pairs so that he explains the purpose of the exercise very clearly. Despite this, the individuals may not have the necessary interviewing or counselling skills to make the event work completely and to obtain all the information relevant to the exercise. There is also the possible problem of selecting incompatible pairs.

Questionnaires

Interviews which are performed effectively usually yield a large amount of high quality information and data on which to base an analysis. However, in some cases this information may be suspect, as in the case when the information sought relates to the training needs of an organization or a large group, rather than just the individual from whom the information was obtained. If the series of interviews was to be extended, it would be costly and time-consuming. If cost and time are at a premium, the interview approach may not be acceptable and the use of a questionnaire might be considered. The questionnaire approach will certainly be useful in determining levels of knowledge.

Where the analysis of skill is concerned, the use of a questionnaire is even more subjective than the interview and certainly more subjective than observation plus an interview. There are occasions in evaluation when we have to accept subjectivity and make the best use of it that we can.

A skills analysis questionnaire will be quite different from one used to assess knowledge. The only real variation possible in a knowledge questionnaire is in the method of response: a yes or no answer, a multiple choice, or an open response. In the case of skills there are also options possible in the form of the questions posed.

One approach will be to list the skills (and perhaps knowledge and attitudes) required for the job or task and ask the individual to state by a tick which skill is required in his or her opinion. The skills listed might be obtained from a job specification or even from an alternative questionnaire approach. The alternative approach is basically a plain sheet of paper on which the individuals are asked to list the skills (knowledge or attitudes) required for the job. He or she could also be asked to rank them in order of importance or even to indicate his or her individual level of skill against each of the items.

Returning to the predetermined data questionnaire, instead of a simple yes or no against the list of items, the completer could be asked to rate his or her own skill level against each item. This is particularly useful with a fully validated questionnaire where the individual's responses can be related to a norm.

Questionnaires used in skills analysis are quite different from those used in knowledge analysis. In the latter, the answers are usually either right or wrong. In an assessment of skills by questionnaire, other than skills which are almost synonymous with knowledge (for example some aspects of mathematics), the replies will be highly subjective since they are based on the views of the completer and could vary considerably, almost to extremes.

An attempt can be made to reduce the subjective element by extending the completion of the questionnaire to the subject's boss, colleagues and, if possible or desirable, subordinates. It must be established, however, that the other levels see enough of the subject's operation to make an objective assessment. Particularly in the case of the subordinates one must be certain that they have sufficient knowledge of the skills and functions on which to make an assessment. I have had subordinates whose assessment of my interpersonal skills on the basis of their criteria would not have pleased me and, on reflection, the same applies to some of the bosses I have had. Others could have similar views about me! The inherent dangers of this approach are therefore very real.

Questionnaires have other dangers. In particular they are not easy to construct in a readily understandable form, nor are they easy to produce in a universally valid and reliable format. They can, however, if necessary, reach a very wide sample of people and the large response is capable of relatively easy statistical analysis.

DELPHI TECHNIQUE

An extension of the questionnaire approach is afforded by the Delphi technique. In this approach the questionnaires, on return from a number of people, are tabulated and the distribution of the responses is demonstrated statistically. The distribution analysis is circulated among those who completed the questionnaire and they are asked, particularly those outside the middle range, whether they wish to reconsider their answers. The responses usually show a swing towards the middle range. The modified responses are again analysed according to the distribution and the completers of the questionnaires are again given another opportunity to revise their views. This approach is intended to ensure that all give the questionnaire their fullest consideration and that the opportunity is available for respondents to change their minds.

AUDITS

A further modification of the use of the questionnaire involves an approach known as an audit, for example, 'Management Development Audit'.

The purpose of an audit is to provide a clear picture of the state of affairs in a particular area of work prevailing in an organization. If a picture of this nature is obtained, any deficiencies or training needs will show up as part of the audit. For example, if I wished to determine with regard to each management development system in an organization:

1. To what extent it is practised
2. An indication of its effective operation
3. An indication of where training or further training is seen as necessary,

an audit would supply most of this information.

The key to the difference between an audit and a straightforward questionnaire approach lies in the fact that the initial stages of an audit are linked with the objectives for the exercise.

Audits in this form have been pioneered by the Durham University Business School and they suggest that the area examined by an audit will produce analyses of:

- involvement of the employee in the process
- communication of information
- planning
- assessment
- activity level.

The process starts when the organization's senior management are interviewed in order to provide a clear picture of the organization and its policy as determined by the management. This determination is essential so that the information subsequently obtained can be weighed against the stated policy. If no policy on particular aspects exists, it must be determined how assessments of effectiveness are made in practice and there must be a discussion of the audit so that top management is fully committed.

Once the base lines have been cleared, decisions are made about the practicalities of using the audit questionnaire. Pilot interviews are held with people in the organization at the level at which the audit will be conducted so that the questionnaire can be constructed with a minimum of possible misunderstandings and adverse reaction.

The final construction of the custom-made questionnaire can now go ahead and decisions made as to whether the audit shall extend to all at a particular level in the organization, to a sample of the audit population, how large a sample, and so on. The questionnaire, with an accompanying introductory letter and a glossary, is then sent out as agreed. The completed questionnaires are then analysed by computer first in general then in specific area terms, the extent of this analysis having been agreed at the contract stage.

Questionnaires can obviously be used as straight alternatives to structured interviews, whatever the approach. However, if used for this purpose there are even more dangers. Predetermined questions which would have been posed at an interview are written into the questionnaire, such as:

- What problems do you encounter in your work?
- Which aspects of your work do you like most?
- Which aspects of your work do you like least?
- What do you feel have been your major accomplishments?
- How could your work be improved?
- What goals do you have?
- What training needs do you feel you have?

It is essential that the questions are open and can be answered by more than a few cryptic words. The problems which relate to such a questionnaire are all those cited as being related to the interview, in addition to the fact that:

- there is even less flexibility
- the answers cannot be challenged
- the respondents may answer perfunctorily
- the questionnaire may not be returned.

Diary method

An individual, or group of individuals, is requested to maintain a diary at work over an agreed period of time. The entries in the diary must relate to their activities during the agreed period. Depending on the use which is to be made of the analysis of the diary, either only the activities are noted (or additionally the time involved is shown), or certain categories are selected for noting whenever they occur. At the end of the agreed period the diary entries are analysed and conclusions drawn for immediate use or amalgamation with information obtained by other approaches.

This method has been used very successfully, but to ensure that it is effective, the people completing the diary must be fully committed to the completion since it is easy to forget to enter items or, if you are not a 'diary' sort of person, to fail to complete it over the required period. The diary is also very susceptible to the inclusion of entries which fill it up 'because there should be an entry about that' or 'I'd better put something in for that period, otherwise it will look bad.'

On the positive side, however, diary analyses have shown aspects of work to recur when this was not appreciated, or take up more time than was realized, or to have been given too high a priority.

Critical incident technique

The critical incident approach can be used with either groups or individuals, both situations requiring similar techniques. The individual is asked to identify and record each day or week an incident or activity which was the most difficult to do that day or week. In this respect, as in the subsequent analysis, it is rather like the diary method, but since it does not require constant or continuous attention it is more likely to be acceptable.

An alternative method of dealing with groups is to use the critical person approach. Here the group is asked to identify a 'bad' manager for whom they have worked and to write down words which describe the aspects which in their view made him 'bad'. The various views are collated to produce a combined description of the areas in which problems can occur. This approach can be considered the negative approach. A similar exercise can then take place but this time identifying the factors which made a 'good' manager they have known – this is the positive side of the analysis.

This latter approach is similar to the performance questionnaire which is a questionnaire in which the respondents discriminate between two statements – one of effective operation, the other of ineffective – applied to a number of skills and attitudes. There is the risk that this type of questionnaire will become lifeless, so respondents are asked to complete it in terms of someone effective they have known, and then somebody ineffective.

Brainstorming

Brainstorming has long been known as an effective problem-solving technique, but it can be readily adapted to produce an analysis of training needs when the analyst has a group of people who are willing to work with him in this way.

Brainstorming has its basis in the lateral thinking approach of creative thinkers such as Edward de Bono. A meeting is organized with the objective of producing as many ideas as possible but without evaluating them at that time. The discussion of any idea generated is banned so as to ensure that free-thinking is not dampened and so that what might appear to be a wild idea may in fact turn out to be perfectly operable.

The group leader, perhaps the analyst in this case, presents the brainstorm topic such as 'The training needs of a newly-appointed supervisor', and asks for ideas. These usually come slowly at first and then more quickly as the group relaxes and enters into the spirit of the exercise. Initially the ideas which emerge are usually traditional but become more radical when the group starts thinking laterally instead of only logically and rationally; they may become very radical towards the end when the members feel they may be throwing in ideas only to make the numbers up. It is often these later ideas which can become the most important, perhaps not as proposed but with modifications.

The list of ideas produced during the brainstorm is later analysed or evaluated by the same or another group, or by the individual whose responsibility it might be to make the decision. The results can be much more extensive and wide-ranging than from many other methods, but it has the disadvantage that the whole process can be lengthy and time-consuming.

Mirroring

Mirroring is an extension of intergroup, interactive processes which brings problem issues out into the open and produces effective solutions as a result of this openness. In the same way, the technique can be used in evaluation by encouraging the surfacing of negative, ineffective and inappropriate views and attitudes.

One example could be when two or three conflicting groups are brought together and are required to ask the question of each other: 'What do you think that *we* think *your* opinion of us is?'

This question asked of, say, the marketing group by the production group might produce the answer: 'We (the marketing group) think that you (the production group) think that we (the marketing group) consider you (the production group) as a bunch of dirty-nailed labourers without any other thoughts ... (and so on).'

The way is now open for the other group to comment on this view, but without direct threat as all that has been said is what somebody else thinks that you are thinking. Consequently with this once-removed statement there is considerable room for discussion and misconceptions can be clarified so that the real outline of a job and its characteristics can be determined to everybody's satisfaction.

Psychological tests

The climate favouring the use of psychological tests varies very widely and even when it is highly supportive there are many individuals and organizations who will not even consider their use. The opposite situation applies in times when such approaches are out of favour – many will still want to use them.

Psychological tests are not commonly used in job analysis since they are intended principally to test the person rather than the job. However, because the person has a strong influence on the job in so many cases, particularly in the non-technical types of work, the tests must be an instrument supporting the analysis. The word 'support' is significant as it is in this role that the tests and their results will be most useful – as an aid to other job analysis approaches. One useful approach to which psychological tests can be put in job analysis is in the identification of a person profile for that job. If the people who are performing the job effectively are tested and a common profile emerges, this can then become a profile for the job; a tool which can be particularly useful in selection processes. However, if an individual differs considerably from the common profile, such a difference suggests that it is worth investigating this individual who may have some training needs; training needs which have created a different profile.

Using psychological tests in job analysis requires caution since, even with a reliable and validated test, results are not guaranteed 100 per cent.

4 Techniques of analysis: the Repertory Grid

Within the analysis approaches described in the previous chapter, the ways in which they are used and the methods employed are very varied. In the observational approach the methods can range from simply observing without a plan to a very rigidly structured method. Similarly, the techniques of interviewing can vary considerably. One of these is known as the Repertory Grid.

Aims of the Repertory Grid

The technique of repertory grids for use in interviewing and obtaining views, information and attitudes arose from Kelly's clinical work in 1953 on what are termed the 'personal constructs' of people. Kelly suggested that our minds construct maps of what we see about us in both material and people terms and these maps, which are highly individual in nature, guide our behaviour. From this basis two assumptions are made:

1. If we can identify an individual's 'construct' map there is a strong possibility we can predict that individual's behaviour.
2. We may be able to modify an individual's map, and therefore behaviour, by some form of training.

There is little quantitative evidence to support these assumptions but qualitative evidence abounds. As far as the first assumption is concerned, we know that when we get to know a person well we also discover 'how they think', and in most cases we can predict how they will react to a given situation. Should the second assumption not be true, there has been considerable time and money wasted training people to behave differently!

The Repertory Grid uses the concept of the individual possession of personal constructs in an interview situation and from this is determined the individual's views of the subject. The principal value in the use of the grid compared with a number of other techniques is that the interviewer can have a minimal role and consequently the respondent's views are less susceptible to external contamination.

This technique exposes two aspects of the Repertory Grid:

1. *Elements* are the objects of a individual's thinking and to which they relate their concepts or values. These elements may be people – 'an effective manager I know, an ineffective one, an average one' – or they may be objects or abstract or concrete concepts – 'the Repertory Grid technique, the in-depth interview, the psychological test'.

2.   *Constructs* are the qualities we use to describe the elements in our personal, individual
     world. 'He is an effective manager because he has a humane relationship with his staff'
     reflects one personal construct as applied to the element of a known, assessed effective,
     manager.

During the Repertory Grid interview a relatively simple approach which relates an
individual's constructs directly with the elements is used.

First, the elements are listed and, as suggested earlier, these usually include a range of
effective, ineffective and average performers, or other elements related to the subject being
investigated.

When these elements have been listed the range of qualities which the individual uses
to describe the elements is encouraged to emerge and these qualities are rated over the range
of elements. From these views a matrix of comparisons is produced, usually with scored
ratings for each element against each construct.

Most problems and difficulties occur when all the data has been gathered: it has to be
analysed and, as there may be more than 50 items of information or ratings multiplied by
the number of individuals involved in the exercise, the problems can be extreme. To aid the
analytical process a number of pre-written programs for computer use have been produced
and these can certainly speed the production of an end result. Some analysis is possible,
however, by manual methods, although this is necessarily time-consuming.

The Repertory Grid in practice

Let us use as an example to demonstrate the grid, an analysis of the qualities required in a
management trainer, with a view to writing a behavioural job description. In order to obtain
a representative view a group of existing management trainers and a group of managers who
have undergone a reasonable amount of training will be used. The grid, of course, can be
used with an individual if the intention is to analyse that person's views only. The procedure
followed is the same whether with groups or with an individual, but the use of groups
means that:

1.   A greater sample view is obtained
2.   More grids have to be analysed

whereas when the grid is applied to an individual:

1.   The results relate to that individual alone
2.   Only one grid has to be analysed.

A grid scoring form is used and a typical example of such a form is reproduced as Figure 4.1.
The number of vertical columns depends on the number of elements used.

The number of horizontal columns is not critical as more than one sheet can be used
for the constructs if this should become necessary. In this example, six elements will be used
to ensure that everybody knows in sufficient detail the same number of people. Nine or
more elements are preferable, but this number is not always possible. The process of
producing the Repertory Grid can be broken down into nine steps.

REPERTORY GRID SCORING SHEET

	1	2	3	4	5	6	7	8	9	

Figure 4.1

STEP ONE

The members of the group identify six management trainers whom they know quite well. If possible, these management trainers should fall into the categories of two effective trainers, two not very effective trainers and two roughly average ones.

STEP TWO

Each member is given six pieces of card or paper on which they write the names of the people they have identified in step one. These are the elements described earlier. A number can also be added to the card, the number being related to that at the head of the column on the scoring sheet. Alternatively, the name itself can be entered on the scoring sheet as well, as in Figure 4.2.

REPERTORY GRID SCORING SHEET

(Pairs similarity)	JOE 1	FRED 2	MARY 3	HARRY 4	JEAN 5	EDDIE 6	7	8	9	(Singles description)
Fat	X 1	X 5	X 2	3	4	1				Thin

Figure 4.2

STEP THREE

Three cards are selected, for example 1, 2 and 3, and each member is asked to identify some aspect related to management training effectiveness which makes two of the three people selected different from the third. As a very simple construct this might be 'fat' for the pair.

The construct word or phrase, in this case 'fat', is written in the top left-hand space of the vertical columns. In the top right-hand space of the vertical columns is written the description of the singleton, the 'odd one out of the three'. In this case it will probably be 'thin'.

This process of obtaining constructs from the three people is continued until no further constructs can be elicited.

STEP FOUR

Once the constructs have been elicited and entered on the sheet, the cards are returned to the pile.

Each 'element' person is then given a score of, for example, 1 to 5. A score of 1 or 2 is allocated to those who fit or nearly fit the description in the left-hand column, the column with the description of the pair. Scores of 5 or 4 are allocated to those who fit or nearly fit the description in the right-hand column, the description of the singleton. This completion is shown in Figure 4.2 for one construct.

STEP FIVE

A different set of three cards is then selected, say cards 4, 5 and 6 and the process in steps 3 and 4 is repeated, always ensuring that the pairs description is recorded in the left-hand column and a score of 1 or 2 relates to the pairs similarity and 4 and 5 to the singles description. A score of 3 is an average or middle-of-the-road score. It helps if at least one 1 and one 5 are allocated – these will usually be from the set of three people for whom the constructs are being elicited.

STEP SIX

Step five is repeated so that the various combinations of the elements can be covered or until the participants run out of constructs to enter.

A suitable series for 6 or 9 elements would be:

6 elements	9 elements
1 2 3	1 2 3
4 5 6	4 5 6
1 3 6	7 8 9
2 4 6	1 3 5
1 2 4	2 4 6
3 5 6	3 5 9
2 3 5	4 6 8
1 4 6	1 8 9
and so on	1 2 9
	and so on

The grid consideration is now complete and the grid scoring sheet of each participant records their views of each element against each construct which has been offered. Obviously much data has been generated and the problem arises of analysing the data. As suggested earlier, the analysis can be produced on the computer, using one of the pre-written programs, but not everybody has recourse to a computer and this may lead to the danger that the grid approach is ignored or rejected.

However, there is a manual approach which can extract a substantial amount of information from a grid. We can continue our example to see how this is done. Steps 1 to 6 are carried out and part of a possible scoring sheet of one of the participants is shown in

Figure 4.3. In this case the constructs are those related to the behavioural aspects of the management trainer. The person conducting the exercise must be careful not to contaminate the results by suggesting constructs – these must be the result of the thoughts of the individual participants and expressed in their own words. However, the constructs must be understandable, particularly if a number of people are involved, so the analyst can help to clarify the wording of the construct – without changing its meaning.

Once the constructs have been listed against the elements as far as is possible or desirable, the grid results can be scored to produce a ready to use analysis.

STEP SEVEN

In this example we are considering the behavioural aspects of a management trainer related to his overall effectiveness, therefore at the end of the grid the participants are asked to rate the elements in a single, given construct over a scale effective to ineffective. This rating is shown at the bottom of Figure 4.3.

The scoring for overall effectiveness can then be compared with individual aspects to highlight differences and provide effectiveness indicators. In order that a check on scoring can be made the overall effectiveness scores are reversed. This reversed rating is also shown at the bottom of Figure 4.3.

STEP EIGHT

The scorings for each construct line are obtained by producing and noting the difference for each element against the overall effectiveness figures. For example, for the first construct we find:

Runs courses with many activities	1^{-}_{4}	1^{-}_{4}	2^{-}_{2}	4^{1}_{1}	3^{1}_{1}	5^{-}_{4}	$^{2}_{16R}$	Most of course consists of lectures.
Effective		1	1	2	3	4	5	Ineffective
Effective reversed		5	5	4	3	2	1	Ineffective reversed

The larger figures are the original scorings, the small figures the difference (it doesn't matter whether + or –) between these scorings and the effectiveness ratings, both direct and reversed. The direct differences are the upper, small figures and the reversed differences the lower, smaller figures. The differences have been added to the scoring sheet and are included in Figure 4.4.

If the total scores for a construct show the reversed score difference to be smaller than the direct, effective score, the construct descriptions should be reversed. An example of this is shown at the bottom of Figure 4.4.

REPERTORY GRID SCORING SHEET

	JOE 1	FRED 2	MARY 3	HARRY 4	JEAN 5	EDDIE 6	7	8	9	
Runs courses with many activities	x	x				x				Most of course consists of lectures
	1	1	2	4	3	5				
Uses a wide range of aids in lectures			x	x	x					Just talks in lectures
	3	2	1	2	5	3				
Has an empathy with students	x		x			x				Has a stand-offish approach
	1	2	2	5	3	5				
Is a swashbuckler in arrangements		x		x	x					Has careful approach to training arrangements
	3	1	4	2	5	5				
Prefers learner-centred training	x		x	x						Prefers tutor-centred training
	1	4	5	2	3	5				
Is knowledgeable over a wide range of methods		x			x	x				Limited knowledge of methods
	2	1	3	3	5	2				
Has an easy articulation	x	x		x						Explanations are unclear
	1	2	3	5	4	3				
Always presents a good professional appearance	x	x	x							Can often be over-casually dressed
	1	5	2	3	1	5				
Prefers to work unaided				x	x	x				Always wants tutor support
	1	3	2	1	3	5				
Activist	x	x			x					Reflector
	2	1	3	4	5	3				
Effective	1	1	2	3	4	5				Ineffective
(reversed scores)	5	5	4	3	2	1				

Figure 4.3

STEP NINE

We are now in a position to analyse the various constructs on the basis of the lower the score, the more significant is that aspect in the effectiveness ranking, at least in the view of the person completing the grid. From the example used, the aspects which go towards the behavioural skills of a management trainer, in descending order of effectiveness, are:

Runs courses with many activities	2	
Has an empathy with students	5	
Prefers to work unaided	5	More
Is an activist	6	effective
Articulates easily	6	aspects

Is knowledgeable over a wide range of methods	6	
Always presents a good professional appearance	7	
Is a swashbuckler in arrangements	8	Less
Prefers learner-centred training	8	effective
Uses a wide range of methods	8	aspects
Trained externally	11	

Of course these are the views of only one individual and may, on their own, represent an extreme view. If, however, as large a group as possible is asked to complete the grid, a more representative picture should emerge, even if this is based on a majority view. When analysing the views of a large number of people, it may be useful to sort out the views into tops and tails – say the four lowest scoring and the four highest – from each participant. Although different words may have been used by different people, the same general views can usually be expressed in one category, but beware of categorizing with one's own bias in view. At least two other people can be brought into this process to avoid contamination of the categorization, either on a discussive basis to decide on overlapping statements or as independent categorizers. The top set of categories can then be stated as the most effective aspects necessary.

Even the widest approach in this way can still introduce bias – namely that of the trainers themselves who may see the role of the trainer in a completely different way from the people they train. So, in order to reflect these possibly different views the exercise can be repeated with a group of people who are the normal training population of the trainers concerned. The two final lists can then be compared to identify any different views and to take these into account in the final analysis.

Interviewer intervention

The procedure above describes the role of the analyst as a provider of a description of the method and pieces of paper; a monitor of the correct operation of the process; and as the subsequent principal analyst, although steps 7, 8 and 9 can be performed by the grid participants themselves. Any further intrusion, particularly in suggesting constructs, will contaminate the exercise. Obviously the grid results can be analysed in much greater depth than suggested in the analysis described above, but it will be in such an extension that the computer will become necessary.

The practical intervention of the analyst, although always attempting to avoid contamination, may consist of the selection of element headings for consideration. The analyst may also *help* the participant to produce constructs or clarify them by asking questions designed to aid the individual, but must never suggest constructs except the final comparison ranging from effectiveness to ineffectiveness.

REPERTORY GRID SCORING SHEET

	JOE 1	FRED 2	MARY 3	HARRY 4	JEAN 5	EDDIE 6	7	8	9		
Runs courses with many activities	$\frac{x^-}{1_4}$	$\frac{x^-}{1_4}$	$\frac{-}{2_2}$	$\frac{1}{4_1}$	$\frac{1}{3_1}$	$\frac{x^-}{5_4}$				Most of course consists of lectures	2 R16
Uses a wide range of aids in lectures	$\frac{2}{3_2}$	$\frac{1}{2_3}$	$\frac{x^1}{1_3}$	$\frac{x^1}{2_1}$	$\frac{x^1}{5_3}$	$\frac{2}{3_2}$				Just talks in lectures	8 R14
Has an empathy with students	$\frac{x^-}{1_4}$	$\frac{1}{2_3}$	$\frac{x^-}{2_2}$	$\frac{3}{5_2}$	$\frac{1}{3_1}$	$\frac{x^-}{5_4}$				Has a stand-offish approach	5 R16
Is a swashbuckler in arrangements	$\frac{2}{3_2}$	$\frac{x^-}{1_4}$	$\frac{2}{4_-}$	$\frac{x^1}{2_1}$	$\frac{x^3}{5_3}$	$\frac{-}{5_4}$				Has careful approach to training arrangements	8 R14
Prefers learner-centred training	$\frac{x^-}{1_4}$	$\frac{3}{4_1}$	$\frac{x^3}{5_1}$	$\frac{x^1}{2_1}$	$\frac{1}{3_1}$	$\frac{-}{5_4}$				Prefers tutor-centred training	8 R12
Is knowledgeable over a wide range of methods	$\frac{1}{2_3}$	$\frac{x^-}{1_4}$	$\frac{1}{3_1}$	$\frac{-}{3_-}$	$\frac{x^1}{5_3}$	$\frac{x^3}{2_1}$				Limited knowledge of methods	6 R12
Has an easy articulation	$\frac{x^-}{1_4}$	$\frac{x^1}{2_3}$	$\frac{1}{3_1}$	$\frac{x^2}{5_2}$	$\frac{-}{4_2}$	$\frac{2}{3_2}$				Explanations are unclear	6 R14
Always presents a good professional appearance	$\frac{x^-}{1_4}$	$\frac{x^4}{5_-}$	$\frac{x^-}{2_2}$	$\frac{-}{3_-}$	$\frac{3}{1_1}$	$\frac{-}{5_5}$				Can often be over-casually dressed	7 R11
Prefers to work unaided	$\frac{-}{1_4}$	$\frac{2}{3_2}$	$\frac{-}{2_2}$	$\frac{x^2}{1_2}$	$\frac{x^1}{3_1}$	$\frac{x^-}{5_4}$				Always wants tutor support	5 R15
Activist	$\frac{x^1}{2_3}$	$\frac{x^-}{1_4}$	$\frac{1}{3_1}$	$\frac{1}{4_4}$	$\frac{x^1}{5_3}$	$\frac{2}{3_2}$				Reflector	6 R14
Effective	1	1	2	3	4	5				Ineffective	
(reversed scores)	5	5	4	3	2	1					
Trained externally	$\frac{x^-}{1_4}$	$\frac{x^1}{2_3}$	$\frac{x^3}{5_1}$	$\frac{2}{5_2}$	$\frac{3}{1_1}$	$\frac{4}{1_-}$				Trained internally	13 R11

Figure 4.4

Problems of the Repertory Grid

The grid technique is obviously not without problems – few techniques are – and contamination by the analyst as described can certainly be a possible problem, particularly when the participants are having difficulty in providing constructs.

Time is a particularly significant problem since the completion of the grid is not always straightforward. The larger and therefore more reliable the grid, the longer it takes to complete and the greater the risk of loss of interest on the part of the completer. If the completer is involved in all the stages the risk of loss of interest will be minimized, but with a resultant increase in time involvement. Even a relatively simple grid as used in the example will take the major part of an hour to set up and complete the constructs. The scoring then has to be completed, and the simple analysis. From start to finish the time necessary can range between a minimum of an hour to more than two hours.

If there are a number of interviewees involved, more time will be needed and certainly more time will be necessary for analysis. The location of interviewees is linked with time. The problems associated with location are eased if those people who have to be interviewed are all together in one place. If they are scattered throughout the country obvious problems of time, availability, travelling and cost are introduced.

An initial problem of definition, particularly in the setting and wording of the objectives and the relevancy of the elements to these objectives, can negate the remainder of the exercise. Smith and Ashton cite the case of a list of dog vaccines used as elements in an analysis which involved vets. Unfortunately the vets had insufficient knowledge of all the vaccines put forward as elements and the construction of the grid was very difficult as a result. It may therefore be necessary to restrict to some extent the range of elements and constructs used. However, if too much control is imposed, the results can be unreliable through contamination or reaction by those participating. If there is no control, the choices made by the participants can be so wide and individually centred that any comparisons are impossible.

In spite of the problems suggested in the use of the Repertory Grid technique, particularly in the eliciting of constructs, there can be little doubt that it is a method which has a low risk of contamination by the views, values and attitudes of the interviewer. It is a very time-consuming method and consequently there is a risk that the individuals may lose interest during the grid construction. A particular, common problem is the difficulty of finding constructs. This can be caused by the recommended method of using three elements and determining differences between two of them compared with the third. It is often difficult to find an aspect which is common to only two of the elements. Sometimes there can be a difference between two of the elements which cannot be identified with the third element. I have discovered through experience that the problem is solved by asking the participant to produce comparisons between two elements. After all the basic principle of eliciting constructs is to obtain comparisons between elements: if the participants can produce constructs by producing comparison between two elements, the objective has been achieved.

5 Techniques of analysis: observational methods

The Repertory Grid described in the last chapter involved directly those people performing or receiving the work under consideration, and asked them to do something practical, even to the stage of the final analysis. However, there are other approaches which exclude the direct involvement of the people being analysed and require only the involvement of the analyst. These approaches are concerned with job analysis by observation and provide objective and quantitative assessments. The various approaches can be classified roughly as process observation and behavioural observation. Process observation is strictly concerned with what is done in the job in functional terms such as turning a tap, picking up a pen and so on. Behaviour observation is interested in what is said, how it is said, the manner of the person and so on.

Process observation

Most jobs or tasks involve the practitioner in doing something which is visible to the observer, either all the time or most of the time. The observation of these practical activities is called process observation and gives us most of our information about most jobs.

Process observation can range from simple, unstructured work observation to highly sophisticated approaches. It exists even in the situation where Auntie Flo, on a coach trip to a pottery works, having watched the potters at their tasks for a while, turns to Auntie Mabel and says 'I didn't realize that the job was so complicated!'

At the other end of the spectrum is someone such as the work study expert who observes the performance of a job against a check list of all the tasks to be performed. They note such things as which tasks are or are not performed, how often they are performed, how long each operation and task takes and so on. The results are then analysed to identify superfluous operations, and solutions are offered to tasks which take too long to perform. These observations and analyses are timed within seconds and fractions of seconds.

The more commonly practised approaches lie between Auntie Flo and the work study expert approach and involve a relatively simple observational tool. This process or job content observation sheet lists the range of specific tasks involved in a job or sub-tasks in a task. The observer watches the worker and logs a scoring mark on the sheet each time a task or sub-task is performed. For example, if we are observing the activities of the hotel receptionist, we are aware from the job specification or some previous observation, that a range of tasks are performed within the job. These tasks, such as answering the telephone, responding to customer enquiries, issuing receipts, are listed and scored as the receptionist performs the task. At the end of the observational period or periods, the observation sheets are analysed and this analysis can determine how often each task is performed, at which time of the day the tasks are performed most, and so on. An example process observation sheet is shown in Figure 5.1.

Behaviour observation

The methods of behaviour observation have many similarities with those of process observation, which is natural since it is the observation of someone performing an activity. But on this occasion the interest lies in the behaviour of the performer rather than the practical functions of the job.

Behaviour observation is based on the selection of categories of behaviour which may or may not be involved in the job, observation of the incidence of these behaviours and an annotation of this incidence and subsequent analysis of these annotations. The selection of the behaviour categories is relatively simple if it is known beforehand which behaviours are needed to perform the job and which behaviours are not. If, however, the observation is general in its approach or the analysis is investigatory, the range of behaviours chosen may have to be extensive. The criteria for the selection of the behaviour categories will relate to the type of operation being observed and the reasons for the observation. If the activity is that of a group leader or a chairman, the categories will be different from those required in the observation of a one-to-one interview.

Let us use the example of an appraisal interview which we wish to analyse by behaviour observation. We are generally aware of the behaviours used in such an activity, but we wish to analyse how often each behaviour occurs and relate this to the effectiveness of the interviewer.

Behaviour categories

We must first decide which behaviours to observe and analyse. The interviewer will naturally have to ask questions, give information, make suggestions, support or disagree with the interviewee, and so on. Some of the categories can be subdivided in order to define more closely the behaviour. For example, questioning can be divided into various forms such as closed, multiple, and leading. Similarly proposals or suggestions can be subdivided into effective and ineffective proposals, content and procedure proposals, suggestions as opposed to proposals and so on.

The range of categories can also be determined from previous observations of interviews in which the interview is analysed first in terms of the categories used and how frequently they occur.

The final decision on the number of categories is based on the physical restrictions of the observer: how experienced the observer is in conducting analyses and how many categories can be controlled to a reasonable level of accuracy of observation. In general, the more experienced the observer, the greater number of categories can be observed.

A basic list of categories would probably consist of:

- Asking questions
- Giving information

Hotel Receptionist

Time periods

									TOTAL

Answers telephone

Makes telephone call – internal

                  – external

Answers customer enquiry – rooms

                  – meals

                  – other

Figure 5.1   Process/content analysis

- Suggesting/proposing
- Supporting
- Disagreeing
- Interrupting
- Other behaviours.

This list is capable of giving a reasonable analysis of an interaction yet is short enough to be coped with by a relatively inexperienced observer. But most experienced observers should be capable of handling more categories, particularly as the interaction involves the observation of two people only, or even one if the interviewer alone is being observed. This is quite different from observing a group in which an observer has to score the category contributions of a number of people.

A realistic list of categories under these circumstances could consist of:

- Suggesting/proposing
- Open questions
- Closed questions
- Multiple questions
- Leading questions
- Reflections
- Giving information
- Disagreeing (without reasons stated)
- Disagreeing (with reasons stated)
- Testing understanding
- Summarizing
- Open
- Supporting
- Attacking/blocking
- Interrupting.

Definitions of categories

Most of these categories are straightforward in their meaning but some have definitions which extend their usefulness. It is obviously essential that the observer understands completely the definitions of the categories so that there can be no confusion. This requirement also demands that the categories themselves must be clear and capable of unequivocal definition, be capable of identification, and sufficiently different from each other to warrant a separate category, and meaningful.

SUGGESTING/PROPOSING

These are the ideas put forward for discussion or agreement leading to a positive end result of the interaction. They can take various forms and will range from ideas put forward for consideration to directives to perform in a particular way. Examples of this range can be:

'I suggest that we ... '
'I propose we do ... '
'Let's do ... '
'How do you feel if we ... '
'I think your approach should be ... '

OPEN QUESTIONS

These questions are usually prefaced by 'what?' 'why?' 'how?' and leave the way open to the respondents to give detailed answers limited only by the depth which they are willing to disclose. Such a question might be: 'What did you think of the event?'

CLOSED QUESTIONS

These can be answered by a simple 'yes' or 'no' and have to be followed up to elicit fuller information. A question such as: 'Did you enjoy that event?' might lead to the answer 'No', which in turn would lead to the further question 'Why did you not enjoy it?' The eventual information could usually have been obtained by asking an open question in the first place, thus saving a number of questions. However, there are occasions when a closed question is the appropriate approach.

MULTIPLE QUESTIONS

Unless the respondent has a particularly astute mind and can handle three or more questions at the same time and will answer them all unprompted, the multiple question is dangerous. If one asks: 'Well now, I want to get your views on the present situation, so can you tell me what you think is happening with x. Of course, this has an effect on conditions in y. What do you think of this effect? And I see you have recently come back from z. What were things like there?' Assuming the respondent has not been completely confused, an answer is most likely to be given to only the last question, as that was the last one heard. The respondent will select this area to answer because it was the last subject, and also because it is a question which poses the least threat. If you need to know the answer to all three subjects, pose them as three separate questions.

LEADING QUESTIONS

Whether the intention is deliberate or not, a question from a boss to a subordinate couched in the terms: 'Don't you feel it is time we ... ?' will tell the subordinate first that the boss feels that it is time and secondly that the *boss* feels that the subordinate should also feel that it is time. Of course the *subordinate* can ignore the leading implications, treating the question as a closed one and answering 'yes' or 'no' (the latter perhaps at their peril!).

REFLECTIONS

These are restatements of what the speaker has just said, usually made with the intention of encouraging them to continue with that topic. 'You feel that it is time that you did something about ... ', expressed as a statement not as a question is such a category.

GIVING INFORMATION

This is the category used to describe statements offering either information or views, thoughts or opinions, feelings or attitudes.

DISAGREEING (WITHOUT REASONS STATED)

As a category this is used to denote bald, blunt statements of disagreement such as 'I disagree', 'No, I don't agree with that' or 'No, I can't go along with that.' The disagreement is stated without reasons being given. It can elicit a variety of responses ranging from 'Why do you disagree?' through non-reaction to 'Who do you think you are to disagree with me!'

DISAGREEING (WITH REASONS STATED)

This is much more likely to produce a positive response since, although the disagreement is still there, the basis for it is explained.

TESTING UNDERSTANDING

This is a category in which one interactor questions whether what has been said by the other person has been understood correctly. 'If I got it correctly, you feel that you ... Is that right?'

SUMMARIZING

This is the collective statement usually, although not always, made by the chairman or leader, which summarizes what has been discussed and what has been agreed during the interaction up to that particular stage. Interim summaries are valuable so that all parties are clear about progress through the various stages, with a summary at the end to tie everything together. A summary can, of course, occur at the beginning of an interaction if it is the continuance of a previous meeting: in this case it is concerned with recounting the stage reached by the previous meeting.

OPEN

An open contribution is made when an error or mistake is admitted or regret is expressed, such as 'I'm sorry. That was my mistake. I should have noticed it in the report.'

SUPPORTING

This category of behaviour occurs when an overt, direct, verbal statement is made supporting another person's views, feelings, opinions, ideas or proposals. It can take the simple form of 'I agree' or 'Yes, I'll go along with that', or can be a long statement repeating what has just been said, but in different words.

ATTACKING/BLOCKING

These two categories are put together as they are both negative rather than supportive. The 'attacking' category is used when the statement is openly aggressive or abusive and has an emotional context. For example 'I might have expected *you* to suggest that' will readily be seen as an attack on the proposer, eliciting the likely response of an equally attacking retort, and so on along the attack/defend spiral.

Blocking occurs when a contribution is made which adds nothing of positive value to the interaction. The classical block is 'Oh, we're just going around in circles.' This may indeed be true, but stating it so bluntly only halts the interaction. Someone else then has to take a positive step to move the interaction forward.

INTERRUPTING

When one or more persons interrupt a speaker while he or she is speaking, very clear messages are being given which are important indicators of the effectiveness of the interaction. Among other things, the interrupter is saying to the speaker:

'Shut up'
'I'm not listening to what you are saying'
'What I have to say is more important than what you are saying.'

Behaviour observation forms

If we wish to observe an interaction in detail and make notes on it, the last thing we want is a complicated observation instrument. Our observation form must be as simple as possible yet be capable of producing results suitable for analysis.

Figure 5.2 illustrates a useful form of observational and analytical instrument which can be used to observe the appraisal interview we are using as an example. It lists the 15 categories previously defined, each category occupying a horizontal row, with vertical columns for the participants.

As the interaction proceeds, a stroke is place in the column relating to the person making the contribution, and against the identified category of that contribution. Figure 5.2 shows that the interviewer made the first contribution of the interaction by describing to the interviewee the form that the interview would take. This is shown by a stroke against the category 'giving information'.

More strokes are added as each participant makes a contribution and the completed observation sheet appears in Figure 5.3.

Analysis of the interaction

The analytical observational record of the appraisal interview shown in Figure 5.3 demonstrates the behaviour pattern of a not very effective interviewer. It can be seen from the number of proposals made by the interviewer and the lack of proposals made by the interviewee that the interview took a very prescriptive line. This pattern is reflected throughout the record of the interview and it is obvious that the event was far from being

	INT'ER	INT'EE	TOTAL
Suggesting/proposing			
Open questions			
Closed questions			
Multiple questions			
Leading questions			
Reflecting			
Giving information			
Disagreeing without reasons			
Disagreeing with reasons			
Testing understanding			
Summarizing			
Supporting			
Open			
Attacking/blocking			
Interrupting			
TOTALS			

Figure 5.2   Behaviour observation form

an effective appraisal. The record shows that the majority of contributions have been made by the interviewer stating their own opinions, asking closed questions, disagreeing and other negative behaviour. The effects of this approach by the interviewer can be seen in the contributions of the interviewee. The interviewee offers little information and is forced to disagree with the interviewer by interrupting frequently when the interviewer was talking.

Neil Rackham and Terry Morgan have undertaken research into appraisal interview behaviour by using behaviour analysis to assess effective behaviours. In order to examine the behaviour of expert appraisers it was first necessary to identify criteria for effectiveness. The criteria identified included whether the appraisees judged the interviews to have been worthwhile and useful; whether the appraisee's performance improved following the interview; and whether there was effective action by the interviewer following the interview. Using these criteria, 117 appraisers were judged as 'expert' and a further 61 were considered on a random choice basis and classified as 'average'. The expert group was eventually reduced to 93, 61 of whom produced two tapes each of appraisal interviews they had conducted, and 32 of whom who produced one tape each, resulting in a total of 154 interviews.

	INT'ER	INT'EE	TOTAL
Suggesting/proposing	7	1	8
Open questions	2	5	7
Closed questions	18	5	23
Multiple questions	9	–	9
Leading questions	12	–	12
Reflecting	–	–	–
Giving information	28	5	33
Disagreeing without reasons	2	1	3
Disagreeing with reasons	14	14	28
Testing understanding	–	–	–
Summarizing	1	–	1
Supporting	1	1	2
Open	–	–	–
Attacking/blocking	8	6	14
Interrupting	8	18	26
TOTALS	110	56	166

Figure 5.3   Behaviour observation form completed

On analysis these interviews produced a behaviour pattern which showed significant differences between expert and average appraisers. This information is shown in the table.

| | % of total behaviour | |
	Expert appraisers	Average appraisers
Proposing	8.1	16.2
Building	4.7	1.8
Supporting	11.7	8.3
Disagreeing	7.2	6.8
Defending/attacking	0.2	1.3
Testing understanding	8.3	3.1
Summarizing	6.4	2.3
Seeking information	15.1	12.7
Seeking proposals/solutions	6.4	2.0
Giving internal information	14.9	12.0
Giving external information	17.0	33.5

(Reproduced from *Behaviour Analysis in Training* by Neil Rackham and Terry Morgan (1977) by kind permission of the authors.)

Behaviour analysis is probably one of the most objective methods of observation and analysis and has a wide and varied use. Observational research with this base has identified a number of appropriate approaches defined in behaviour categories. This research data can thus be compared with the results of other observations and the necessary conclusions made. It will be seen later that behavioural observation and analysis can be introduced at the initial analysis stage, during training events to determine continuous change, and at the end of the training to identify any terminal change from the initial state.

6 Now we're ready to train

Preceding chapters have suggested that it is of little value even to consider validation or evaluation if the initial groundwork has not been laid in order to determine the extent of the change, or training, necessary.

It has also been suggested that, if it has not already been obtained, data as quantitative as possible should be determined about:

1. What the job requires in terms of knowledge, skills and attitudes;
2. What knowledge, skills and attitude levels are currently possessed by the potential training population.

From this data the gap between 1 and 2 should be determined: the level of existing knowledge, skills and attitude produces the training need. The information required in 1 and 2 above can be obtained in a number of ways such as through job descriptions, job analysis, job specification and job/task observation.

By this stage the needs of an individual or group should be clear, and from what level they need to start. If at the end of the training event, or subsequently, new levels of knowledge, skill or attitude are found to be higher than at the start, the training is validated and the organization will be receiving some benefit. At least one can make this *assumption* and in some cases it must be an assumption.

If the training need and the existing level are determined both immediately before the training event and immediately afterward, there can be little doubt about the role played by the training. It is claimed, sometimes as an excuse for not taking any positive action, that pre-training assessment of learners is not always possible for a variety of reasons. Perhaps there are situations when it is not always possible to assess each individual's starting level in absolute and objective terms, but this is not an excuse for doing nothing at all. If evaluation is to be possible two 'measures' must be available – the level of knowledge, skill or attitude immediately at the start of the training programme, and the level immediately at the end of the programme. If the training and the learning have been successful, a positive change will have taken place and it is this change that evaluation must identify. But the criterion must be that to assess/measure this change, the starting point must be known.

In some cases tests of knowledge, skills and attitude will be possible to measure the change from pre- to post-situations. In other cases the assessment will be based on the experienced judgement of the trainers. In yet others, the trainers' judgements will be supported by self-assessment of their own levels. These last two methods can be highly subjective and are sometimes rejected by evaluation purists because of this subjectivity. But if subjective assessment only is possible in a subjective situation, this is the only option and must be accepted as such. After all, so much training and learning is subjective in nature and it would be ridiculous to try to require only objective testing. If subjective evaluation only is possible, take this option and evaluate subjectively. Failure to take any action at all on the grounds of rejection because of subjectivity, particularly at the start of any training programme, is to accept that this type of evaluation has no value whatsoever. This also means that as there are no indicators of any change over the training period, then evaluation of any form is impossible. Certainly subjective assessment is inferior to objective measurement, but we must work with what we have available.

In subjective assessments, use whatever means are available, obviously the closer to objectivity the better. Even though they may be subjective, if the assessments are applied in a consistent format and manner, a considerable weighting can be given to them, particularly if a number of different types of subjective assessment is applied.

The interests of evaluation are best served by an assessment of the extent to which the learner puts the learning into operation at work – given the opportunity to do so. But even this aspect of evaluation can fall if there is no initial evidence that the learner did not possess the skills, etc. prior to taking part in the training programme. We can identify implementation some time after the training, but without an initial assessment we must recognize that contamination of these identifications are possible. It is possible that the learner possessed the skills, etc. before the programme, or may even have learned without the training!

Line manager involvement

Any form of validation or evaluation has little or no intrinsic value, other than as an academic exercise, unless the learners themselves and the organization, or at least the immediate line manager, are involved and immersed in the process. The learners must be involved to a greater or lesser extent, depending on how the validation approaches are introduced by the trainer. We shall see in Chapter 8 that the learners are invited/required to take an active part in providing end of event validation information either verbally or in writing, and also to produce personal action plans. If these actions are presented seriously as a part of the training and learning processes, rather than something trainers do at the end of a course (for *their* purposes and not the learners'), they can form part of the learning process itself. Given encouragement, time, explanations and so on, the processes involved in taking part should help the learners to concentrate on what they have (or have not) learned, how and why they have learned, and what they are going to do with the learning.

Success may not be achieved if it is left to the trainer to encourage the learner to become deeply involved, rather than pay lip service to the validation process. This may occur if, in spite of good training, the trainer is unable to motivate the learner, perhaps because of inter-relationship conflict or antipathy, or for a variety of other reasons.

Success is much more likely if all the possible forces are brought to bear to ensure a full realization of the potential of the situation. This *must* involve the learners' higher management, and in particular the learners' immediate line managers. Although they may know little or nothing about the training, they are in a very strong position of influence over the learner to ensure that good training is put into practice, and even something is gained from poor training. One cry frequently heard from managers whose staff have been on training events and return fired with enthusiasm and intent to perform the new, good practices they have learned, is that they cannot afford to let the learners loose on these new methods because they know nothing about them and consequently cannot support their introduction. There is a simple answer! The managers should themselves be trained in the 'new' methods, preferably before their staff attend the training.

The purpose of training is not to satisfy the trainer or the training function, although this of course must be an effect, but to provide the learners with the opportunity to improve their skills *for the benefit of the organization* (it is a bonus as far as the organization is concerned if the individual also benefits).

To aid this motivation and commitment, the line manager must make clear to the learner the extent to which he/she and the organization value the purpose of the training and the expectation that the learner will extract the maximum benefit from the training. In return they will help the learner back at work in any way which is appropriate and possible. Awareness of this supportive attitude has the by-product of ensuring that the learner's full attention is on the training and hence its effectiveness. Although it is not generally recognized, these actions are part of the validation process.

The open and overt interest of line managers is exhibited in the early stages by their (hopefully real) interest in the training and development of the learner. Even with the best intentions, this overt interest can quickly be lost, or appear to be, and any diminution of commitment soon reflects on the learner. The managers must maintain any interest they show.

The starting point is the identification of the individual's training and development needs and agreements/arrangements about how these needs might best be met.

Confirmation of programme suitability

As soon as the TNIA (Training Needs Identification and Analysis) has identified a training need in the organization and the members of staff in a department have been identified as requiring the training, action will need to be taken to select a suitable programme of training. This may of course be one or more of the varied methods of training and development discussed elsewhere (e.g. Rae, 2000), and will include consideration of such learning events for the individuals as:

- Coaching at work
- On-the-job training
- Off-the-job training courses organized by the organization's training department
- Off-the job training courses run by external consultants
- Reading suitable texts
- Open or Distance Learning packages
- Computer packages including CD/DVD programmes
- Internet-available training packages
- Learning via the organization's Intranet using the Internet programmes, CD/DVD packages, internally produced programmes, etc.

and so on.

Decisions will have to be made about which form or forms of training are likely to be the most suitable in the particular case (and more and more programmes are now using an integration of various methods). It is the responsibility of the training department to ensure that the maximum number of types of training could be available and the line managers are made aware of these possibilities. It is, in many cases, the line manager who has the final say about how and where their staff are trained, and these decisions must be made on a wide knowledge of the above (with trainer advice where relevant), but will not be made only on training/learning grounds, but also on responses and resources' availability, and containment within the available budget. This latter aspect must always be balanced against the anticipated ROI and the sanctions for not enabling the change – it must not be assumed that this as easy task!

PROGRAMME APPROPRIATENESS

A set of questions can be used by the line manager to help in assessing the appropriateness of any particular programme or approach, and the line manager must always remember that the final decision (with discussion and advice) is theirs. Another essential element in these decisions is the involvement of the learner in the choice as, after all, they are the people who are going to have to take a committed part in the programme. Consequently there must be significant discussion with all the people involved – this is not abdication of responsibility by the line manager, but the effective use of all supportive facilities available.

A useful set of questions is shown in Figure 6.1 and, with some editing, can also be given to the potential learners for them to assess the appropriateness and ready themselves for the discussion described above.

---

1. Is a training course the most effective way of meeting the learning need, or can this be achieved in another way – coaching, mentoring, peer help, team development programmes, Internet or Intranet programmes, etc.?
2. Which members of the staff need to go forward for the training – everyone, selected individuals, those identified for improvement or change, etc.?
3. Will the person(s) attending the programme be able to pass on this learning to other members on their return to work?
4. How committed is the learner to the training and to the aims and objectives of the training programme? Are these latter known to you and the learner?
5. Has the programme been developed as a direct result of a TNIA in the organization or elsewhere?
6. To what extent am I aware whether the training programme is an effective one for the organizational and individual objectives that have been identified?
7. To what extent is the programme known to be value for money?
8. What pre-programme work does the programme require and how much time will be required to perform this? Can this be supported at work?
9. Is finance available in my budget or that of the organization for the training programme costs (in virtual or real terms)? If this is not known, how can I seek to obtain the budget and what is the likelihood of this being made available?
10. Will the training increase the profitability of the business following effective implementation of action by the learner on their return to work? How will this correlate with the assumed ROI?
11. Has the training programme been designed, planned, resourced and provided with materials based on researched and validated learning principles, models and theories?

---

12. If the training is held elsewhere than at or close to the individual's place of work, have the associated costs (travelling, travelling time, accommodation, social funds, etc.) been taken into account in an assessment of the ROI?
13. Where does this training programme stand in relation to the ratings of similar events?
14. Can I ensure that the learner completes an Action Plan for the implementation of the learning at the end of the programme?

Figure 6.1   Questions to help in assessing training appropriateness

SUPPORT IN THE PRE-PROGRAMME STAGE

A frequent requirement prior to the training programme is that by the training organization for the learners to complete some pre-programme preparation. This might be in the form of:

* Reading relevant books, articles or papers
* Watching and assessing, in a provided format, recommended or supplied videos or DVDs
* Following programmes on provided CDs or DVDs or on recommended Internet sites
* Undertaking work-based research and obtaining local data, case studies, etc.

These tasks are intended to prepare the learner for the training programme and to try to ensure that all the participants are roughly at the same level of knowledge at the start of the programme. Co-operation of the line manager is most valuable at this stage.

Other pre-course work for the learner can be related to the longer-term evaluation process and might consist of:

1. General questionnaires relating to the course to assess the level of knowledge held by each participant;
2. A specific question questionnaire that will include queries about the key aspects of the course and the views of the learner about their existing level of knowledge or skill;
3. A self-awareness type of reactionnaire designed to make change comparisons for analysis at different stages (e.g. the first completion of the three-test described in Chapter 8);
4. Similar questionnaires to those in (2) and (3), but for completion by the line manager about the individual. If both (2) or (3) and (4) are used, it can be difficult on occasions to resolve the differences between the self- and boss-assessments owing to different viewpoints or scales of reference.

Whichever requirement or request is made for pre-course work, the basis for the complete evaluation process, the line manager must be prepared to make time and other resources available and actively support the learner. The learners must commit themselves to completing the work fully if they are to benefit from the training.

THE TYPE 2/3 QUESTIONNAIRES

These, particularly the Type 2, are the most common form of pre-course assessment and they require the completer to be as honest and open as possible in their responses. The questionnaire is not only used to give the trainers (to whom it is returned prior to the course) information about the levels of knowledge and self-assessed skill of the participants, but is used as the benchmark for comparison at the end of the training course. As mentioned above, Type 3 questionnaires specifically require multiple action at the end of the course (see Chapter 8).

In the light of the pre-course responses, the trainers may decide to/have to vary the content and level of the proposed material for the course.

TYPE 2

Questions that might be posed in this approach could be:

1. How confident do you feel about starting a negotiation initiated by the other party? Please answer as fully as you can, giving reasons.

and so on.

The responses by a number of learners approached could vary considerably and would require the trainer to assess and analyse them – in a larger size group this could take a substantial amount of time owing to the textual nature of the responses, but they could disclose valuable and significant items of information.

TYPE 3 QUESTIONNAIRE FORMAT

This is the three-test evaluation aid referred to earlier and described in detail in Chapter 8, but basically it is formed from the same type of questions as in the Type 2 questionnaire. However, instead of requiring textual comments, the learners are required to rate themselves, on a scale of 0 to 10, on how they see themselves and their skill levels at that time. For example, question 1 of the Type 2 questionnaire would emerge in the Type 3 questionnaire as:

1. How confident do you feel about starting a negotiation initiated by the other party?

Not at all   0   1   2   3   4   5   6   7   8   9   10   Completely

Some of the advantages of the Type 3 questionnaire approach are its wider applicability so that it can include the more subjective forms of training, easier comparison in a course validation process, and less time-consuming comparisons.

Item 10 in Figure 6.1 is linked to the crucial question, namely, 'What effect is the training and development of your staff going to have on the efficiency level of your business?', for, after all, the principal assessment of any training is the bottom line. Similar considerations will apply to non-profit organizations as their well-being similarly depends on their effectiveness. What increases can be expected in product production and sales, services, people management, customer services, and so on?

Before going down a long, hard road of attempting to calculate, assess or guess a ROI in financially calculable terms, it may be worthwhile to ask whether you need to achieve this level of 'ROI'. Some training results in a change from 'doesn't know' to 'know' or 'can't do' to 'can do' – these changes that can be observed may need no further investigation. For example, with a group of staff sent on a training course to learn a set of new regulations and who come back capable of operating the regulations as a result of this new knowledge, can one calculate the benefit of this or need one simply accept that the training has done what it was asked to do and the learners have returned improved people?

The approach to the answers to these questions can be:

1. Define what the outputs of the organization are and need to be, e.g. what is essential in the generation of achievement or income for the survival and development of the organization?
2. Try to define as accurately as possible the value, if necessary, of the existing business outputs of, for example, the people who are attending the training for improvement.
3. What added value in relevant terms is likely to come about from the trained people?

and so on.

Pre-course briefing

At the least, in the immediate period before the training takes place, the manager must hold a pre-training briefing meeting with the learner. It is a common experience for learners – and I have certainly been through this myself in the past – to leave work to attend a training event with the feeling (real or imagined) that nobody, including the manager, knows or cares where they are.

A pre-course discussion will let the learners know that their managers are aware of their needs for development and is, preferably, actively involved in this development.

Ideally the pre-course discussion would follow agreement that the learner should attend the training programme and take place a few days before the event. Discussion should not take place too far in advance of the event, else it will seem too remote from it, nor too close (say the morning of the event!) to give the impression that the manager has just remembered about it. Two or three days prior to the event would seem about right.

The interview should include as a minimum the items listed in Figure 6.2.

1. Final agreement that the particular skills involved in the training event are necessary either for the learner's job or his development;
2. Final agreement that the learning event is the most relevant vehicle to satisfy the learning need;
3. A discussion relating the objectives of the event to the needs of the organization and in particular the local part of the organization;
4. A discussion relating the event's objectives to the personal needs of the individual;
5. A consideration of the possible approach which will be taken by the learner to the training, e.g. concentration on certain parts, requests to the trainer for some inclusion of particular topics, and so on;

6. A guarantee by the line manager that, provided the learner has benefited from the training, any action necessary and possible will be taken to help the learner put the training into effect;

7. Agreement on a time and date on which the line manager and the learner will meet on the learner's return to discuss the training:

    - Impressions of the effectiveness of the training and the trainer(s)
    - An impression of the value effectiveness of the training
    - Discussion of the aspects from which the learners feel they have most benefited
    - What the learner intends to do with the training;

and so on.

Figure 6.2   The pre-course briefing session

A discussion of this nature will reinforce in the learners' minds the interest of their managers, will help them concentrate on particular aspects of the training, prepare them for the course and the aspects of learning, and let them know that on their return action will be taken relating to the course. Any trainer will readily acknowledge that a group containing individuals with this motivation and interest in the training will produce a learning event which is fulfilling for both the learner and the trainer, and will almost certainly be a very enjoyable experience for both.

Attention to the training will help learners to evaluate its usefulness. Both the line manager and the learner want to assess the effectiveness of the training, not only for the learner in question but for future learners. At the end of the event, learners with these positive attitudes will consolidate their views of the training. In this way the trainer, the learner and the line manager all benefit from validation.

Control groups

One approach which attempts to take into account the element of learning that would have taken place without training is the use of what are known as control groups; groups which are as similar as possible to the group which is being trained. Ideally they must be a complete match in terms of job, age, experiences, skill level, education, intelligence and so on. It is the realistic application of this matching which presents the greatest difficulty in the use of control groups: matching is simple to state in theory but difficult to put into practice, and a number of subjective assessments may have to be made.

In the simplest control group approach where one control group is compared with the training group, the control group receives no training but is given the pre- and post-training tests as if the members had undergone the training. The training group, of course, has the training and the pre- and post-training testing.

The use of control systems involving more than one control group is possible, and in many ways desirable, since the greater the number of control groups the more objectively valid will be the measurement of change or no change. However, the larger the number of control groups, the greater the administrative problems.

It is essential that any pre- or post-training tests administered to a control group are exactly the same tests as those given to a training group, and given under consistent and similar conditions, preferably at the same time. As suggested earlier the results must be treated with some care. If the non-training group shows a similar change over the period to that of the training group, serious doubts must be expressed about whether the training is necessary. If the non-training group, however, shows no change whereas there is substantial change within the training group, this supports the view that the change has been due to the training. If the result lies some way between these two extremes, the trainer must question whether all the training is necessary.

Initial assessments

Sometimes it is necessary to make assessments at the start of a training event. This is essential if for some reason, as happens in so many cases, there has been no pre-training investigation. At the very least trainers require to know the level of the participants in order that they can adjust the training to this level. Unless pre-training assessments have been made, the starting level needs to be determined in order to assess any change following the training. Consequently there is a wide range of approaches and many of the methods are also those in use at other stages of validation. The more common approaches used at this stage are:

Knowledge/skill assessment
Skill/knowledge self-assessment
Skill determination
Knowledge tests – Open answer
                   Binary choice
                   Multiple choice
                   Short answer
                   True/false choice.

Knowledge/skill assessment

This approach has obvious limitations, but it can be useful to the trainer if no pre-training information is available, since it can:

- warn of deficiencies in the training group
- warn of problems in the training group
- suggest the range of knowledge/skill/attitude of the group.

Most training events open with a session during which the participants introduce themselves. Usually the introductions are very superficial with names, locations, jobs and career histories being given. This type of information is not in itself particularly helpful, but at least the session acts as an ice-breaker by giving each trainee an opportunity to start talking

– sometimes it is unfortunately the only time some individuals speak! The value and use of this form of introduction can be increased by controlling the content of the introduction.

For example, at the start of a course concerned with job appraisal reviews (JAR), the participants could be asked to introduce themselves in terms of:

- Name
- Location
- Number of staff on whom they report
- Experience of JAR – types, numbers, etc.
- Problems experienced or envisaged
- Personal objectives for the course.

Part of these comments will be subjective, but they will at least offer some starting material relevant to the training. Notes should be taken of the information so that comparisons can be produced at the end of the course, particularly relating to problems and their resolution, and the satisfaction of the personal objectives of each individual. If these objectives are relevant to the training and have not been satisfied by the end of the course, the training has obviously not been valid for that individual.

This purely oral expression of needs can be extended by having the participants write down their personal objectives and the problem areas they would like to see covered during the training. These written aims, either retained as a personal document or posted up round the walls of the training room, can serve as the basis of a partial validation discussion at or near the end of the course. Have the personal objectives been satisfied? If not, can action be taken now or can plans be made to do something about unresolved problems?

Knowledge tests

CONSTRUCTING QUESTIONNAIRES AND TESTS

Although many tests and questionnaires have specific rules relating to the construction of their questions (see later), there are some general rules and comments which are worth considering at this stage.

The critical items for consideration before constructing any test or questionnaire are: 'Why do you *need* a test?'; 'What do you really *need* to know?'

Notice that the significant word in each of these questions is 'need', rather than 'want'. It is only too easy to include tests and questions because it would be 'nice to have the information' or 'it would be useful to have that information' without specifying the 'use'. Tests and questionnaires are difficult enough to construct effectively without having to produce extraneous questions in addition to the essential ones. A further problem with the 'want to know' questions is that they tend to deviate the test/questionnaire from what should be a consistent theme.

It is necessary to be careful with duplicated questions. In some cases, duplication in a different form is necessary to ensure that the correctness of the answers is not due to chance. From the experience I have had with questionnaires – both in completing and controlling them – when duplicated questions were noticed, which is almost inevitable, the first reaction is one of suspicion, followed by the decision to make the duplicated answers consistent. In some cases this is achieved by returning to the previous questions to check the answers that had been given, even though instructions might have been given to avoid doing that. If possible it is advisable to avoid duplication for this purpose. However, it is not always possible, but the test constructor must be fully aware of these dangers.

The language used in tests and questionnaires is referred to later when specific tests are described, but one golden rule must be to relate the language level to that of the participating groups, the learners. Naturally during the training itself, the trainer's language will have been adjusted to take account of the level of the learners. This adjustment must be retained for use in any test. So many people believe that there are two forms of language – the spoken and the written. Certainly, when writing, care should be taken to ensure that the grammar is correct, spelling must be in accordance with the relevant culture, and the text must be controlled much more than with the spoken word. But these are mechanics. The language itself is still the same – or should be. Unfortunately many 'speakers' seem to believe that they should write in a completely different language. In their writing, nobody ever 'has' anything – they 'possess', 'own', 'have permanent recourse to'; they never 'do' something – 'the relevant and necessary action is taken'; they don't 'breathe' – they 'have a life supporting respiratory condition', and so on. These same people, when speaking, use 'has', 'do' and 'breathe'. In the case of tests, if the learners have been trained with a particular vocabulary and language reference, this should be continued as far as possible in framing the test questions.

Reliability and validity of tests

In the background of the construction of all tests, whether of skill, knowledge or attitude lurk two aspects that appear to have, if not paramount then major importance. These are the aspects of *reliability* and *validity* of the tests being applied. Although I believe that these aspects have more relevance in the fields of academia, education and research, they must be considered as formidable parts of evaluation. The meanings of both these words when applied to testing are not straightforward and although the basic definitions appear to be relatively uncomplicated, their application is much more complex.

RELIABILITY

The general description of reliability when applied to testing refers to a test that is sufficiently consistent to give approximately the same results in subsequent tests. If a person or group is tested and very little happens in the intervening period before the second application of the test is made, the scores should be very much the same. This similarity states that the test is reliable. If the test results are significantly different, then the test is unreliable.

One of the principal factors in determining reliability between the two successive tests is that 'very little happens in the intervening period'. This is far from the case in practical training and development where the intent is to introduce a major element of change from before or at the start of the programme to the end of the programme. This change equates to effective training when applied to the training or learning objectives. In the basic definition of reliability, if I applied a test at the start of a programme and applied the same test at the end, with very similar results, I would come to the conclusion that my training had failed by not producing the essential change.

In practice the reliability is demonstrated by a significant change, provided the same test is administered under the same sort of conditions to the same group that has followed a common programme. These should be the criteria for reliable pre- and post-tests.

VALIDITY

The term validity is concerned with a test effect that is even more difficult to describe accurately and to ensure that it is applied in practice. Validity describes the extent to which the test in question is in fact measuring what it sets out to, or is claimed to, measure. The validity, therefore, is the argument used for applying a particular test.

There are several types of test validity, variously described by different 'authorities'. The principle one that the practical trainer will encounter is known as 'content' or 'face' validity – does the test reflect the material that is included in the programme and is it representative of the skill, knowledge or attitude presented in the programme? A high content validity for a test will be one in which the well-balanced majority of items included in the programme are included in the test. A face-valid test must measure what it says it intends to, otherwise it will create suspicion and rejection by the people being tested.

Some guidelines that will help the test constructor to ensure a more valid instrument include:

- A significant or substantial number of questions relating to a full range of learning topics form the test. This must be the right balance as too few will not support the validity and too many will make the test cumbersome
- The questions should be phrased in a neutral manner so that the people being tested cannot introduce bias because they respond in the way they think the tester wants them to do
- The way in which the test is administered must be consistent and objective, with no indications of bias in any way given by the tester
- As far as possible the questions should be put so that the responses will not be ambivalent. This is particularly possible in the case of behavioural training when there is frequently misunderstanding on the part of the learners between behaviour, attitude and personality.

Information obtained from tests will only be as good as the tests themselves, so, within the constraints of the need to demonstrate effective training, i.e. change, the tests must be constructed with both reliability and validity in mind.

QUESTIONNAIRE FORMAT

Whichever form of test or questionnaire is used, the constructor will reap benefit from considerable pre-planning. The guidelines described above should certainly be taken into account, but thought should also be given to other aspects, many of which can be forgotten in the rush to construct the main part of the questionnaire.

Ideally, the questionnaire should begin with a clear statement, however brief, explaining to the learner the purpose of the approach and what the constructor hopes to achieve by it. If the purpose is clearly understood, the learners will be more likely to complete it accurately and honestly. The aim must be to demonstrate what the learners *know*, not what they *don't* know. The reason for the test should be followed by clear instructions about its nature and how to complete it correctly. These instructions need to be placed not only at the beginning of the questionnaire. If it is a long test with a number of pages, it is helpful to repeat the instructions at the top of each page, or at least a summary of the important points. If interim instructions need to be placed in the middle of the questionnaire, or the instructions are changed at that point, they should be positioned and/or printed in such a way that they cannot be missed.

Although it is not always possible, because of the nature of the test or questionnaire, every effort should be made to progress the questioning from the general to the specific, the easy to the difficult, from the 'should be known' to the 'must be known'. The test should start with two or three questions to which the learner should know the answers. Care should be taken, however, that this does not conflict too much with another essential part of the format: the test sequence should follow in general the sequence of the learning. This sequence will make sense to those completing the questionnaire and they will see the relevance of the test.

Most of the specific rules are described later, but there are one or two general points worth making here.

1. Group related questions together rather than scattering them randomly throughout.
2. The general rule (found in interviews) about asking open questions rather than closed ones does not apply to test procedures, unless it is a probing questionnaire in which opinions rather than facts are sought.
3. Never assume that the people under test will understand your questions. *You* might understand them, because the meaning originated in your mind, but there is no guarantee that this meaning will be readily transferred into an understandable written form. With a newly-created format, it is always useful to try it out on a test population, preferably similar to the one that will be taking the test.
4. Ensure that any question you pose is a single question only. Again, as in interviews, multiple questions (not 'multiple choice') can confuse because the respondent will not know which one to answer, may answer none or may answer the last one only. It is even worse if the multiple components concern unrelated subjects. Similarly, leading questions should be avoided otherwise there is the danger of suspicion that the test is part of a manipulation.

SUMMARY

The following is a list of the most important questions to ask yourself when you are constructing your test/questionnaire.

1. Do I really need to set this test/questionnaire?
2. Why do I need to set it?
3. Am I using the correct format and type of test/questionnaire?
4. Are my questions
   * worded – as simply as possible
                   – as briefly as possible
                   – as directly as possible?

- unambiguous for the group?
5. Do my questions
    - involve one idea only?
    - influence the response in any way?
    - keep clear of negatives?
    - avoid leading the response?
6. Is the sequence logical?
7. Are the instructions clear and accurate?
8. Do adjacent questions *not* influence each other?
9. Is space used effectively with adequate space between
    - questions
    - questions and the place for the responses?
10. Have I tested out the questionnaire on myself and others?

Types of knowledge tests

At the start of a training course the participants, unless they are completely new entrants to the occupation or industry, will each possess some knowledge. If this knowledge is tested at this early stage, it will enable the trainer to:

1. Assess the general level of the group and pitch the training level accordingly;
2. Provide the information which will be compared with a later test to determine the changes which have taken place.

OPEN ANSWER

The most widely known test approach is the examination question approach which sets a question to determine the amount of knowledge possessed. This knowledge is shown in the reply to the question. The problems of this approach is that the answer, which can be expressed in a variety of ways, has to be assessed or even interpreted. The format of the question determines the generality of the answer. A typical question would be 'Compare in as many ways as you can the ... and the ...' Formulating questions requires considerable skill as well as knowledge on the part of the tester, and enough time to complete the assessment and interpretation if a comprehensive examination is to be set.

BINARY CHOICE

The knowledge element can be tested by methods which do not require as much time and staff resources as the full examination method. One method is to pose questions related to the subject under consideration and supply alternative answers from which a choice can be made. The selection answers may consist of simple Yes or No, if this is all the question demands, or some short phrases. Examples of these approaches would be:

	(Delete inappropriate answer.)
1. Does your company offer annual job appraisal reviews?	Yes/No
2. To whom would you look for your annual job appraisal review?	Your boss/Your boss's boss

This approach has the obvious advantage of simplicity and ease, not only in the answers but also in the assessment of the correctness of the answers. However, this very simplicity must limit the approach to some extent since the ability to simplify accurately demands excellent knowledge on the part of the subject and the ability to phrase unambiguous questions on the part of the test conductor. For example, if you were completing the answer to the *yes/no* question posed above, how would you interpret the word 'offer'?

The advantage of this approach is that it is simple to administer and simple for the trainee to understand. It is also speedy in operation. The questions and answers have to be carefully selected if they are not to be too obvious or too unclear. The principal problem is that because there is a choice between two answers only, the trainees may be tempted to guess the answer and they have a 50/50 chance of each answer being correct. There will be a diminution of this effect based on the laws of probability, but whatever the statistical basis, the validity of the test could be reduced in the mind of the person tested in addition to the tester.

TRUE/FALSE CHOICE

A similar binary choice test prone to the same probability errors is the true/false test in which the trainee is asked to score a statement in either of these states. For example:

The machine operator only is allowed to press the stop button.	True/False?

Although this test appears simple, as in the case of the yes/no test it is most difficult to construct and administer since most statements require considerable qualification to ensure that they are clear. The criticism can also be levelled that yes/no, true/false, or the alternative answer approaches give no reasons 'why'.

There are a number of rules which must be followed in the construction of binary selection and true/false choice tests and many of these rules apply to other questionnaires. Seven important rules are:

1. The question must consist only of one question and that question must be clear to the reader so that it does not have to be puzzled over for its meaning, otherwise the person being tested may be confused. The intention is to test the knowledge of the person, not to test their ability to interpret ambiguity.

2.   One of the answers given in the alternative answer approach must be correct and there must be no doubt or ambiguity about it as the correct or true answer.

3.   Keep the statements short and use simple language. This will increase the likelihood that the question is clear to the reader. Long and complex questions tend to assess the ability to understand written questions rather than knowledge of the topic.

4.   Use negatives sparingly. Because 'no' and 'not' can so easily be missed when the question is being read under circumstances of stress, as far as possible construct the statement so that it can be written in a positive form. If a negative must be used, underline the negative word. Avoid double negatives.

5.   Avoid words which may give a clue to the correct response. Statements which include such absolute words as 'never', 'always', 'all', 'none' tend to be false statements, whereas qualifying words such as 'usually', 'may', 'sometimes' tend to accompany true statements.

6.   In spite of the advice given in 5, avoid the use of words such as 'frequently', 'most of', 'regularly' and 'sometimes' which can mean different things to different people and can confuse.

7.   The statement should be sufficiently plausible not to appear obviously false (if this is so) so that the risk of forcing guesswork is reduced.

MULTIPLE CHOICE

One way of avoiding some of the problems cited above is to extend the range of answers from which the choice has to be made. This approach is often used in television programmes, and a 'silly' answer is frequently included in the list of options. The difference between the multiple and the binary choice approach is that three or more possible answers are provided, usually up to a maximum of 5. For example:

The Job Appraisal Review interview is:
1.   Mandatory
2.   Voluntary for all staff up to age 60
3.   Voluntary for all staff.

In this questionnaire the responder has to choose from the answers offered and either tick the selected answer, or ring the number of the chosen answer. The greater the number of optional answers offered, the less chance there is of random selection producing a high score, as is the situation in the binary choice. However, the multiple choice approach is much more difficult to construct because of the need to produce a wide range of optional, incorrect answers.

One variation of the multiple choice is given in the example above. It can be described as the incomplete answer test as the stem of the test is completed by one of the answers – 'The Job Appraisal Review interview is voluntary for all staff'.

An alternative is to pose the stem as a question rather than an incomplete statement. For example:

What are the recommended tyre pressures for a Zucat 327?
(a)   28 lbf/in^2 front and rear
(b)   30 lbf/in^2 front and rear

(c) 28 lbf/in^2 front, 30 lbf/in^2 rear
(d) 30 lbf/in^2 front, 28 lbf/in^2 rear
(e) 40 lbf/in^2 front and rear.

One variation which is often used, more to establish attitudes based on knowledge and experience rather than to obtain correct answers, is a multiple choice in which the tester has a preferred answer in mind. The other answers are not wrong, only less preferred by the tester, the organization, research or some other body. For example:

Practical practice interviews are best performed with:
(a) Real-life case studies
(b) Case studies based on real life
(c) Constructed case studies for the interviewer only
(d) Constructed case studies for the interviewee only.

Obviously in a test such as this it has to be made clear by the tester that the best or preferred answer is required of the responders.

In the same way that there are rules for binary and true/false choice question construction, there are some specific ones for multiple choice approaches.

1. Ensure that the question is phrased in simple, clear language which can be understood immediately and without reference to the multiple choice answers for guidance.
2. Try not to repeat much of the same wording in the various alternatives – put as much in the question as possible.
3. Avoid using negatives and double negatives – this rule is common to question formation in any approach. If you have to use a negative, emphasize this is some way, e.g. by underlining, upper case letters, etc.
4. Ensure that the correct answer is the only correct one possible, but do not make the other alternatives too obviously the wrong answers.
5. Avoid giving clues to the correct answer. Clues are usually given by repeating wording in the multiple choices from the question; by making the correct answer obviously correct in the way it is expressed; and by giving greater detail to the correct answer.
6. Make the incorrect choices as likely as possible and use the same type of language for all choices, both right and wrong, and make each choice answer more or less the same length.
7. Vary, in a random manner, the position of the correct answer from one question to another.
8. Keep each question independent of the others, since an obvious association might help in answering another question.
9. Number each question, but use letters – upper or lower case – before each alternative to avoid confusion with any numbers which might appear in the answer.
    • If the 'question' is in the form of a question, close with a question mark and commence each alternative, indented, with an upper-case letter and end with a full stop. Do not end with a full stop if the answer is numerical, to avoid confusion with a decimal point.
    • When the main 'question' is an incomplete statement, the alternatives should begin with a lower-case letter and end with the relevant punctuation mark.

Although the above rules help towards clarity in the question and the choices, do not be slaves to them, provided that what is used does not confuse.

Examples of both major forms described in 9 above are:

1. By which convention from the following is a footpath shown on an Ordnance Survey map?
    A. A single broken line
    B. Two parallel broken lines
    C. Dots and dashes in a line
    D. An unbroken line.

2. The recall of factual information can be best measured with:
    A. matching items
    B. multiple choice items
    C. short answer items
    D. essay questions.

SHORT ANSWER

Similar in many ways to the binary and multiple choice answer tests is the one which requires the respondent to write a short answer rather than select one from a provided list. This approach is more difficult for the respondent who has to search for not only the answer, but also the words with which to phrase it. For example 'The minimum stopping distance for a car travelling at 40 mph in dry conditions is …'.

This short answer approach is probably the most effective of the knowledge tests as it is the one which, apart from the full examination approach, requires the respondent, without help from optional answers, to demonstrate knowledge or lack of it. It also requires considerable work on the part of the tester who has to construct the questions in such a way that they are clear and unambiguous.

The rules for constructing a test in this format include many of those described for binary and multiple choices. In addition:

1. Check that the question can be answered with a short answer, although, provided it is correct, a longer answer should not reduce the validity of the answer.
2. Use a direct question in as brief and clear a form as possible.
3. Require the response words only. Do not word the question so that non-essential words need to be supplied – 'a', 'an', 'the', 'some'.
4. Keep the blank space for the required short answer at the end of the question as far as possible, or in the same place in all the questions. Varying the position of the answer space slows up the test completion and can confuse the reader.
5. Maintain the same length of space for each answer to avoid giving clues to the type of word or words.
6. Ensure that the question can be answered correctly with only one answer.
7. Where a numerical response is required indicate the necessary (mpg, fps, mph, AU) units. The danger, however, is that the unit may act as a clue or trigger for the response.

Skill determination

In a similar way to the assessment of the participants' level of knowledge/skill from their verbal introductions, some approach can be made to the assessment of their actual skill levels in the subjects being considered. This can be handled by asking them to take part in an activity or set of activities in which they have to use as many as possible of the relevant skills in which they are already capable. A useful method is to start with a simple activity in which the participants should be able to succeed; then follow up with an activity that includes one or two of the key learning points in which the learners may not have much or any skill. If necessary, a further, more complex activity can then be set to start the learning process. It is not advisable to throw the learners in at the deep end by giving them the complex activity as the starter. In some circumstances a relevant alternative to an activity might be the requirement to perform a practical demonstration of, for example, a machine operation.

However, many skills, particularly those at management level, are more difficult to test and assess, and any initial assessment must be necessarily much more subjective if the individuals have not been observed *in situ*. It may be suggested that if any attempt at validation has to rely on a subjective assessment, the assessment has little value. But it has been noted earlier that in spite of any difficulties it is always worth trying to produce *some* assessment rather than none at all. Also, there are other validation approaches, even though themselves subjective, which may support the initial assessment.

The approach in circumstances such as this is to have a questionnaire completed by the participants themselves at the start of the training event, a questionnaire related to the training content. In this questionnaire the individuals are asked to rate on a scale how effective they think they are in a number of aspects which will be included in the training event.

Skills self-assessment

SEMANTIC DIFFERENTIAL QUESTIONNAIRE

One common type of questionnaire is based on a semantic differential and in a questionnaire of this nature the participants are asked to rate the aspects on a scale between opposites. For example, a questionnaire for people attending a meetings' management course could include such items as:

Preparation of agenda
Skilled | | | ✓ | | | | Unskilled

Control of meetings
Well | | | | ✓ | | | Badly

Handling of difficult members
Well | | | | | ✓ | | Badly

Use of summaries
Frequent | | ✓ | | | | | Rare

| Complete | | | | ✓ | | | | | Incomplete |

| Fully accurate | | | | ✓ | | | | | Inaccurate |

and so on.

Each individual will complete a questionnaire of this nature and the questionnaire can be held until the end of the course and used for assessment, whether this might be tutor based or learner based. It can also be used immediately as a discussion base to start the training course by bringing into the open the different views of the course participants about the levels of their skills.

The semantic differential assessment method requires the individuals to make a subjective assessment of their skill using scale divisions ranging from a minimum of three divisions to as many as the trainer feels the individual can handle: a scale with six or seven divisions is about the norm. A mark is placed in the space on the scale which represents the level at which the person feels they are, relative to the descriptions at each end of the scale with the shades in between. There is considerable discussion in scale questionnaire circles as to whether an odd or an even number of divisions is the most effective. If an odd number is chosen, say seven, then there will be a mid division which will at best be treated as the 'average' division and at worst a safe marking which can be given without having to make a real decision. The even division of, for example six, means that the assessor has to be positive in the assessment when away from the extremes, and mark a division on either side of the middle line showing 'satisfactory plus' or 'satisfactory minus'.

THURSTONE SCALE

One way to avoid the problems of allocating a numerical weighting to a subjective view is to use a Thurstone Scale. This presents the individual with a number of statements related to the training event and requires either agreement or disagreement with each statement. A variation of this approach, which most people seem to prefer, is for the individual to state whether there is agreement or more agreement than disagreement, or disagreement or more disagreement than agreement. This does away with the need to have a choice between the extremes of agreement or disagreement only.

A questionnaire in this form might require answers in the form of: A = You agree or agree more than you disagree; D = You disagree or disagree more than you agree.

1.	A manager's first responsibility is the care of her staff	D	A
2.	A manager must be able to do all the jobs of her staff	D	A
3.	A manager is closer to her staff than to her manager	D	A

The principal advantage of this type of scale is that specific items which require answers can be included in the list and consequently the scale can be used extensively. The tester must, however, be prepared for comments from the group completing the questionnaire who may be attempting to rationalize or defend their answers and who say that:

- various interpretations can be placed on the wording of the statement
- they could not be so definite about agreeing or disagreeing, even when taking into account the broad definitions of A and D.

The first objection can in fact be used by a trainer to make the group discuss fully what a question means to all of them before they answer. The second objection can only be handled by stressing that they are not required to answer extremes only.

LIKERT SCALE

Another method of countering the second objection to the Thurstone Scale is to offer a wider variety of answers. The Likert Scale normally offers a range of five choices:

- Strongly agree
- Agree more than disagree
- Uncertain
- Disagree more than agree
- Strongly disagree.

An example of this type of scale would be:

1.	I always listen carefully to the instructions	SA	A	U	D	SD
2.	It is better to listen than to talk	SA	A	U	D	SD
3.	People always listen to what I say	SA	A	U	D	SD

The same arguments may be raised against this scale as with the Thurstone Scale but, again, any assessed ambiguity can be used as a group discussion item. As far as the second objection is concerned, there is a greater choice of answers. The choice may still not be sufficient, but there is doubt whether people can be more specific over a subjective element.

RANKING SCALES

In this format polarized statements are not involved and the skill necessary for producing the content of ranking scales is much greater than in the case of the polarized scales. The ranking scale is particularly useful for encouraging the emergence of attitudes without making this objective obvious to the learners. The scale is particularly susceptible, however, to being answered in the 'correct' way, especially if the learners have 'read the right books'.

In ranking scales, the learner is required to place a number of statements in order of priority or importance. For example, if one of the statements is considered to be the most important or significant, this will be ranked 1. The one identified as having the next importance will be ranked 2, and so on. Without any external influences the rank responses should represent the views of the learner at that stage. Subsequent completion of the instrument will show, by comparing the rankings, to what extent the learner's views have changed during the learning event (note that any change does not necessarily occur *because* of the learning event – the change may be purely coincidental or reliant on other effects).

Although a ranking system appears to be even more mathematically based than a polarized version, it is in fact more subjective. Some problems of completion can arise when the learner is unable to separate the ranking. There are two possible solutions to this dilemma. If, in a list of ten statements to be ranked, two at position 5 cannot be separated, both can be given the position 5 and the next ranked item described as rank order 7 (not 6). An alternative is to use the rank median approach. In this method both would be ranked at

5.5, the median point between 5 and 6. This latter method is more logical and mathematically useful, particularly if more than two statements have to be placed at the same position. In the case of three statements, in the first method each would be ranked 5, with the next statement at 8. In the other approach, all three would be ranked 6, the median of the three. In general terms this may not seem to have much significance, but if the rankings are to be analysed statistically, the second method is likely to be more useful.

A typical ranking scale which might be used on a management course would be similar to the following.

KNOWLEDGE TEST 1

The following are aspects of good management. Rank them in order of their importance as far as *you* are concerned at this stage. Rank them according to what you actually feel, rather than how you think the trainer might want them ranked. Put a 1 against the statement you feel is the most important, 2 against the next important and so on. Rank all the items. It you cannot decide which of one or two items ranks higher than the other, give them both the same rank and rank the next item at its real numerical position. For example, if two items fall at position 5, both are ranked 5.5 with the next item at rank order 7; if three items fall at position 5, all three are ranked 6 with the next item at rank order 8.

ITEM   RANKING

Support for his/her subordinates
Loyalty to the organization
Coaching her/his subordinates
Making training opportunities available

and so on.

This type of questionnaire is very versatile. In addition to determining the learners' individual judgements at various points in an event, it can also be used as a group training activity instrument. In this case the individual learners are asked to rank the statements, then the group, by means of discussion, influence and negotiation, are required to produce an agreed group ranking. The group ranking can be compared in discussion with the original one produced by the individuals. The activity can involve communication skills, influencing, negotiating, coping with disagreement/ conflict, reaching agreement through consensus, minority reporting, and so on.

SELF-ASSESSMENT OF ATTITUDES

Apart from the specific knowledge determination test, most of the assessment approaches described so far require the learners to give an assessment of their own skills. This assessment must by necessity be subjective and can approach 100 per cent inaccuracy if the completer has little skill in self-assessment. The assessment is likely to be more objective if the questions relate to specific skills, rather than to attitudes and feelings.

One method of reducing the subjectivity is to administer the same questionnaire, not only to the learner but also to the learner's boss, and if possible to the learner's subordinates.

It might be assumed that if these additional assessments are obtained, the final combined assessment must be complete. This is not necessarily so, however, for a variety of reasons. The assessment by the boss may be very biased due to value judgements or simply because the boss sees the learner so rarely that his views are almost worthless. Subordinates are more likely to know the learner better, but they may have weak judgement or knowledge levels upon which to base their assessments.

In such an event, and particularly in cases where we are trying to assess attitudes or feelings rather than specific skills, the subjective views of the learners themselves may be the best we can hope for. Certain tests can, however, reduce the subjectivity.

A typical, initial self-assessment questionnaire, Figure 6.3, is one which I use in connection with the interpersonal skills training I offer. Any views expressed by individuals about themselves in this area must necessarily be highly subjective. The subsequent use of the same questionnaire will be discussed later when we consider immediate and longer-term outcome evaluation.

The format of this questionnaire is intended to provide a base level for each learner's skills or attitudes at the commencement of the training, or prior to the training, as the questionnaire is commonly completed prior to the learners attending the course. One has to assume that the questionnaire is completed honestly and with the maximum awareness by the individuals of their own feelings. I have tried using parallel questionnaires with the learners' bosses and subordinates, but with unreliable results for the reasons cited earlier. The scale of ten is used in order to encourage the completer to assess the level as accurately as possible, or at least make them think hard about the rating, and it does not permit any assessment at an 'average' level. It has a further advantage, at a later stage, because it permits any movements to be expressed as a percentage increase or decrease.

Whatever the method used, and however subjective the approach may be, it is essential to obtain as extensive an initial assessment as possible about the learner's level. Without this assessment, further validation or evaluation has little meaning.

Evaluation contracting

Before leaving the aspects of actions prior to a training programme, it is worth considering contractual arrangements between some of the parties of the Evaluation/Training Quintet. Evaluation does not simply just happen! Someone must take positive action to agree, initiate and implement the process. This should be part of the organization's strategic plans, but, unless there has been positive action of this nature for assessment under Investors in People, such a statement or even intent is not always present.

The aims and aspirations of most trainers, internal and external to the organization, are to provide training that enables the required learning and, hopefully, to know that the learning will be evaluated and implemented when the learner returns to work. The ROI can then be assessed. It is dangerous, however, to make assumptions about the practice of these actions and the responsible trainer will make moves to resolve the strategy and set action in operation when a new training and development situation is developing.

A friend of mine is the Training Manager for the Avon and Somerset Constabulary and he has advocated that, prior to the training, what he terms a 'definitive statement' is agreed by the trainer/training manager with the stakeholder (preferably at the highest senior management level) and the agreement broadcast to all levels. Hopefully, this encourages the

NAME _____   DATE _____

BEHAVIOUR SKILLS QUESTIONNAIRE   1 2 3 4

Please enter a tick in the space against each item on the scale 1 to 10 representing where you consider your present level of skill might be.

IN A GROUP AS A MEMBER OF THE GROUP

LOW   HIGH

1   2   3   4   5   6   7   8   9   10

1. Controlling amount of talking I do.
2. Being brief and concise.
3. Supporting others' ideas.
4. Building on others' ideas.
5. Being aware of my behaviour.
6. Initiating proposals and suggestions.
7. Explaining my disagreements with the points of view of others.
8. Controlling amount of giving own views.
9. Stressing feelings of others.
10. Thinking before talking.
11. Controlling amount of interrupting others.
12. Being aware of behaviour of others.
13. Controlling a tendency to outdo others.
14. Being positive in the group.
15. Bringing out others' opinions.
16. Controlling how much I try to dominate the group.
17. Getting others to listen to my view.
18. Withstanding silence.
19. Telling others what my feelings are.
20. Being helpful to others.

Where would you rate your general, overall level of interpersonal skills?

1   2   3   4   5   6   7   8   9   10

Figure 6.3   Self-assessment questionnaire

clients in the organization to state their aims and objectives for change and how they see their resolution.

A 'definitive statement' of this nature that clarifies what success means for them could read:

> At the end of the training, or other project, programme (*a specified target group*) will benefit themselves and the organization by being able to/being more effective at/having a complete knowledge of/etc. (*the change subject relevant*). The training programme will be validated (*by*) and wider evaluation including support for learning implementation will be carried out by the learner's line manager.

Trainers who are external consultants or training providers are in a more difficult situation than internal practitioners when it comes to a question of evaluation for a client. It is rare, although becoming less rare, for the subject to be raised between the consultant and the client and for the process to be included in the consultancy contract. This can leave the consultant unaware for some time about how the programme has been received and whether their actions have helped the learners in the practical situation, and even more so the organization's reaction to an assessment of ROI (if any).

Trainers/Consultants can, and many do, conduct programme start, interim and end of programme validation of the training effectiveness. But pre-programme and post-programme actions are usually out of their hands. The simplistic reaction can be, 'Well they are being paid for what they do; what more do they want?' But training practitioners usually have wider interests in the people they help to learn than the immediate learning event, for a variety of reasons, not least of which being that they want to do the best job possible for their client and also to know if/where they might be going wrong. These problems can be alleviated somewhat by the 'definitive' statement and its implications that the pre- and post-actions will in fact take place. Faith is all there is, unless it is included in the contract for the trainers/consultants to take action themselves; this, however, is not always the most appropriate approach, particularly by an external provider.

7 *Assessments during the event*

Validation and evaluation are concerned with identifying the change which takes place from the state existing before the training event to that evolving after the training. But the trainer often needs to know *during* the training to what extent the training is having an effect. If the required changes are not taking place, it may be necessary to modify immediately the approach or the material. The acceptance of the need to modify the training, and the ability to do so, reflects the flexibility of both the trainer and the training event and is itself a measure of validation.

Most of the direct tests of knowledge and skill described previously can be used at this interim stage, either as a repetition of the original test or an updated test related to what has occurred on the course so far. The tests may be administered formally or informally. If the formal approach is used, depending on what needs to be assessed, a written test of knowledge may be set or a practical activity tested. Assessment of the answers given in the knowledge test or the result of the practical test will give an objective indication of the progress of the learning.

The testing need not, of course, be formal or even obvious. Knowledge development can always be assessed by discreet questioning during a discussion. If all the learners have the opportunity to answer questions, their replies will reveal the extent of the learning.

Similarly, the specific test required can be included as part of a practical activity and its performance observed.

Observation must play an important part in assessment of learning during a training event, particularly in training other than for specific skills and knowledge. There is always a major danger in introducing interim validation that is intended to obtain feedback on how the learners see the training progressing: **if the feedback shows that all is not progressing as it should, you *must* do something about it.** Doing something as a result of this feedback can be time-consuming and you must ensure that you have authority and are in a position to build in this time: **if you are unable to take the necessary action as soon as possible, perhaps because there is no free time, there is little point in seeking the feedback. You might only antagonize the participants.**

Activity observation

The exact nature of the observational method will depend on the type of activity involved and, if observational aids are used, these too will vary with the activity.

At its simplest, observational assessment is practised by the trainer who has in mind a standard towards which the learners will be moving. The trainer's observation of the progress of the learners towards this standard will furnish an assessment of achievement. The observation of experienced and skilled trainers who can compare a group or individual with other learners with whom they have worked should not be discounted. However, whatever the experience of the trainers and their attempts to make any assessment as objective as possible, there is always the danger that a considerable amount of subjectivity will remain. The level of subjectivity can be reduced if a quantitative or objective form of observation is used.

If the observation of an individual is open to accusations of subjectivity, these problems can be reduced by having more than one person make the observations and by using the multiple observations as the basis for assessment. This approach could of course be achieved by the use of a number of trainers, but it is rare for any training event to have such a luxury. Instead, if the training involves group training activities, the group itself can provide the multiple observations. However, unless we are dealing with a very experienced and advanced group, even multiple assessments may not compensate for reduced observational skills.

At its simplest the group performing the activity will also act as its own observers and will be responsible for analysing the group's performance. This approach is fraught with many difficulties and, although it is used extensively to train a group to be more aware of its own activities, it has less value as an assessment approach. If the group has been actively involved in a group task either the task or the observation can be simplified because of the dual requirements on the individuals. We can observe a parallel of this effect with the leader or chairman of a real-life group who, becoming too involved in the task being performed by the group, finds that their control over the group will be reduced.

Some of the group can be withdrawn to act as observers and this approach can often increase the value of the observations. In what is commonly called the 'Fishbowl Approach', about six members are taken from a group of 12 to act as observers while the remaining six are required to perform a task. The advantage of this method is that the observers can concentrate on observing and the participants can concentrate on performing the task.

After the event, the activity can be assessed by a combination of the views of the participants, the observers and, if necessary, the trainer. Variations of the sequence are possible and it is sometimes desirable to use different approaches at different stages of a course. For example, the participants can be asked to comment on how they assess their own performance before allowing the observers to come in with their views. Finally the trainer can tie up any loose ends, perhaps arbitrate on any disagreements and comment on the favourable aspects of the activity since it is almost certain that the comments of the others will have concentrated on the less favourable aspects. Alternatively, the sequence with the participants and the observers can be reversed, giving the observers the first opportunity to comment. There is one almost invariable rule: the trainer must not be the first to comment. Depending on the trainer's power position, the trainer's views could contaminate those of the others, or the others could react against those views and thus introduce conflict.

The skill and experience of the observers will determine the value of the observational assessments. Even with observers who have little skill, improvements can be obtained by the use of observational guides or *aides-mémoire* which will at least concentrate the observers' attention on the areas requiring information. Many group observational guides are based on the Action Centred Learning approach of looking at the needs and actions relating to the task, the group and the individual. Figure 7.1 shows a typical *aide-mémoire* for observers looking at a group decision-making activity.

OBSERVATION OF LEADER

Observe the leader closely during the activity and make short notes about any significant incidents related to the subject headings below.

Did the leader

TASK	Achieve the task? How successfully?
	Analyse and define the problem?
	Work to a plan?
	Test ideas, proposals and solutions?
	Make the best use of resources?
	Use all the information available or obtainable?
GROUP	Brief them effectively about the task?
	Reach agreement on the objectives?
	Agree the group process – timing, standards, decision procedures?
	Summarize progress? How often? How well?
	Encourage the group to work together?
	Control the group?
	Keep the group on the track?
	Involve all the members?
INDIVIDUAL	Give each member a job to do?
	Check the understanding of each individual about the job and the task?
	Investigate special skills and knowledge?
	Confirm the progress of each individual?
	Bring each person in as necessary?
	Ignore anybody?
	Visibly upset anybody?

Figure 7.1   Activity analysis

This type of observational *aide-mémoire* can be modified in many ways to suit the activity and its requirements. If the training is concentrating on the effective role of the chairman or leader of a meeting, the items for observation will relate to this role. For example:

- How much were members brought in?
- How effectively were members brought in?
- How much did the group become involved in the decision-making?
- How much use of summaries was made?

and so on.

Similar approaches can be used in the observation of one-to-one interactions or interviews. Figure 7.2 shows an *aide-mémoire* which can be used to observe an interview practice, but, of course, other modifications can be made to suit other types of interaction.

Structure

How did the interviewer start the interview?
Did the interviewer follow a structure?
Was this structure explained to the interviewee?
How did the interviewer terminate the interview?
Was the interviewer aware of the interviewee's reaction to the interview?
If so, how was this achieved?

Behaviour

How quickly was rapport established?
Was the interviewee encouraged to talk?
How prescriptive was the interviewer?
Did the interviewer appear to listen?
Did the interviewer appear to be interested?

General

What were the three best aspects of the interview?
What were the three worst aspects of the interview?
How would you rate the interview as a whole?

Figure 7.2   Interview observation form

In the same way that we found reporting back could vary when assessing the performance of groups, so can variations be applied to the assessment of an interview practice.

The approach commonly used after an interview practice is to ask the interviewer to comment first on his own performance. This quite often brings out most of the learning points which can be confirmed by the observer, who is the next to report. The observer may be able to reduce the self-criticism of some aspects of the interviewer and introduce some positive aspects. The interviewee can then be asked to comment from the viewpoint at the receiving end of the interview – a most important viewpoint in any interview.

Finally, if anything remains to be said, the trainer can come in. Perhaps the trainer's role will be to summarize and clarify the comments and to add any omitted aspects which are sufficiently important to warrant comment.

If there are a number of interview practices, the comments of the observer, the interviewer and the interviewee can take place in any combination of all three provided that the trainer is always the last to come in, other than helping the assessors make their comments.

Aids to observation

In many cases the use of the participants themselves, with or without the addition of observers, is preferable to other forms of observation since they:

- learn how to analyse an event by (painfully) working through one of their own
- gain practice in giving feedback to themselves and others
- learn how to use an analytical resource they always have available, themselves.

But it is sometimes necessary to consolidate the information available by observation and modern technology has given us two approaches we can use to support or replace the more traditional methods.

AUDIO EQUIPMENT

The simplest equipment approach to observation is the use of the tape recorder. This equipment can record an event for later replay, when critical incidents can be identified, or the particular use of words or tones checked with the participant. While the event is being taped, the trainer or other observers will look out for incidents which need comment and will make a note of the position of the incident on the tape.

Audio recording is usually most effective in a one-to-one training situation, not when recording a group event. The recording equipment and the microphone(s) must be unobtrusive and as a result the sound quality of a group recording may be poor, particularly at times of very high activity. The voice levels of different people may vary from distortion at one extreme and sound loss at the other, unless the microphones and equipment are highly sensitive and reactive, or there is an equipment operator available to monitor and maintain the balance.

VIDEO EQUIPMENT

Video equipment is more versatile than audio equipment as it incorporates both sound and vision facilities. Two approaches are possible – as a visual aid only or to provide a permanent recording.

One of the major problems encountered in observation, as active birdwatchers will be aware, is the physical presence of the observers. This presence can affect the performance of learners practising an interaction or task. If we remove this observational distraction, however, by removing the observers, we also remove the facility of giving observational feedback.

But if we remove the observers to another room and replace them with a TV camera linked with a receiver in the observation room, we have gone some way to resolving this problem. The observers can see and hear everything taking place but cannot themselves be seen or heard. In theory this is an ideal solution but, unfortunately, we have introduced another contaminatory factor – the camera. The participants are aware of the presence of the camera and there is the danger that they will over-act or over-react because of it. In practice, they do usually react at first, but eventually become less camera conscious and more natural as the event or the course progresses. Notice must be taken of this possibility and its effects taken into account in the appraisal. Afterwards, the observers and participants can come together in the traditional way to discuss what has happened.

A useful addition to the basic equipment which will help in the post-event discussion is the video recorder. This can be used in the same way as the audio recording, but it has wider possibilities and more impact as the participants are able to see themselves.

The ability to see oneself on a video recording has both advantages and disadvantages. Some people can become so obsessed with watching themselves that this gets in the way of seeing and hearing what they are doing. A disadvantage of video recording and audio recording is that feedback from its use can take much longer than when it is not used. And it *must* be used. There can be a very unfavourable reaction from trainees if television is used but the opportunity is not given to see the result.

As with audio recording, video recording is more effective with one-to-one or very small groups, for the same reasons – the constraints of sound and vision. Obviously a larger group can be recorded if there is perhaps a director, with three or more cameras to take in the whole group and different parts of the group. A compromise can be obtained using two fixed cameras and with the trainer operating a vision switcher, but the trainer can do little else while doing this.

The time problem can sometimes be reduced by letting the participants watch the recording in their own time or when they can be excused from an activity. For example, on a self-presentation course I have recorded an individual's presentation and used the recording minimally in an appraisal feedback immediately after the event. I have also used the whole recording, but when this happens the presenter does not take part in the next person's presentation. They sit elsewhere watching the video recording of their presentation (or as much of it as they can stand!). In this way the video recording is used, but little extra time is expended. A similar approach can be used for recordings on interview training courses, negotiation training, sales and marketing training and management of meetings courses.

BEHAVIOUR ANALYSIS

The use of general observational approaches, with or without observational aids, attempts to reduce the subjective nature of observation and assessment. Other approaches attempt to reduce subjectivity even further and behaviour analysis – described earlier – is one such successful tool. Its use can range from an analysis and feedback of a one-to-one interaction, through the observation, analysis and feedback of a chairman's skills, techniques and behaviours, to the observation of the process and progress of a whole group.

Feedback and discussion of the observations can vary according to the activities being observed. With most observational and feedback techniques it is common, and indeed expected, to discuss interview results immediately following the interaction. The process observation of a decision-making group, a negotiation activity or the skills of chairmanship also need to be considered immediately after an event. But when we are looking at, for example, the development of behavioural skills, it may be dangerous to look immediately at one isolated event.

Whenever I need to observe and analyse the behavioural skills of a group, I delay the publication of the results for as long as possible and certainly resist having to state them after the first activity. The behaviour of people varies considerably, for many reasons, from one event to another: an activity may not appeal to them; they may not know anything about the subject of an activity; the time of day may be having an effect on them, and so on. The publication of the behavioural observation after any activity may thus give a false

Activity / Category	A	B	C	D	E	F	Average
PROPOSING	2 (2%)	6 (11%)			3 (16%)	1 (3%)	2 (5%)
SUGGESTING		1 (2%)					–
BUILDING		1 (2%)					–
SEEKING IDEAS		1 (2%)					–
SEEKING INFORMATION	14 (14%)	9 (17%)	3 (10%)	1 (3%)	4 (21%)	1 (3%)	5 (11%)
TESTING UNDERSTANDING	2 (2)			1 (3)	1 (5)		1 (2)
GIVING INFORMATION	43 (43%)	23 (43%)	19 (63%)	24 (77%)	7 (37%)	16 (43%)	22 (50)
DISAGREEING WITH REASONS	11 (11)					1 (3)	2 (5)
SUMMARIZING							–
SUPPORTING	5 (5)	3 (6)	1 (3)		1 (5)		2 (5)
OPEN	1 (1)						–
DISAGREEING	1 (1)					1 (3)	–
ATTACKING						2 (5)	–
BLOCKING	9 (9)	2 (4)	7 (23)	1 (3)	3 (16)	7 (19)	4 (9)
BRINGING IN	1 (1)	1 (2)				2 (5)	1 (2)
SHUTTING OUT	12 (12)	6 (11)		4 (13)		6 (16)	5 (11)
n Individual / n Group (Group average)	101/396 (59)	53/250 (36)	30/390 (56)	31/249 (35)	19/145 (21)	37/289 (41)	44

Figure 7.3 Profile feedback sheet

94

picture overall, although accurate for that one isolated event. A more realistic behaviour pattern or profile is produced from a number of activities, although it is still necessary to look at the variations from one activity to another.

On interpersonal skills courses with which I am concerned I give the observational data feedback to the participants at the end of the third day, by which time they have performed some seven or more behavioural activities and are also ready to look at the data in terms of any necessary behaviour modification. Figure 7.3 shows a typical example of the profile feedback sheet for an individual on an interactive skills course. The horizontal rows represent the behavioural categories within which the individual has been observed. The vertical columns are used for each observed activity and record the number of contributions, the contributions identified with the relevant category and the raw number of contributions expressed as a percentage. The number of contributions are totalled for each activity and compared with the total contributions for the group expressed as a raw total and also a hypothetical average for the group. The contributions in each category are totalled, averaged and entered in the final vertical column to produce a general pattern or profile for each category.

Normally at this stage in an interactive skills course, the individuals make decisions based on this feedback on whatever behaviour modifications may be necessary. These plans when put into operation can be monitored by continued analysis and the eventual production of a 'Post-modification' profile.

End-of-day assessment

In addition to checking the progress of individuals, the progress of the course and the attitudes of the participants can be monitored with a view to modifying the material and approach if necessary.

This monitoring is often achieved by an audit at the end of the day's proceedings. The participants are asked such questions as:

- What have you learned today?
- What helped the learning?
- Was there anything which hindered your learning today?
- If so, how did this happen?
- Was there anything you would have liked to have
  - spent more time on?
  - spent less time on?
  - omitted?
- Was there anything that you did not understand or agree with?

The course participants are asked to complete an audit sheet containing these questions and are allowed about ten minutes at the end of each day for this purpose. The audit sheets are then given to the tutor who, before the following morning, summarizes and analyses the information. The information is used initially as a discussion base at the start of the next day. This can often produce more than simply discussion, for if the sheets show a common desire for more time to be spent on a particular topic (perhaps because the topic has not been accepted or understood completely) the tutor must take account of these statements.

The normal progress of the course may be suspended so that some time can be taken to remedy the failure or omission; if this is not done the course will not progress effectively.

A simple but effective daily audit can be used without the need for a written statement at the end of each day's training. At the *start* of each training day, the course participants can be asked to each identify three words which reflect their feelings or views about the previous day and its training activities. The words from each participant are posted on a sheet of paper fixed to the training room wall. The words are offered to the group to be challenged or clarified and a lively period of discussion can ensue. Depending on the words and what arises from the discussion, the tutor can take any necessary action to extend the discussion or pursue aspects raised if the three-word audit identifies areas which require further action.

The results of this type of audit relate in many ways to the type of training. The approach is more relevant, but not completely so, to human relations training in some form – sales, negotiating, interviewing, interactions and so on. I have used this method at the start of each day on a team-building course and on one occasion the discussion resulting from the posting of the group's words lasted for the remainder of the morning, resulting in detailed feedback within the group. The method, however, is equally useful to the trainer involved in more mechanical training as it gives him continuous feedback on the attitude of the group to the training being offered and some measure of the understanding being achieved. For example, if the word 'confused' occurs several times in one morning, there are clear indications that the trainer has a problem to solve.

A more extensive reactionnaire/questionnaire can be used instead of the relatively simple one just described, although it is used in a similar way – completion at the end of the day; overnight assessment by the trainer; and discussion/action the following morning as necessary. The questionnaire can cover the complete day either as a whole or with the questionnaire divided into the day's sessions and/or activities. In many cases the form of a full validation may be too restrictive, so a more simple tick list can be used on these non-terminal occasions, particularly if any adverse indications are to be discussed the following morning.

Figure 7.4 shows one of these tick list approaches, and Figure 7.5 a more extended one that can be of greater value and use: here the participants are asked to extend their scoring by making textual comments. The figures demonstrate questionnaires that related to the full day's training: when feedback for the individual sessions/activities is required, the questionnaire will need to be divided accordingly.

End-of-day assessments by the learners also help them to remind themselves of what happened during the day and the learning they achieved as the day progressed. If the completed questionnaires are returned to the learners (with trainer copies taken), they can be used by the learners in the construction of their action plans at the end of the programme.

Spot checks

In addition to the end-of-day assessments and the three-word review described earlier, shorter reviews can be used at different stages through a programme, particularly a longer one. These can include:

- The Thermometer
- The Speedometer

Date ....   Course ....   Name ....

Please circle (*in each session section*) the rating for each item that represents most closely your views.

I feel that the training during today (*the session ....*)

1.	Was clear	6	5	4	3	2	1	Was confusing
2.	Was not too complicated	6	5	4	3	2	1	Was too complicated
3.	I learned a lot	6	5	4	3	2	1	I learned little
4.	I had a lot confirmed	6	5	4	3	2	1	Little was confirmed for me
5.	Was presented effectively	6	5	4	3	2	1	Was poorly presented
6.	Contained the right amount	6	5	4	3	2	1	Contained too much material
7.	Made me think	6	5	4	3	2	1	Didn't make me think
8.	I was actively involved	6	5	4	3	2	1	I was only passive
9.	Was necessary to the course	6	5	4	3	2	1	Was not necessary to the course
10.	The timing was just right	6	5	4	3	2	1	The timing was too short/long

Figure 7.4   End-of-day reactionnaire

Date ....   Course ....   Name ....

(*In this version the preamble and scoring ranges are as in Figure 7.4, but after each item the following request should be entered.*)

• Where your rating score is 3, 2 or 1, please state why you have given that rating.

(*At the end of the scoring table, the following questions should be added.*)

• What have been the major points you have learned?

• What are you going to do with that learning?

• Was anything omitted that you felt should have been included, or you were expecting to be covered?

Figure 7.5   Extended end-of-day reactionnaire

- Faces
- Blobs
- Progressive Interim Review.

A useful approach is to use your selected instrument (for example, the Thermometer), close to the start of the programme after the group has introduced itself and has started to settle down; then, in a course of at least a few days' duration, again at the mid-point, then towards the end of the event, but away from the more formal end-of-event validation exercises. In an extended programme the instrument can be used on a number of occasions during the period, or alternated with one of the other spot checks.

For most of these activities, the intention is for the learners to identify and share their feelings or views at that point and record these views by making a mark on the instrument which is usually displayed on a pre-prepared poster. When the marks have been made, any clusters (good or bad) should be readily recognizable and can form the basis of a discussion, say on the differences between the majorities and the minorities. These variations can be due to a variety of reasons – age, culture, sex, personality, participants from different departments or employers, multi-discipline role holders, and so on. It is also useful to look for any individual differences as these might suggest an individual who is 'feeling out of it'.

The caveat stated earlier of only embarking on interim checks if you will be able to/have time to do something about any problems raised, is also relevant here. The discussion on the feelings expressed must be 'encouraged' rather than 'forced', particularly in the earlier stages of the event – isolated individuals should only be invited to comment if they indicate any wish to do so.

In order that an analytical comparison can be made as the programme progresses, the participants can make their marks as individually recognized ones so that they can recall them at later stages. Of course, with a very open group from the start, or where an intention might be to hurry that process along, the participants can be invited to use their names instead of a mark.

THE THERMOMETER

Figure 7.6 shows a graphic that can be copied on to a poster/flipchart on which the participants will be invited to make their marks against the 'temperature' they feel how they best view the course atmosphere. A different colour can be used on each occasion the activity is completed, using the same poster, and, following any discussion, the poster can be fixed to the training room wall. An effective time to use the activity is immediately *before* the lunch break, rather than afterwards or at the start/end of the day. This gives you time to consider any implications and any activities that might be necessary or desirable.

THE SPEEDOMETER

This spot check is useful to assess the feelings of the participants about the pace at which the programme is progressing for them and their ability to keep up. Their individual marks are entered against the sector in which they identify themselves.

LEVEL INDICATORS

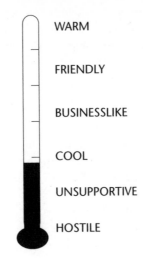

WARM

FRIENDLY

BUSINESSLIKE

COOL

UNSUPPORTIVE

HOSTILE

Figure 7.6   The Thermometer

| TOO FAST | FAST | JUST RIGHT | SLOW | TOO SLOW |

Figure 7.7   The Speedometer

Figure 7.8   Faces

FACES

A variation of the thermometer demonstration of how the learners feel about the programme and its developing atmosphere is shown in Figure 7.8. A range of faces with expressions that range from very happy to very unhappy can be used, but other images are possible, for example cartoon characters or humanized animals.

BLOBS

This instant review format can be contained within a very short period or can extend over an hour or more. In this case the exhibited flipchart lists the key elements of the training programme used to that stage, or, as with the just described spot checks, questions about the views of learners on the training. Figure 7.9 suggests one of these posters, based on the learners' views.

A freer form of this activity is to ask each participant to write down, clearly and briefly, on the poster (or posters) three significant statements they wish to make about the event so far – their views, feelings, opinions. When all the statements have been made, the group is then invited to put their blobs (or marks, etc.) against all the statements with which they also agree. The results of any significant clustering can then be discussed for possible action.

Please consider the programme so far and place a blob — ● — in the box that you feel represents most closely your answer to the question. The boxes in between the extremes are for levels between these extremes.

Interesting	☐	☐	☐	☐	Boring
Clear	☐	☐	☐	☐	Confusing
Simple	☐	☐	☐	☐	Complicated
Time too short	☐	☐	☐	☐	Time too long
Visual aids good	☐	☐	☐	☐	Aids poor
Session should be retained	☐	☐	☐	☐	Session should be omitted
Learned a lot	☐	☐	☐	☐	Learned little
Confirmed usefully a lot	☐	☐	☐	☐	Confirmed little
Pace too fast	☐	☐	☐	☐	Pace too slow
Good interaction within group	☐	☐	☐	☐	Poor interaction within group
Good interaction with trainer	☐	☐	☐	☐	Poor interaction with trainer
Have no problems	☐	☐	☐	☐	Have a lot of problems

Figure 7.9   Blob review – reactionnaire type

A major variation of the straightforward blob review is to use a more extensive, though basically similar, review.

Let us take the example of a training course with 16 participants taking part in a 4-day course which started at the Monday lunchtime. The trainer might decide at the start of the Wednesday morning training that there seems to be a need for a review of the views of the learners at that stage. The first action would be to ask each individual to write down 'three significant statements they would like to make about the course so far'. No further guidance should be given – in fact there is none to give! What they write should consequently be what they see as important. Seven or eight minutes should be allocated to this stage.

The group is then split into eight pairs to decide, from the joint six statements they have brought to the pairing, which three they wish to carry forward. This constraint introduces elements of communicating, influencing, negotiating, dealing with disagreement/conflict and presentational skills. Allow about 10 to 12 minutes for this stage.

When the three statements have been decided upon, four groups of four should be formed and the process repeated with the similar brief – to agree within 12 minutes on three statements.

If time permits, the process can be repeated with two groups of eight. At the end of 12 to 15 minutes three statements from each group are to be selected.

If time is limited, the next stage can be omitted, but it is very useful then to bring the two groups of eight together into one group with the six statements, and give them up to 10 minutes just to discuss the statements. No requirement should be placed on them to reduce the number of statements in this discussion, but no more than six statements should emerge at the end of the discussion.

Of course, this stage may be varied depending on the number in the training group. For example, after either the pairing or the individual considerations, triads can be formed, either by breaking up some of the original pairs, or going straight from the individual stage to the triads.

Whichever path is followed, the full group should be given the opportunity to discuss the final six statements before they are entered on a chart in the form of Figure 7.10.

STATEMENT	SD	D	A	SA

Figure 7.10   Progressive Interim Review chart

The statements should be entered as agreed on the chart which should then be displayed on a board or the wall. The participants are invited to come to the chart and place a mark (x, /, *, etc.) against each statement in one of the columns on the right of the chart. These columns headed SD, D, A, SA stand for 'Strongly Disagree', 'Disagree', 'Agree', and 'Strongly Agree'.

Once all the views have been entered, a pattern will emerge, possibly with agreement or disagreement predominating against various statements, or sometimes even a wide scatter. The statements themselves and the distribution of views can then form first, a basis of discussion on any problems, difficulties or conflicts which seem to be emerging, and second, discussion and agreement about how these aspects will be resolved.

The progressive decision-making stages can last from 45 minutes to an hour or more, depending on the number in the group and the trainer's leniency in the allocation of discussion time, and 10 minutes for the group to enter their views. The number, extent and nature of the problems will then determine how much time is *needed* to discuss and resolve the identified problems. This can commonly take an hour or so, but can take considerably longer if major problems have been identified.

It is essential that if a review is held and problems are identified, time and resources are made available to resolve the difficulties. If there is no possibility of allowing resolution time, it is not only time-wasting, but also dangerous to seek interim views. The commitment of course members can be destroyed if they are asked for their views then no account is taken of them.

Over-use of tests

Trainers who use or see the need to use tests during training to obtain immediate reaction assessments must be aware of a very real danger: the adverse reaction of the learners to the tests or assessments. If they have to complete frequent questionnaires this completion can become boring and tedious and it can become counter-productive to continue the practice. The learners may be too weary to perform yet another task at the end of the training day and may be anxious to get away to dinner, the bar or bed. Consequently, completion may be either superficial or 'chance' answers only may be given. If assessments of a detailed nature are delayed until the following morning, there may have been some memory loss, something which may be significant in itself particularly if a pattern develops.

So the trainer cannot anticipate 100 per cent success or co-operation, but most try to strike a balance somewhere between minimum and maximum use of tests so as to be aware at all of how the training event is progressing and how much learning is being achieved.

8 *End-of-event validation – 1*

The second important validation event occurs at the end of the training programme, the first being any assessments or tests prior to or at the start of the training. The testing during the event is also important but, bearing in mind the dangers of over-testing, the validation scheme would still be successful if the interim stage was omitted.

It is also at the end of the course/event/programme that we must differentiate between reactionnaires and questionnaires in their roles in validation. As we have seen, a reactionnaire seeks from the learners their feelings, views and opinions. However, in validation questionnaires are used for a more objective assessment that is directly related to the learning achieved. The reason for this is that the learning achieved is the only immediate measure that allows some assessment of the training effectiveness, whether knowledge or skills. Attitudes and behaviours are even more difficult to 'measure', but even here some effective approaches are possible.

Effective approaches

Most approaches in validation and evaluation include the completion of some form of end-of-course/workshop/programme questionnaire, reactionnaire or test. The assessments during the event are also important, but attention must be paid to the time available for these and any action resulting, and also the danger of over-testing. These interim assessments can be omitted without upsetting the final validation process.

One complaint made by trainers is that the participants either omit answers to some of the questions posed or that they take little time and care in the completion. I believe that these have a number of causes, many of which can be traced to over-testing, poor questionnaire construction and a number of other possibilities.

Guidelines to end-of-event validation

TIME FOR THE PROCESS TO BE COMPLETED

The criterion at the end of the event when an effective validation is wanted, is NOT, as all too frequently still occurs, to simply hand out the instrument a short time before the end of the event and ask the learners to fill it in there and then. In my view, even worse is to hand the instrument out in the same way, but ask them to send it back. Both these methods will suggest to the learners a low level of importance for the document, gives them too little guidance on various aspects, and, if it is to be sent back, because of these and other factors, the percentage of returned instruments may be low.

In order to facilitate a higher level of effectiveness, sufficient time to consider and complete the validation instrument must be built into the programme. This time can even include discussion about the results or perhaps learner-learner discussion of what each has written. I have attended, and run, programmes that have had a week's duration when most of the final morning has been allotted to various activities including those just mentioned, related to the end of the event.

LENGTH OF THE INSTRUMENT

The length of any questionnaire should be kept to the minimum necessary to obtain the required information. The greater number and more complicated the questions, the less likely it will be that the completers give each question a realistic consideration that the trainer is seeking. There will be, however, times when longer and more complex information is required: in such cases sufficient explanation for the questions and time for completion should be given.

STRESS THE IMPORTANCE

If you feel that validation is important to you and the learners, stress this when the process is being introduced, particularly in relation to what it leads to when they are back at work and for their colleagues who may be attending the programme at a later stage. Let them know what you are going to do with any documents they complete and hand in to you. On a number of occasions I have heard course participants heading back home and saying, 'Why did we complete that form? – this should never happen.

LEAVE THEM ALONE

When you have explained the process – why, when, how, and so on – and ensured that they have understood what they have to do, give them the instruments and let them get on with it. If your introduction has been an effective one and your questionnaire is clearly explanatory, you should have little need for further intervention – don't hover and keep looking over their shoulders!

MAKE YOUR QUESTIONNAIRE OR REACTIONNAIRE CLEAR

1.   Use clear, differential questions   The basic part of many questionnaires and reactionnaires is a scoring bar or a set of boxes along a scale of polarized questions. The questions at the two poles should be different semantically and usually take the form of antonyms, the scales being shown as numbered or unnumbered vertical bars, boxes or symbols that can have ticks or crosses entered, or the numbers ringed, and so on. For example:

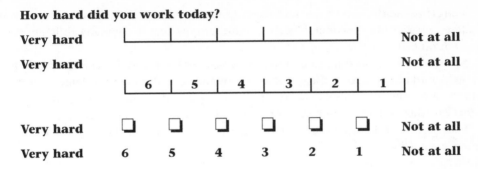

How hard did you work today?

In the first three examples, a tick or cross is placed in the space or box in the position that most closely represents their views. In the numbered example, the relevant position number can be circled. What the completer has to do must be made clear in the introduction to the questions.

2. Keep the scoring system consistent   Throughout the instrument, and preferably in all the instruments used, a consistent scoring format should be maintained. There is no specific research of which I am aware that suggests which is the best system. My personal approach is to use any of the scoring methods, but always (a) being consistent, (b) having the higher/better pole to the left and (c) using numbers with the highest value to the left. For example:

How much did you learn from the course?

A lot	6	5	4	3	2	1	Little

There is always danger with tick lists that the completer may just race down the list, entering ticks without really considering their response, even putting the tick at the same point down the list. Some validators have tried to avoid this by changing the polarized words and/or the scoring numbers at intervals. For example:

A lot	6	5	4	3	2	1	Little
Little	6	5	4	3	2	1	A lot
A lot	1	2	3	4	5	6	Little

and so on.

There is no real evidence to show that this approach avoids the problem and my experience is that it causes confusion (if it is even noticed!).

3. Avoid the 'average' rating   When people do not think about the question they tend to mark at the central scoring point in an odd number rating scale. If this is a common rating, there is always the suspicion that the ratings mean nothing. If you use an odd number of points, you must make it clear that the mid-score does not equal 'satisfactory' – it could mean in the minds of different completers 'satisfactory', 'neutral', 'average', 'don't know' or 'don't care'.

Avoid this possible confusion or misleading responses by using an even-numbered scale, for example 4, 6, 8 or 10 points, there being no mid-score and the completers are put in the position of having to think where they are going to place their mark.

4.   Length of scale   This topic follows on from the question, 'Should there be an even or odd number of positions?' and raises the further question, 'How many scale positions should be offered?'.

At the simplest, the scale can contain two positions – 1 and 2 – corresponding to a Yes/No, A lot/Little, I agree/I disagree response more frequently found in knowledge tests. In most cases, however, this can be too restrictive, particularly in the subjective areas of assessment where the fact is not black or white, but a shade of grey in between.

There are no rules about how many divisions there should be, but there are the following guidelines:

• The more divisions there are, the better defined can be the shade of response

but

• The more divisions there are, the more difficult it is for the responders to make decisions of scale.

Ten divisions, as a maximum, can be used on occasions, but more assessors find a six-point scale both useful and acceptable. This can be considered in terms of the top three scores being in a more acceptable response area; the three lower ones in the less acceptable area. So, on a six-point scale, 6 could equal 'A lot'; 5 'Quite a lot'; 4 'A reasonable/satisfactory amount'; whereas 3 could equal 'Less than wanted/desirable'; 2 'Not a lot'; and 1 'Little or none'.

5.   Questions   The questions related to the desired responses should leave no room for doubt or misinterpretation:

• Unless the response of 'yes/no' or similar is specifically required, always pose the question in an open manner, usually by prefacing the questions with 'How', 'Why' or 'What' – these will usually produce more open responses.
• Relate the questions to the current event only and have reference to the validation sought – it may be interesting and gratifying that the participants enjoyed the event, but how much did this contribute to the learning?
• Keep the questions singular, avoiding multiple ones, for example:

How do you rate the level of the visual aids and handouts?
High   6   5   4   3   2   1   **Low**

When the participants respond to this, to what does the response relate – to the visual aids or the handouts? These, although having similarities, are sufficiently dissimilar to require separate questions. This is particularly relevant if, say, the visual aids were good and the handouts poor.

• Define the words to avoid confusion or ambiguity. If the scale such as the one below is used, what do the responses mean?

What did you think of the visual aids used?
Very good   6   5   4   3   2   1   **Poor**

Do the polarized statements refer to the artistic quality, their clarity, their relevance, when used, and so on? Does the response relate to *all* the aids or only to the ones the learner can remember?

- Do not 'load' the questions. In the so-called 'Happy Sheet' reactionnaires are so worded that the event, trainer, and so on is never given a bad rating, the good responses always being led to these results by a bias in the question. A typical question asked is 'How *well* ...?', suggesting that any response relates to a level of '*well*'. This pitfall is avoided simply by omitting the 'well'.
- Use accepted and understood antonyms in the response poles, as far as the English language allows this, although some relaxations are possible. For example, 'bad' (not 'poor') is the antonym of 'good', although to avoid completers having to rate extremes the antonym might be 'not very good'. Similarly: Very much – Very little; Excellent – Poor (but also Rich – Poor!); Always – Never; Frequently – Rarely; and so on. As suggested, the problems of using direct opposites is that people tend to avoid extremes, preferring to rate, for example '5' rather than '6' and (to a lesser extent) '2' rather than '1', where the lower/higher ratings would have been appropriate.
- When using a rating scale always include a space for textual comments, such as those that can justify the rating or explain why it was given. This is particularly useful if ratings have been given at the lower end of the scale. If a textual response is also given, you are given some indication of what has gone wrong to warrant this rating.

End-of-event approaches

A number of approaches can be used to attempt validation of feedback at the end of a course, workshop or other programme. These can include one or more of the following:

1. **Group reviews** conducted orally;
2. **Knowledge tests**, usually, but not necessarily always, in a written form;
3. **Skill tests**. These can be assessments of learning by means of demonstrations of the skills, behaviours or attitudes by the learners in events provided towards the end of the programme, the learners utilizing the skills, and so on learned during the event. The demonstrations might be practical ones in an event that is part of the training event during which the learners utilize the skills, and so on they have learned;
4. **End-of-programme reactionnaires**. Reactionnaires completed by the participants at the end of the course or programme giving their views, feelings, or opinions about the event;
5. **Learning validation**. An end-of-course or programme questionnaire that identifies the learning achieved by the participants, prepares them for action planning and, in learning terms, identifies the effectiveness of the programme;
6. **Action planning**. A commitment by the learners to implement their learning on return to work.

Group reviews

Although it is not a written instrument, probably one of the most common ways of obtaining feedback about a training course is the group review. At the end of the course, usually the final event, the group of learners is brought together to give them the opportunity of stating verbally their views about the training course. Unfortunately, although relations may have been good between the trainers and learners (and this is not always the case) it is unlikely that the verbal comments will be completely forthright and comprehensive.

An approach that is more likely to produce realistic results is when the full course group is divided into small groups, each small group being asked to review the course. People are more likely to say what they have on their minds when in a small, self-led group than in a full session, usually led by the trainer. Some leads might be given to the groups by the trainers about the aspects on which they should concentrate or include, but care must be taken not to contaminate the views with an excess of direction.

Once the small groups have identified the main comments they wish to make, the groups are brought together for a full group review. Spokespersons should be appointed within each group so that the comments made in the full group can be done on behalf of the group rather than individuals.

The principal advantage of this method is that feedback from the group is immediate and can be questioned for clarification, provided that the trainer does not give the impression of being defensive in the questioning.

There are, however, a number of disadvantages to the approach. As the event is at the end of the training course, the members may be legitimately anxious to get away and, as a result, may not put much effort into the activity. So timing is important and, if validation is accorded the importance it deserves, sufficient programme time should be left for this purpose. There is also the danger that a vocal minority might exert undue pressure and influence over the majority and full views may not be expressed. Division into the small groups may reduce this danger, but the vocal objectors may still exert undue influence either at that stage or when the groups come together again.

One interesting variation that can make the feedback less formal and possibly more open, is 'The Review', when an activity is introduced in which feedback is obtained as part of the activity. For example, the learning group can be divided into two sub-groups, each being asked to review the event, agreeing as far as possible each item within the sub-group, and being ready to present their views to the other sub-group. When the groups reconvene, each one presents to the other the views they have agreed and these are discussed, perhaps to try to obtain an agreed common statement.

Knowledge tests

At one period in the history of training, if tests were applied they were usually ones testing the participants' knowledge increase resulting from the training. These have little use in present-day training programmes unless they are specifically and intentionally restricted to the giving and receiving (including remembering) of items of knowledge. An example of this may be a short programme concerned with a company's new products, detailed knowledge and understanding of which is required by the sales force, retention of this knowledge being essential when the agents go out to customers.

In most cases it is ideal, and usually practicable, to repeat the test as it was posed at the start of the programme. The test results can then be compared directly with the earlier ones, showing in as objective a manner as possible the changes over the training period. If this training has been continuous or not open to contamination in other ways, the improvement shown by the change can be fairly readily attributed to the training.

Skill tests

The majority of training programmes nowadays are skill learning events and, as with knowledge, if the change as a result of the training is to be assessed, there must be some form of test early in the programme and near its end. Skills presented on training programmes will be concerned with either objective practices or the more general, 'softer', skills.

The more objective events will include training in operational aspects of the job – setting up and operating a machine; wiring an installation; using a computer to produce documents or data banks; and so on. In the majority of these cases, the operation is either right or wrong and practical tests or demonstrations can be produced for the learners to show the extent to which they have learned the skills within the limits agreed. In such cases, the observing trainer will have a checklist against which the operations by the learner are observed and cleared, failure to reach the agreed standard requiring further learning and/or retesting.

However, the greater part of skills training is directed at much more general, subjective skills. Assessment of these learning aspects can be approached in similar ways to those of the operational training events, although with varying degrees of reduced quantitative assessment. In, for example, negotiation skills training, the first series of practice negotiations are observed and the skills of the learners assessed against a model of effective negotiation. Subsequent training puts forward skills and techniques in negotiation and the final series of negotiations, when observed using the same criteria for the earlier series, should demonstrate to what extent the participants have taken the learning points. These results will obviously be more subjective and less complete than practical demonstrations and knowledge tests, but, if the approaches are as consistent as possible, a reasonable degree of comparison is achievable.

Reactionnaires

Reactionnaires are lists of questions to the learners and are concerned with their views, opinions or feelings about various aspects of the training event, rather than the specifics of their learning. The 'Happy Sheet' referred to earlier is an example of the worst type of reactionnaire. But well-constructed reactionnaires can be valuable in a number of ways. Again, unfortunately, reactionnaires are frequently handed out indiscriminately at the end of every course for immediate and swift completion, often only given cursory attention and introduction. Once completed, these reactionnaires are simply filed away in the training office and never referred to again. In these cases, why were they ever even issued? On one occasion I asked the Training Manager about the massive file of these that was retained in this way, and the response suggested that it had always been done that way!

THE INITIAL CASE FOR REACTIONNAIRES

The four-stage model for evaluation introduced by Kirkpatrick (1996) is widely used, but certain aspects have been challenged strongly by a number of researchers. One of these, Kirkpatrick's Stage 1 – Reactionnaire Level – is challenged on the grounds that is is neither validation nor evaluation and therefore has no place in a model of evaluation. The four reasons cited by Kirkpatrick for using reactionnaires are:

- They provide valuable feedback on a lesson
- They show that the trainers are there to help the trainees to do their jobs better
- They provide quantitative information about the training for management review
- They provide quantitative information that can be used to establish standards for later classes.

All these suggested benefits have been challenged, the basic argument against them being that reactionnaire responses are individual, subjective views, opinions and feelings that can change from individual to individual, time to time and are dependent on the individual's internal circumstances. Responses of this nature answer the question, 'Has the learner enjoyed the programme?', but do not show objectively whether they have learned anything. One of the most favourable supports that can be made is that if the participants (or some of them) have 'enjoyed' the training, they are more likely to have learned something. In the following section, a substantial list of arguments against the use of reactionnaires as evaluation instruments is discussed.

THE LIMITATIONS OF REACTIONNAIRES

Reactionnaires are used extensively by trainers who often do not realize their diminished value in validation and evaluation. It is important for users to recognize not only these limitations, but also some of the real dangers in the use of some of them, the 'Happy Sheet' or its equivalent being the main culprit, particularly if scoring scales or tick lists alone are used. In the light of these potential problems, the question can be asked why trainers continue to use them. Some of these reasons are:

- The sponsors of the training like to see these sheets, particularly if they support the training well
- The trainers believe that they tell them clearly and honestly how they are performing as trainers
- Good reactionnaire responses, even if they have been manipulated by the phrasing of questions, 'demonstrate' a good training programme that is well liked
- They provide quick answers and, if tick lists alone are used, take up little time on the course, however flawed the responses may be
- Opinions given in this way satisfy, for some reason, for some trainers, a morbid reason for knowing how the participants responded to the programmes.

Dr John E Jones, well-known author of training material and of Organizational Universe Systems in the USA has written a paper for *Training and Development Journal* entitled 'Don't Smile about Smile Sheets' (available as a reprint from http://www.ous.iex.net). He lists a non-exhaustive description of 26 faults with end-of-course reactionnaires, five of which were cited in the first edition of this book. Some of the 26 faults in Jones' list (plus some additions) are (reproduced here with permission):

1. **Ratings don't correlate with transfer of training**   No available research shows a clear relationship between end-of-course ratings and the extent to which participants apply training on the job.

2. **Many raters are unqualified**   Training participants do not have the background to supply valid judgements about the effectiveness of a training course. They know what they like, but they are usually uneducated about educational and training theory and methods.

3. **Participants have uneven comparative histories**   Participants usually have highly varied training experiences with which to compare a given course. What one person considers to be outstanding may appear ordinary to another; both may have valid reasons for their opinions.

4. **Data are retrospective**   End-of-course ratings suffer from all the faults of retrospective data. What we remember may be highly inaccurate; our judgements about it may vary across time. Asking participants to rate the opening session on the last day is usually useless.

5. **Responses are judgemental or subjective**   Most end-of-course reactionnaires ask respondents to make value decisions. Such ratings are, of course, judgemental and subjective. What one person sees as useful another may see quite differently.

6. **Ratings are sensitive to mood**   The activities that immediately precede the end-of-course ratings can affect the data. For example, a celebratory atmosphere in the room may improve ratings.

7. **Trainees fear reprisal, even when surveys are 'anonymous'**   Some participants almost always leave blank the demographic items on end-of-course questionnaires. In general, the more demographic items that are included, the more the fear of reprisal on the part of respondents.

8. **Trainees do not complete surveys**   Participants don't want to complete long questionnaires from which they will not personally benefit. End-of-course evaluations, then, usually compromise in favour of brevity.

9. **Ratings are sensitive to wording nuances**   If you change a key word, the ratings change. Using loaded language or controversial terms can have serious and unknown effects on patterns of response.

10. **Surveys set expectations for change**   The act of asking for people's input raises expectations that something will be done with the results. Training participants often ask later to hear how the staff used their ratings and suggestions. Be wary of asking about things that are not going to change.

11. **Surveys are quick, taken at a time when people want to leave**   Many training participants approach the task of validating a course in a cursory manner. After all, it is not their course. Their motivation is often to 'get out of here' rather than to improve the course.

12. **Statistical trends depend as much on group composition as on design and delivery**   Comparing average ratings across sessions is not an 'apple to apples' practice. The particular mix of participants – or even the presence of a difficult participant – can skew ratings.

13. **Statistical trends are not comparable when design and delivery change**   When a course takes place over a long period, there should be continuous

improvements to its design and delivery. That makes end-of-course ratings apply to non-comparable experiences; the statistical trends can be misleading.

14. **Not all instrument items are equally important, and often some of them do not even match the rating scale** How a respondent interprets an item is a function of her or his experience base; no two training experiences are exactly alike.

15. **Ratings of different parts of training (such as the opening, lectures, and hands-on activities) are always uneven and non-synergistic** For example, adults tend to rate lectures lower than they rate experimental training exercises. In addition, rating a presentation is a contaminated act. Reactions to different aspects of the training – the style of the trainer, interest in the content, use of audiovisual aids, and so forth – may co-mingle in the act of rating.

16. **The emphasis is often on excitement** People like to have fun in training courses. Many resent it when the trainer asks them to work hard, even for compelling business reasons. Training that resembles 'rest and recreation' often gets high marks. End-of-course ratings may reflect the extent to which people simply 'had a good time'.

17. **Surveys may confuse 'like' and 'worth'** Instruments that use rating scales that include words such as 'like' and 'satisfying' promote this confusion. What we need is a clear index of the usefulness of the session, not whether it made people smile.

18. **Surveys tend to focus on what is wrong** On the basis of end-of-course ratings, training-design specialists may inadvertently change what is really working in the course. If a questionnaire only solicits data for improvement, 'critiques' may become negative criticism.

19. **When a course 'raises the ante' regarding taking responsibility for being an organizational leader, a trainee may arrive at the closing session with doubts about the future ('Do I want to say?' 'Do I have what it takes?')** Such concerns can depress end-of-course ratings.

20. **Self-confrontational experiences can have temporary effects** In courses that include self-disclosure, feedback, risk taking, confrontation and divulgence of personal values, people may experience a lack of validation of their self-concepts. The experience can be temporarily upsetting, and may result in low ratings.

21. **Survey 'report cards' put pressure on staff** There is a strong tendency to 'play the ratings'. If training managers use survey results in evaluating staff, trainers may choose not to confront participants and may even slip into entertainment postures. Many trainers see end-of-course ratings as a threat.

22. **When the numbers come out of the computer, many trainers pay the most attention to the negative results** They remember the one or two 'cheap shots' that participants wrote on the questionnaires and discount the positive feedback.

23. **Reactionnaires give a very limited indication of learning** Where 'learning' is mentioned this fails to either justify or quantify the extent and depth of the learning.

24. **Make no mention usually of transfer of learning** Usually comments by the participants about what and how they are going to transfer their learning to work and to implement that learning.

25. **Is not a mathematical approach**   When tick boxes and scoring ranges are used, these give every indication of being a mathematically-based approach, but the essentially subjective basis of the responses do not enable objective results, however much they may appear to do so.

26. **Give only an impression**   They provide *at best* an impression of what the learners *think* they have learned.

THE VALUE OF REACTIONNAIRES

Although reactionnaires are generally subjective, they have their uses and, indeed, value. These can be summarized as:

• They can provide useful material for programme publicity by the use of the quasi-arithmetical analyses possible
• They provide information that is perhaps the highest level of views that can be obtained for some programmes – a criterion for validation is that objective training should be capable of objective measurement; subjective level training can only be assessed by subjective means
• They can provide a warning signal where something has gone badly wrong in a programme
• If broad objectives have been stated at the beginning of the programme by the learners, the broad brush of the reactionnaire can be used to test the reaction satisfaction of these objectives
• Responses to questions seeking useful reactive data can be sought in this way – how effectively the training need was identified; whether there was a pre-course briefing and views on its effectiveness; environmental factors that worked against full learning during the event; programme design that the learners could identify as unhelpful; the acceptability or otherwise (as opposed to value) of the learning methods used; and so on
• They demonstrate, particularly in out-of-organization courses, the important aspect of customer satisfaction with the training and development programmes.

As commented earlier, the value of a reactionnaire increases if it is improved beyond the simple tick list, with the opportunity afforded to the learners to justify their scorings, comment fully on these scorings, compare and contrast levels of information, and so on. But in the end, the responses are views, feelings and opinions only, and must be seen as such in an overall assessment.

Forms of reactionnaires

THE BLANK SHEET REVIEW

This is the simplest form of reactionnaire and avoids the use of suspect rating-scale reactions. Unless it is constructed with extreme care, the rating scale questionnaire can be so ineffective, if not dangerous, that many would-be validators are very suspicious of the validity of the approach. The popular relationship of this type of questionnaire with 'happiness sheets' discourages them from using them at all. The alternative suggested here is a freedom of approach given to the learners. This will, in many ways, produce much more acceptable results. The freedom is achieved by asking the learners to comment on the course, its value, their learning, their intentions, without giving any other specific directions about the type or amount of content. In this case, the 'validation questionnaire' is simply a headed, but blank, sheet of paper which the learners are asked to complete. At the time of issue, the validator should introduce the 'questionnaire' to the learners by asking them to enter any comments they feel are important to make about the course, the training content, the trainer or anything else related to the training. The ultimate approach would be to give the learners the validation sheet and simply ask them to comment without even giving any directions whatsoever. Usually, the learners will ask for some direction, but if this is given it should be minimal. An example of this type of validation sheet is given below.

There are, as with every validation instrument, arguments for and against the use of this approach. On the plus side, it is argued that the learners, if they enter comments without direction, are motivated to state what they feel to be important, and the trainer must take notice of what they have said. By giving the learners this free rein, however, the validation is placed completely into the hands of the learners. This in itself is a good move, but the comments may not include those aspects of the training in which the trainer is particularly interested. Parts of the course from the early stages will not be recalled as well as the later subjects, but the trainer may be very interested in the learners' reactions to them. In using the undirected approach, the validator/trainer must be prepared to accept this learner-orientated validation. If the trainers require comments on specific elements of the training, they must use one of the questionnaires which direct the learners' answers.

The trainer must recognize that if comments are not made about certain aspects of the course, at whatever stage in the event, they may not have made a sufficiently strong impact on the learner. If the trainers feel that comments on these aspects should appear on every sheet, but appeared on none, they must analyse very carefully the possible reasons for this omission – unimportant, badly presented, old material, emphasis wrong, timing of the session, and so on.

Another barrier is common to other questionnaires, but may be even more significant with the blank sheet. This concerns the amount of time allocated at the end of the course

---

ELLRAY ASSOCIATES
COUNSELLING TRAINING PROGRAMME

Please make any comments you feel should be made about the training course or anything related to it. Be as open as you wish and make your comments as extensive as you wish. Please add your name to the sheet, but this is not obligatory. Thank you.

THE BLANK SHEET REVIEW

for the completion of the validation, and the overt importance given to it in its introduction. The time factor is crucial here, because if the learners are to make significant comments they must have sufficient time to consider what they want to include and to express these on paper. Scoring questionnaires require consideration of the answers to the questions, but need less time for completion; in some cases the learners are asked to write comments, but they are directed towards the subject.

The validation must be introduced so that its importance to the learners, the trainer and others interested is made clear. Without this, the completion of the sheet will be at best fragmented, unclear, and may be with an absence of important comments, and at worse no comments at all.

The inclusion of the completer's name must be discussed with the group during the introduction, and the trainer must be completely open about its purpose – it may be required by the organization, for analysis purposes according to occupation, location, and so on, or any of the other legitimate reasons. The confidentiality of the completed sheet must also be discussed openly. These comments will help the learner to appreciate the importance of the document, and make meaningful comments more likely. If there is no analytical reason (or organizational demand) for the completer's name, the learners should not be pressed to enter their names.

A validator who wishes or needs to correlate and analyse the validation comments relating to a session or course may encounter problems if few or no comments have been made on the session the trainer wishes to validate. It will be impossible to validate a complete course from this approach, because the likelihood is virtually nil that *all* the learners will have commented on *all* the aspects of the course. This presents no problem if the interest is solely in one individual, but real difficulties arise if the learning has to be related to that of a group.

After the sheets have been completed and collected, the group can be given another training task to perform, one which will last for sufficient time for the trainer to make a swift, superficial analysis of the comments. This analysis would, for example, identify where a number of the learners were not satisfied with a particular aspect; alternatively if a small number from the group had selected a particular event or events on which to comment – either favourably or unfavourably – the question would be raised why they had selected that aspect, whilst the other learners had not; and so on. Following this 'analysis' the group is brought together for a probing discussion on the picture emerging from their validation. It is essential that the trainer does not give any indication of defensiveness or disagreement with any adverse comments. The purpose of the discussion is to find out why the adverse comments were made; why only some members made these comments; what do the others think about it; and so on.

As with other validation questionnaires, the 'blank sheet' can be given to the learners at the end of the event to take away with them and return it after consideration. There is an even greater likelihood of non-return of this type of validation sheet than almost any other, because of the requirement to write original comments rather than just score or answer questions.

FEELINGS REVIEW

The compromise between the blank sheet approach and the structured questionnaire is particularly valuable when we are considering validation of very general forms of training such as we find in the human relations area. The structured approach is very satisfactory when attempting to validate training which is highly structured, such as a series of specific knowledge inputs or discrete skill activities. However, when the training is unstructured or is very learner-centred, this structured approach runs into difficulties of definition in what is to be validated. The structured, specific approach is the nearest one can get to a quantitative, objective assessment of objective training methods, an impression being heightened by the apparently mathematical nature of the instrument. But, if the training is itself of a subjective nature, then the best we can hope for is a subjective assessment – in fact, for subjective training the most appropriate method of approach may be the subjective approach. Facts are objective, feelings are subjective, so an assessment of feelings will necessarily also be a subjective one.

The feelings review approach is commonly used in human relations training where feelings rather than facts abound. This is particularly so in interpersonal or interactive skills training. The questionnaire following the sense of the training elicits the real feelings and attitudes of the participants in the terms used during the training itself. In this approach, free and far-ranging comments are obtained. However, the format does not allow an easy comparison between the answers of individuals as is possible with a numeric scale. Perhaps there is much to be said for this 'disadvantage' in that the validation answers have to be read more closely than a set of simple numbers.

One example of this approach is shown in Figure 8.1 which shows a feelings questionnaire used at the end of an interpersonal skills course. This questionnaire demonstrates the range and variety of questions which can be asked if the training had led to this level of openness between the participants and the tutor.

The end-of-course recommended reactionnaire

In Chapter 7 two end-of-day forms of reactionnaire were suggested, the questions and their formats, particularly Figure 7.5 reflecting effective forms of general reactionnaires. These forms can be adapted as end-of-course reactionnaires and a full example is shown in Figure 8.2.

It must be reiterated that a reactionnaire even of this recommended nature is:

* intended to obtain feelings, views and opinions only
* intended to be used on selected occasions only and not at the end of every event. Such occasions might be:
  – For the first two or three events of a new programme
  – Where there are indications/suspicions that something is going wrong with a training programme.

Specific reactionnaires

More to the point and usually more effective and useful is the specific form of reactionnaire that seeks information from participants about their views of certain aspects of an event – for example the training environment. Figure 8.3 shows an example of this with the hotel accommodation for the training for investigation.

Name _____   Date _____

INTERPERSONAL SKILLS REVIEW

1.   The major feeling I have about this learning event is . . . . . .

2.   If this course had been a film, a play or a book, the title would have been . . . . . .

3.   The part(s) of the event I enjoyed most . . . . . .

4.   The part(s) of the experience I can make most use of . . . . . .

5.   Something I learned, or had usefully confirmed about myself is . . . . . .

6.   Something I learned, or had usefully confirmed about other people is . . . . . .

7.   The part(s) of the event I enjoyed least was(were) . . . . . .

8.   The part(s) of the event I can make least use of is(are) . . . . . .

9.   If I were starting this experience again I would . . . . . .

10.   One thing I regret having done is . . . . . .

11.   One thing I regret not having done is . . . . . .

12.   Right now I am feeling . . . . . .

Figure 8.1   Feelings review questionnaire

Name   **Date**   **Course**

Please consider the course that you have just completed and against each item circle the number that most closely represent your views about the programme. The spaces in between the two extremes are to enable you to give your rating at stages between the extremes.

I feel that the course/workshop/programme was:

Clear   6   5   4   3   2   1   Confusing
If you have circled 3, 2, or 1, please comment why you have given that rating.

Not too
complicated   6   5   4   3   2   1   Too complicated
If you have circled 3, 2, or 1, please comment why you have given that rating.

Well presented   6   5   4   3   2   1   Poorly presented
If you have circled 3, 2, or 1, please comment why you have given that rating.

Contained   Contained
right amount   6   5   4   3   2   1   too much
If you have circled 3, 2, or 1, please comment why you have given that rating.

Essential   6   5   4   3   2   1   Of little use to me
If you have circled 3, 2, or 1, please comment why you have given that rating.

Timed just right   6   5   4   3   2   1   Time too short/
                                                                       too long
If you have circled 3, 2, or 1, please comment why you have given that rating.

Very active   6   5   4   3   2   1   Very passive
If you have circled 3, 2, or 1, please comment why you have given that rating.

Demanding   6   5   4   3   2   1   Undemanding
If you have circled 3, 2, or 1, please comment why you have given that rating.

Challenging   6   5   4   3   2   1   Unchallenging
If you have circled 3, 2, or 1, please comment why you have given that rating.

I learned a lot   6   5   4   3   2   1   I learned little
If you have circled 3, 2, or 1, please comment why you have given that rating.

Confirmed a lot   6   5   4   3   2   1   Confirmed little
If you have circled 3, 2, or 1, please comment why you have given that rating.

It made me think   6   5   4   3   2   1   It didn't make me
                                                                       think
If you have circled 3, 2, or 1, please comment why you have given that rating.

My objectives were   6   5   4   3   2   1   My objectives
fully achieved   were not achieved
If you have circled 3, 2, or 1, please comment why you have given that rating.

I would recommend this programme/course/workshop to a colleague   YES   NO

Any other comments:

Figure 8.2   End-of-course reactionnaire

SEMANTIC DIFFERENTIAL QUESTIONNAIRE

When we are attempting to validate learning which is most wholly concerned with behavioural and attitudinal skills there are many difficulties in the way of producing an objective test. In fact, as we are dealing with almost completely subjective aspects it may be too much to seek an objective assessment.

If self-diagnosed attitudes have been obtained at the start of a course by means of diagnostic reactionnaires constructed with Thurstone or Likert scales, the reactionnaire can be repeated at the end of the course. Any differences between the two can be discussed and assessed as evidence of change, usually, however, in conjunction with other assessment aids.

It must be recognized that we are dealing not only with highly subjective results, but also with reactionnaires which are highly susceptible to false answers, whether deliberate or not.

These reactionnaires are more difficult to compare than those based on semantic differentials to which a numerical weighting can be added easily. Again one has to be careful and not assume that this makes the approach really quantitative and objective. This is not

TRAINING ACCOMMODATION

Name   **Date**   **Course**

Training accommodation address

Please ring the score number that is nearest to your views.

BEDROOM COMFORT
Good   6   5   4   3   2   1   Poor
If you have scored 3, 2, or 1, please state the reasons why you have given that rating.

BEDROOM FACILITIES
Good   6   5   4   3   2   1   Poor
If you have scored 3, 2, or 1, please state the reasons why you have given that rating.

MEALS QUALITY
Good   6   5   4   3   2   1   Poor
If you have scored 3, 2, or 1, please state the reasons why you have given that rating.

TRAINING ACCOMMODATION COMFORT
Good   6   5   4   3   2   1   Poor
If you have scored 3, 2, or 1, please state the reasons why you have given that rating.

TRAINING ACCOMMODATION FACILITIES
Good   6   5   4   3   2   1   Poor
If you have scored 3, 2, or 1, please state the reasons why you have given that rating.

Any other comments:

Figure 8.3   A specific form of questionnaire

so: all it does is to make comparisons easy and thus help identify significant changes.

The form of the semantic differential reactionnaire used at the end of the training is exactly the same as the one used at the beginning of or before the training. Both forms are then compared and analysed for indications of change. This is the classic pre- and post-test approach. However, when we are looking at behavioural and attitudinal changes there are serious shortcomings to this simple approach.

If we are assessing a course on supervisory or management skills, one of the aspects we would want to look at would be the learner's use of time. Consequently, at the start of the training we could ask a question related to the learner's management of time and ask for a self-rating on a scale of ten. A typical approach could be:

Use of time at work

Badly controlled   1   2   3   4   5   6   7   8   9   10   Well controlled

At the start of the course an individual might self-rate at scale 7, that is to say self-assessing as quite skilled, though not exceptionally skilled, in the use of time. As the assessment is self-generated the rating must necessarily be subjective, but at least if we use the reactionnaire on more than one occasion, the subjective judgements are all made from the same base.

If the same reactionnaire is used as an end-of-course validation test, the traditional pre- and post-test approach has been fulfilled. As the reactionnaires are identical we can compare the results on an apparently reasonable basis. At the start of the course the time use element was rated at 7; let us assume that at the end of the course it is rated at 8. This is not an exceptional increase in skill, but remember that the initial assessment was 7 – not a bad level of skill to start with.

However, there are several other possibilities which might be usefully considered. The assessment of 7 may have been an accurate one and therefore the increase of 1 in point skill may be realistic. But there may have been some aspects of self-delusion in the initial rating, and, though the end rating may be more realistic than the initial rating, the increase in skill of 1 point may not reflect the true increase.

This result will almost certainly be because of contamination of the individual's assessment by the training: the learners will almost certainly have had their awareness and perceptions heightened as a result of the training.

The three-test approach

One way of attempting to test the results of this possible contamination is to introduce a third completion of the same questionnaire. After the questionnaire has been completed for the second time, at the end of the course, the learner is asked to complete it again, a third time. But on this occasion they are asked to complete it *as if they were completing it at the beginning of the course but with their current perception of their skill* – in other words, knowing what they know now. Let us assume in this example that the score of 7 was at a higher level than it was in reality. Consequently when the learner completed the questionnaire for the third time with new awareness, a true initial level gave a score of 3. This showed that the increase in skill from 3 to 8 was a significant 5 points. When this increase was compared with other observations of skill practice and the learner's own views of skill increase, an increase of 5 points seemed to be a more realistic validation of the training.

I have used this three-test approach on a number of different training courses, particularly those concerned with human relations training. At the start of an interpersonal skills training course the learners complete the self-assessment questionnaire shown in Figure 8.4. This completion is designated completion 1. The same questionnaire is used again at the end of the course and on this occasion is designated completion 2. Finally, in order to obtain the more realistic assessment without training contamination, the questionnaire is administered again as completion 3.

From these three questionnaires comparisons can be made through use of the rating scores, but the warning must be repeated that although we are dealing with numerical ratings, the base data is still highly subjective. The comparisons can be made to show differences not only between completion 2 (the end-of-training completion) and completion 1 (the original initial completion) but also between completion 2 and completion 3 (the reassessed starting level).

Figure 8.5 shows a summary of the completed questionnaires with the comparisons added. The figures show that when the end-of-course assessments (column 2) are compared with the initial assessments (column 1) there has been an increase in skill in some elements, no change in others and a slight decrease in skill in others, within a range –2 to +5 points. When the individual changes are totalled the result is an overall increase in skill of 19. However, as we are considering a course which is concerned with increasing awareness, it is safe to assume that the initial assessment was incorrectly made by learners who have awareness problems. The end-of-course results can therefore be more realistically compared with a reassessed starting position, since by the end of the course it is again safe to assume that awareness has increased. Consequently when we compare column 2 with the reassessed view of completion 3, certain changes are observable. There are still some decreases in skill, but these are smaller and fewer in number: some decreases have become increases, some of the 'no changes' have now become increases and many of the increases have become bigger increases. The sum of the changes has now become a total increase of 46 points compared with the pre/post test of 19 points.

However, one has to be very careful in an interpretation of comparative assessments such as those under discussion, since a successful validation can produce widely different results from those described above.

Some situations can result in the end results being significantly poorer (lower scored) than the initial scorings, even when the revised figures are taken into account. These occasions can suggest to the trainer that the event has been a learning failure. But what usually emerges is that the learners have realized that their initial self-assessments were hopelessly unrealistic. A similar change can occur when learning in fact has not occurred to the anticipated extent – this can often be explained by the learners realizing that their initial assessments were far too high and that consequently they had too much to learn in the time allotted to the event: so far from being a failure, the event has highlighted what they need to do.

My experience has been that the three-test approach produces much more realistic results (not necessarily 'better') than the pre-/post-test approach, although it must be recognized that the method is still sensitive to subjective treatment. This subjectivity, of course, is found in any form of self-assessment.

NAME _____   DATE _____

BEHAVIOUR SKILLS QUESTIONNAIRE   1   2   3   4

Please enter a tick in the space against each item on the scale 1 to 10 representing where you consider your present level of skill might be.

IN A GROUP AS A MEMBER OF THE GROUP

		LOW							HIGH		
		1	2	3	4	5	6	7	8	9	10
1.	Controlling amount of talking I do.										
2.	Being brief and concise.										
3.	Supporting others' ideas.										
4.	Incorporating others' ideas.										
5.	Being aware of my behaviour.										
6.	Initiating proposals and suggestions.										
7.	Explaining my disagreements with the points of view of others.										
8.	Controlling amount of giving own views.										
9.	Stressing feelings of others.										
10.	Thinking before talking.										
11.	Controlling amount of interrupting others.										
12.	Being aware of behaviour of others.										
13.	Controlling a tendency to outdo others.										
14.	Being positive in the group.										
15.	Bringing out others' opinions.										
16.	Controlling how much I try to dominate the group.										
17.	Getting others to listen to my view.										
18.	Withstanding silence.										
19.	Telling others what my feelings are.										
20.	Being helpful to others.										

Where would you rate your general, overall level of interpersonal skills?

1   2   3   4   5   6   7   8   9   10

Figure 8.4   Three-test approach: self-assessment questionnaire

Category	COLUMN 1 (Initial)	COLUMN 2 (Terminal)	COLUMN 3 (Revised initial)

In a group as member of the group

	Category	COLUMN 1 (Initial)	COLUMN 2 (Terminal)	COLUMN 3 (Revised initial)
1.	Controlling amount of talking	4	7 (+3)	4 (+3)
2.	Being brief and concise	4	4 (–)	4 (–)
3.	Supporting others' ideas	5	5 (–)	5 (–)
4.	Building on others' ideas	5	6 (+1)	3 (+3)
5.	Being aware of my behaviour	5	7 (+2)	4 (+3)
6.	Initiating proposals and suggestions	7	6 (–1)	5 (+2)
7.	Explaining my disagreement with the points of view of others	7	6 (–1)	5 (+1)
8.	Controlling amount of giving own views	5	5 (–)	3 (+2)
9.	Sensing feelings of others	4	7 (+3)	3 (+4)
10.	Thinking before talking	4	7 (+3)	3 (+4)
11.	Controlling amount of interrupting others	5	6 (+1)	3 (+3)
12.	Being aware of behaviour of others	6	8 (+2)	2 (+6)
13.	Controlling tendency to outdo others	7	7 (–)	7 (–)
14.	Being positive	6	7 (+1)	8 (–1)
15.	Bringing out others' opinions	7	7 (–)	4 (+3)
16.	Controlling how much I try to dominate the group	6	4 (–2)	3 (+1)
17.	Getting others to listen to my views	7	8 (+1)	8 (–)
18.	Withstanding silence	4	7 (+3)	3 (+4)
19.	Telling others what my feelings are	4	7 (+3)	2 (+5)
20.	Being helpful to others	8	8 (–)	7 (+1)
	General overall level of interpersonal skills	6	6 (–)	4 (+2)
			(Total 19)	(Total 45)

Figure 8.5   Summary of questionnaire answers

Category	Column 1	Column 2	Column 3
1	4	7 (+3)	7 (+3)
2	4	7 (+3)	7 (+3)
3	4	7 (+3)	6 (+2)
4	3	6 (+3)	4 (+1)
5	3	7 (+4)	5 (+2)
6	3	6 (+3)	5 (+2)
7	3	4 (+1)	5 (+2)
8	3	8 (+5)	3 (–)
9	3	7 (+4)	6 (+3)
10	3	5 (+2)	5 (+2)
11	3	6 (+3)	3 (–)
12	4	6 (+2)	5 (+1)
13	5	4 (–1)	3 (–2)
14	6	4 (–2)	3 (–3)
15	4	5 (+1)	5 (+1)
16	3	4 (+1)	6 (+3)
17	3	5 (+2)	3 (–)
18	3	7 (+4)	3 (–)
19	4	5 (+1)	4 (–)
20	6	7 (+1)	6 (–)
Overall	3	5 (+2)	4 (+1)
		Total 45	Total 21

Figure 8.6   Statistical comparison of questionnaire answers

BEHAVIOUR ANALYSIS

Assessment of change is even more difficult when the training is concerned with attitude and behavioural skills changes. Most observations in these cases will be subjective. However, where there is the need to observe behaviours with a view to effecting a change or modification in them, a more objective instrument of observation can be used. We have seen earlier that behaviour analysis can be used throughout a course to plot the development of a behaviour pattern. It has also been shown how this pattern can be brought to the attention of the learners in a matrix form, with the suggestion that the data can be used to plan any behaviour modification necessary. Behaviour analysis can be continued and any modification recorded as some validation of change. The statement is qualified by use of the word 'some' since, although the behavioural observation may be accurate, the observation may not necessarily represent only real learning. The individual or group may behave in the way which is appropriate to the behavioural model which will be the basis of the training, but performance at the appropriate level on the course need not necessarily mean that this performance will be transferred to work – the learners may simply be pandering to the trainer. However, it is all we are in a position to observe and we have to be satisfied with it as being all that is possible to judge at this stage.

REPERTORY GRID

It was suggested earlier that attitudes, feelings and the attributes of various jobs can be determined prior to or at the beginning of training by an interview utilizing the Repertory Grid approach. As with many of the other approaches suggested, the Repertory Grid can be repeated at the end of the event. The differences can then be compared with the earlier completion and analysed. The Repertory Grid approach has an advantage over some other other interview methods in that the interviewer has much less direct involvement and hence there is less likelihood of interviewer contamination.

9 *End-of-event validation – 2*

There are three principal documents connected with the end-of-course validation of training. The first, used frequently in training, albeit not specifically – 'validation' – is the reactionnaire in its various forms described in Chapter 8. The other two will be discussed in this chapter and are:

- The Learning Questionnaire
- The Action Plan

Both of these documents relate directly to real validation of a programme and form the link between the training and learning and the implementation of this learning at work, and hence an approach to the training ROI.

The Learning Questionnaire

Unlike the reactionnaires used during and at the end of a training course/workshop/ programme, the Learning Questionnaire (LQ) concentrates on validating the achievement of the objectives of both the training event and also those of the learners. Although the statements made on this document can still, pedantically, be termed views or opinions, they are immediately checked against the objectives and also at the later stage at work when the stated learning is to be implemented. The LQ can follow on from, and support/confirm, any tests of knowledge or skill used near the end of the event, and it identifies in a summarized form this learning and any other not tested in any way.

A properly designed LQ concentrates on obtaining full textual responses from the learners rather than an, often, facile tick list. It also, in addition to its function in the validation/evaluation process, helps to consolidate in the learners' minds what they have followed during the programme, what they have learned from this content and prepares them for their eventual action planning.

On the occasions mentioned earlier, the LQ can be supplemented by a reactionnaire as suggested in Figures 8.2 and 8.3, namely in a new programme or an ailing programme.

The construction of scoring ranges, if included in the questionnaire, should follow the advice given for similar reactionnaires. There may be reasons, however – for example, requests by senior managers for tabular information – why the scoring ranges should be summarized and analysed as quasi-mathematical products. These must be viewed with some suspicion, since the completion of many range scores or tick lists are at the reactionnaire level of views, opinions and feelings.

Figure 9.1 suggests a form of end-of-event LQ that I have used in different forms over a number of years and found to be a useful questionnaire both from my viewpoint and that of the learners. This questionnaire leads to an assessment of the learning achieved, both as new and confirmed learning, and consequently can be related to the objectives of the programme and the learners. The entries, following reflection, are both a further reminder and reinforcement, and consolidate in the learners' minds what they are going to do with the learning on their return to work, the LQ comments preparing the learners for the completion of their action plans. The final part of the questionnaire seeks their views on any learning aspects that they were expecting to be raised in the event, but were not raised, and any related aspects that they needed that were not touched on. The strength and frequency of these latter comments are particularly useful in alerting the trainers to a need to review the programme.

Name   **Date**   **Course**

Please consider and reflect on the learning programme you have just attended and complete the following in as much detail as possible. On the scoring ranges, please ring the score number you feel most closely represents your views.

Part One: Learning

To what extent do you feel you have learned from the programme?

A lot   6   5   4   3   2   1   Little

If you have given a rating 3, 2, or 1, why have you given that rating?

What have you learned?

What do you intend to do with this learning on your return to work?

Part Two: Confirmation of learning

To what extent do you feel your previous learning (perhaps some you had forgotten) has been confirmed in a useful manner, or has been usefully brought back to your memory?

A lot   6   5   4   3   2   1   Little

If you have given a rating 3, 2, or 1, why have you given that rating?

What has been confirmed, etc?

What do you intend to do with this learning on your return to work?

Part Three: Non-learning

What have you *not* learned on the programme that you needed to and/or expected to learn? Please describe fully any items.

What can you do about this?

Part Four: Any other comments

Figure 9.1   A Learning Questionnaire (LQ)

Immediate or delayed validation

A much-discussed topic in training circles is whether end-of-event LQs and reactionnaires should be completed at the end of the event and handed in then, or given to the participants before they leave and they are asked to return them after a few days back at work.

The arguments *for* completion at the end of the event include:

- The event and its contents are fresh in their minds and any comments will come without difficulty
- Certain aspects of their learning will stand out above others and these will be obviously important aspects on which they comment
- There is the opportunity for the learners to discuss their views with each other
- The trainer is given immediate feedback
- Unclear statements can be clarified immediately
- Questions raised can be cleared or promised an early response by the trainer
- In normal circumstances, 100% response is guaranteed.

The arguments *against* completion at the end of the event include:

- Going home is uppermost in their minds
- The participants may be in either a state of euphoria or a state of depression depending on whether the event was successful, exciting or a failure
- The trainer was a very well-liked personality, or the trainer was not liked or respected, and this might contaminate immediate completion
- Dominant members exert an influence on the views of others
- Some people prefer to delay their views until they have had a longer period to reflect/until they can relate the learning to their work.

The arguments *for* delaying completion until after the participants have returned to work include:

- The learners are given time to consider the value of the event and their learning and to what extent this has been real learning that can be implemented at work
- The debriefing meeting has taken place with their line managers and further thoughts have emerged from this discussion
- Completion takes place away from the artificial atmosphere of the training event with the possible contaminations mentioned above
- Comments, particularly personal ones relating to the trainer, or reflecting on the trainer, might be embarrassing to make with the trainer present.

Arguments *against* delaying completion until after the participants have returned to work include:

- Return cannot be guaranteed unless a foolproof method is installed
- The immediate pressure of work on return takes on a priority, and as a result, in some cases completion is simply forgotten.

- The learners have no intention of completing the questionnaire
- The learners do not wish to commit comments to paper
- There is a reduced/reducing commitment to support the trainers with feedback.

Whichever argument appears to you to be the strongest, always remember that the environment can play an important part in the decision, some of the factors being:

1. The time available at the end of the event to enable a full completion (and discussion where possible);
2. The organization's culture (if all the participants come from the same organization) that can allow the trainer ready contact with the participants when they have returned to work, the trainer has sufficient authority to require return (but care must be taken over any overt indication of pressure), and the culture encourages these actions.

Otherwise, if completion is delayed for, say three or four days after they have returned to work, there can be strategies to ensure return:

1. An arrangement with the participants' line managers to ensure returns
2. Follow-up by the trainer by telephone or in writing (including e-mails) reminding them of the importance and value of the documents
3. Giving the learners a stamped, addressed envelope, addressed to the trainer and noted with the date by which the form should be returned
4. Rather than give the questionnaires to the participants at the end of the event, send them after their return, perhaps routing this through the line manager where (1) is relevant or using a modified (2) approach
5. Depending on the number of questionnaires, reactionnaires, etc. required, these can be separated with the completion of the most important/useful first, say the LQ, then the action plan and finally the reactionnaire, to be completed within a week. Alternatives might be the completion of one of the instruments, say the reactionnaire, if used, at the end of the course, the remainder being delayed, or the most important one, the action plan, being the one to have completed at the end of the event.

E-mails are becoming useful tools with their increasing availability and use as simple, quick and easy contacts with learners and their line managers following an event, perhaps linking with an interactive Internet site, or distribution via the organization's own Intranet. Return can be equally easy and prompt using the same methods.

Trainer assessment

So far, the validations, evaluations and assessments have all been concerned with the training material of the programme and its effects on the training and the learning; no mention has been made of the trainer in this respect. In many ways, to obtain an objective assessment is a more difficult subject to approach than a neutral critique of the training material. Where the learners are involved in assessing in this way, there are also moral and knowledge issues of a) whether learners should assess their trainers, and b) whether they are in a knowledge/skill position to do so.

Depending on the circumstances and the reasons for trainer assessment, the people who might at times be concerned in this assessment include:

- The trainer's line manager (e.g. the Training Manager, HRD Manager) for appraisal reasons
- The learners to assist with a complete validation of the training programme – after all, a programme constructed from the best material possible can fail if the trainer is unable to help the learners to learn from this material
- The trainers themselves: in many cases there is nobody available/willing to perform an assessment of their skills, so the only people that can even try to approach this are themselves
- Co-trainers or peers who have agreed with a trainer to observe them and give feedback on their performance.

This subject is summarized here, as for fuller guidance about trainer assessment reference should be made to *Trainer Assessment* (Rae, 2002).

Assessment of trainer practice by observation

BY THE LEARNERS

An assessment of the skills of the trainer can only be made by direct observation of them in a practical working situation – neither an easy task for the observer, nor for the person observed, as anyone who has been in a similar position of being observed and knowing about it will confirm. Many people feel that the learners are in the best position to observe and assess the trainer, since:

- The learners on a training course are on the direct receiving end of the approach to training and learning by the trainer
- Only the learners can say how much what the trainer did and with what skills helped them in their eventual learning
- The participants on a training course may be the only ones who might be interested in assessing the trainer (they are doing this mentally from Day 1 in any case!).

However there are arguments that are raised against learner assessment:

- If the trainers know that their learners are going to assess them, this can have a significant effect on how they approach the learners, the training taking a second place to their public image
- People assessment is always open to contamination, the views on the trainer being skewed by how they talk and are received as talking to each individual; the learners preferred or did not prefer their out-of-class socializing; some individuals felt the trainer was being particularly hard on them or soft on others; some participants simply liked or disliked the trainer; and so on
- The learners, even if they have attended several training courses, are unlikely to have much skill in assessing the skills of a professional practitioner. Their views may be inappropriate from a lack of understanding of the techniques used

- Individuals or groups may be biased if they felt that the trainer either supported their views or disagreed with them (and said so).

The for and against views should be considered before it is decided to enable the learners to assess their trainers. This reflecting may result in the decision that more effective validation might be obtained by using the end-of-course LQ – if a lot of learning has been achieved there is a very good chance that the trainer was a successful (effective) one personally, although this can be a very subjective view.

BY A CO-TRAINER OR A LINE MANAGER

An assessment for feedback made in this way will usually be an agreement between co-workers on a training programme and will also more often than not be on a knock-for-knock basis – all will observe and assess each other and give feedback in a co-trainer session. The major factors in favour of being assessed by a co-trainer are a) that they have a vested interest in both performing their training roles to the maximum effectiveness, and b) both will have training skills, thus being in a position to be able to comment on the skills of others in a professional way.

Similar favourable comments as above may also relate to assessment by the trainer's line manager, particularly if they are a training manager with knowledge and skills in training of their own. There will be in the mind of the observed trainer, however, an increased element of stress, being aware of this observation and assessment and its (potential) use for practitioner and career appraisal.

The problems, over and above the appraisal syndrome, arise when the line manager is the trainer's manager for administration purposes only, that is to say they are not trainers themselves and are in a similar position to that of the learners on the course. In such cases, other evidence, such as LQs and reactionnaires might also be used in conjunction with the direct observations.

BY THE TRAINERS THEMSELVES

Where it is not possible or desirable for assessments to be made by direct observations as described above, any observational assessments might be supplemented by comments by the trainers themselves on their own performances and skills. These are obviously highly subjective, albeit based to some extent on the comments of others, but they may help to build up a full, composite picture of the trainer.

Whichever method or methods are used, if at all possible, as described in the case of the co-workers, every observation should be discussed with the trainer and others involved. Even a skilled trainer observing another may fall into the trap of not realizing why the practising trainer used a particular technique, until a discussion enables the reality to emerge.

OBSERVATION FORMATS

The observation instruments will in the main be more inclined to the reactionnaire as there will be significant subjectivity involved, although this may be counteracted by several observations. There are two principal instruments, the first of which is a modified Behaviour

Analysis (see Chapter 5) record in which behaviours attributed to the skills of an effective trainer might be identified and compared with the effective model. Another may be a specially designed questionnaire/reactionnaire using relevant questions for the situation (such a questionnaire can be used, modified if necessary, as the trainer's self-assessment document).

Figure 9.2 suggests a format for observation of a trainer presenting an input session and Figure 9.3 where they are facilitating an activity. Both these forms can be readily modified for use by the trainer in a self-assessment mode.

Name of trainer   **Session/Activity**
Date

Please complete the following questions by ringing each rating that most nearly represents your view. In addition to your rating, add comments to support this rating so that the feedback can be complete.

1.   Opening platform presence

To what extent did the trainer exhibit nervousness during the opening stages?

| None | 6 | 5 | 4 | 3 | 2 | 1 | A great deal |

How?

How did any nerves disappear as the session continued?

| Quickly | 6 | 5 | 4 | 3 | 2 | 1 | Not at all |

2.   Opening of session

To what extent did the trainer obtain attention from the start?

| A great deal | 6 | 5 | 4 | 3 | 2 | 1 | Little |

How?

3.   Continuation of the sessions

To what extent did the trainer maintain attention as the session progressed?

| All the time | 6 | 5 | 4 | 3 | 2 | 1 | Lost it |

How?

4.   Eye contact (showing interest)

To what extent did the trainer maintain eye contact with the group?

When speaking

| Most of time | 6 | 5 | 4 | 3 | 2 | 1 | Rarely |

In what way?

When listening

| Most of time | 6 | 5 | 4 | 3 | 2 | 1 | Rarely |

In what way?

5. Sincerity

How sincere and committed to the subject did the trainer appear to be?

Very		6	5	4	3	2	1		Not at all

How did this show?

6. Enthusiasm

How enthusiastic was the trainer's manner?

Very		6	5	4	3	2	1		Not at all

How was this evidenced?

7. General manner

To what extent did the trainer's manner relax you and encourage you to listen?

A great deal		6	5	4	3	2	1		Little

What distracting mannerisms were present?

8. Voice

How clear was the trainer to the whole group?

Very clear		6	5	4	3	2	1		Unclear

If unclear, or tending towards unclear, in what way?

How appropriate was the language used?

Appropriate		6	5	4	3	2	1		Inappropriate

If inappropriate, or tending towards inappropriate, in what way?

9. Visual aids

To what extent did the trainer use visual aids to vary the presentation?

A great deal		6	5	4	3	2	1		None

10. Visual aids relevance

How relevant to the training were the visual aids?

Relevant		6	5	4	3	2	1		Not relevant

In what way?

11. Visual aids quality

What was the quality of the visual aids used?

Excellent		6	5	4	3	2	1		Poor

Why?

12. Visual aids use

How effectively were the visual aids used?

Very well		6	5	4	3	2	1		Badly

How?

13. Subject coverage

How well within the objectives was the subject covered?

Completely		6	5	4	3	2	1		Poorly

What was omitted or unclear?

14. Use of session notes

Was the use of session notes distracting?

Not at all		6	5	4	3	2	1		Very much

In what way?

15. Use of questions

How well did the trainer use questions to the group?

Very well		6	5	4	3	2	1		Badly

How?

16. Response to questions

How well did the trainer respond to questions from the group?

Very well		6	5	4	3	2	1		Badly

How?

17. Learner involvement

To what extent were the learners involved in the session?

A great deal		6	5	4	3	2	1		Not at all

How appropriate was this level?

18. Classroom control

How well were the session and the learners controlled?

Effectively		6	5	4	3	2	1		Ineffectively

In what way?

19. Handouts 1

How adequate were the handouts?

Adequate		6	5	4	3	2	1		Inadequate

How?

20. Handouts 2

How relevant were the handouts?

Relevant		6	5	4	3	2	1		Not relevant

Why?

21. Closing the session

How well did the trainer bring the session to a close?

Well   6   5   4   3   2   1   Badly

What was the cause of this?

Was a final summary used?

22. Timing

How well did the trainer keep within the time constraints?

Completely   6   5   4   3   2   1   Badly

What were the principal causes?

23. Pace

How well did the trainer pace the presentation?

Very well   6   5   4   3   2   1   Badly

How?

24. Appropriate approach

Was this the most appropriate tactical approach for this subject or group? If not, what approach might have been more appropriate?

25. Creativity

To what extent was creativity of approach, methods, resources, etc. practised as required?

Fully   6   5   4   3   2   1   Not at all

In what circumstances?

26. How would you rate the presentation of the session overall?

Excellent   6   5   4   3   2   1   Poor

Figure 9.2   Trainer assessment – input session

Name of trainer   **Session/Activity**
Date

Please complete the following questions by ringing each rating that most nearly represents your view. In addition to your rating, add comments to support this rating so that the feedback can be complete.

1.   Opening of session

To what extent did the trainer obtain attention from the start?

A great deal   6   5   4   3   2   1   Little

How?

2. Sincerity

How sincere and committed to the subject did the trainer appear to be?

All the time   6   5   4   3   2   1   Lost it

How?

3. Enthusiasm

How enthusiastic was the trainer's manner?

Very   6   5   4   3   2   1   Unenthusiastic

In what way?

4. Setting the scene

To what extent did the trainer appear to have prepared the activity area(s) before the start of the activity?

Well   6   5   4   3   2   1   Not at all

How did this show?

5. Introducing the topic

How well did the trainer introduce the activity?

Clearly   6   5   4   3   2   1   In a confused
                                                                manner

What happened?

6. Activity description

How clear was the trainer's description of the activity?

Very clear   6   5   4   3   2   1   Unclear

What was omitted or unclear?

7. Activity stages descriptions

How clear was the trainer's description of the stages of the activity?

Very clear   6   5   4   3   2   1   Not clear

In what way?

8. Activity briefs

How clear were the activity briefs issued to the participants?

Very clear   6   5   4   3   2   1   Unclear

How?

9. Observers

How clear were the roles of the observers made?

Very clear   6   5   4   3   2   1   Unclear

How?

10. Observer briefs

How clear were the observer briefs or observation forms?

Very clear   6   5   4   3   2   1   Unclear

In what way?

11. Trainer interventions

To what extent did the trainer make appropriate interventions during the activity?

Appropriately   6   5   4   3   2   1   Inappropriately

What interventions were made?

12. Activity review 1

How appropriate was the method of activity review?

Appropriate   6   5   4   3   2   1   Inappropriate

13. Activity review 2

How well did the trainer control the review?

Very well   6   5   4   3   2   1   Badly

What happened?

14. Summary

How well did the trainer summarize the key points resulting from the activity?

With skill   6   5   4   3   2   1   Clumsily

What happened?

15. Appropriateness of the activity

How appropriate was the activity for this event?

Appropriate   6   5   4   3   2   1   Inappropriate

Why was this so?

16. Appropriateness of the type of this activity

How appropriate was the type of activity used?

Appropriate   6   5   4   3   2   1   Inappropriate

Why was this so?

17. Timing

How well did the trainer keep the activity within the time constraints?

Completely   6   5   4   3   2   1   Badly

What happened?

Figure 9.3   Trainer assessment – activity facilitating

Action planning

Action planning at the end of a training course/workshop/programme serves several purposes: it helps learners to reinforce their views on what they have learned during the programme, enables them to reflect on this learning and how they will implement it when they return to work. In the last-named aspect, the action plan also acts as the vital link between the training/learning on the training programme and the implementation of the learning, the basic reason for the individual's attendance on the training programme so that the operation of the organization can be improved. It is also the start of the second stage in the assessment of the ROI on training. Consequently, substantial importance should be given to the production of an action plan on *every* training programme, with the obvious planning of time to enable this to happen before the end of the programme.

Without a considered and formulated action plan, the learners may leave the training event with every intention of putting their learning into practice, but, when they arrive back at work, lack of interest by the boss and colleagues, pressure of immediate work, active disagreement with the new ideas by the boss and colleagues, adverse circumstances, and so on, may demotivate the learners who will slip back into their pre-training ways.

So the action plan is a commitment by the learners to implement their learning when they return to work, preferably supported by their boss and colleagues, but with the document to remind them.

The action plan also acts as a further validation of the training, as it shows for the intended action the key training/learning points of both the trainer and the learner. Examination of the plans and comparison between the various plans of all the learners will show in learning terms (the only true validation) to what extent the hopes and expectations have been achieved. Variation between the learners on a programme is a natural event, but some major, common variations, seen from their inclusion or exclusion, can indicate particularly good or bad aspects of the programme.

However, the other principal important feature of the action plan is the link between training and work and the encouragement for the line manager to take an active involvement in the training/learning process. The practical application of this aspect will be discussed in Chapter 12 which leads more and more towards an assessment of the ROI in the training.

THE ACTION PLAN FORMAT

The guidelines for the learner in the production of an action plan include consideration that it should:

- be simple and straightforward
- be clear and unambiguous
- contain items that can be implemented by the learner at work, with or without support or any resources that might be available
- contain comments on the methods to be used, the resource required and the timings – start, finish times or dates – for all the action items
- not contain more items than the learner should be able to implement without too much delay or problem at work. If the action list appears to be too complex or long, more than one action plan should be produced, each plan being dated for progressive introduction.

As far as the last item in the list above is concerned, some practitioners suggest that no more than three items should be included, as this is a number that a returned learner should be able to deal with easily; more than this and the learner could find problems and thus be discouraged from implementing any items. I feel that a more realistic approach is that suggested in the list above: obviously a very extensive list, say 20 items or more, is usually unrealistic, but the final decision must be guided by the type and complexity of the items, and the learner's opportunities and abilities to implement them.

PRODUCING THE ACTION PLAN

There are a number of key steps towards producing an Action Plan:

1. Completion of the action plan should be preceded by completion of the end-of-event Learning Questionnaire (LQ) which consequently links the learning views with initial, intended action thoughts and thence the action plan.
2. Wherever possible, and available, interim documents, e.g. Learning Logs or end-of-day validations, should be used as reminders.
3. The individual learners should then complete their action plans, taking particular account of:
   - the feasibility of implementation of the items
   - materials, resources, help from others that might need timing
   - how they will implement the items
   - how these plans might have an effect on their relationships with their colleagues
   - possible obstacles to the plans
   - likely or possible supports for the plan.
4. When the items they would like to include have been identified, it is useful to prioritize their implementation order, e.g. the least important or simplest first, rather than concentrating on a complex, time-consuming and difficult item which may fail.
5. I have found it a useful practice, following the initial construction of the action plan, for the learners to pair off to discuss their plans, bounce ideas off each other, perhaps pick up ideas they had not considered, and look at implementation and its possible obstacles, alternative implementation methods, etc.
6. The final plan is then prepared with personal commitments to a) discuss it with their line managers on their return to work, and b) implementing the plan.
7. It can be useful for the trainers also to have a copy of the action plan, particularly if there is no likelihood of the line managers becoming involved, or there is to be a parallel contact with the learners and their line managers, with the trainers taking follow-up action. This is particularly important when longer-term follow-up action is to be taken.These of course are 'last ditch' measures when the line manager is not to be involved directly.

Figure 9.4 suggests a basic form of action planning with the major items defined. Figure 9.5 extends this format so that working action plan sheets can be used for each item of the plan – perhaps most realistic when there are only two or three major items.

PERSONAL ACTION PLAN

Action Plan items	How to implement	When and by when
1.		
2.		
3.		
4.		
5.		
6.		

Figure 9.4   A basic personal action plan

Intended action for the learning transfer and implementation of your Action Plan

Complete a separate sheet for each item included on your action plan:

1. What is the item of learning you intend to implement?

2. By which targets will you measure progress?

3. What barriers might impede your implementation?

4. How will you avoid or negate these barriers?

5. Time: when do you intend to start implementing the item?

6. Time: by when do you intend to complete the implementation of the item?

7. Resources: what resources (people, equipment, extra skills, etc.) will you need to complete the implementation of the item?

8. Benefits: what benefits do you hope will result from your actions (including cash value if possible to assess)?

9. Commitment: when will you and your manager meet to review the progress of this action?

10. Any other comments:

Figure 9.5   An extended action plan

CHAPTER **10** *The evaluation of media-based learning methods*

Training and development has approached a decision roundabout with several exits or forward routes during the past decade, and even today there are still many discussions raised from doubts about which direction should/will eventually be taken.

There are advocates for several of the exits and some of their statements are:

- Training in the more traditional way is proven as the best
- The Internet and electronic approaches are the best for the future
- Anything can be taught via the Internet
- Soft-skills can only be taught in the more traditional way
- The Internet and other CBT is only suitable for technical and procedural training

and so on.

What are these alternative methods for modern training and development? The following is a list of the principal media-based training approaches in use today, additional to the more traditional approaches of the training course and workshop, led by a trainer with a group of learners in the training room. The better of these events use modern trainer techniques and attitudes where activity and interactivity are the order of the day rather than a passive audience sitting and 'being taught'.

- Open or Distance Learning packages or self-learning
- Computer-Assisted Training
- Computer-based Technology or E-learning
- Internet learning programmes (various)
- The Internet and Web sites
- E-mail
- The Intranet.

Open or Distance Learning packages or self-learning

These packages have been in existence and wide use longer than any of the other approaches in the list above and in many ways have been very successful in the field of self-learning. Their existence stems from the long-standing correspondence course in which lessons were sent from a central supplier to the learners who completed the task – answering a questionnaire, completing a project, writing an essay or report, and so on. The completed task material was returned to the centre where the work was marked and corrected as necessary. This process continued until the learner had completed the programme successfully – frequently a very extended process, relying on ordinary mail and very occasional reference to the centre by telephone.

The modern equivalent, variously called Open or Distance Learning, has the same self-learning basis, sometimes with reference back to the 'centre' when problems are encountered or answers are to be provided. The basic Distance Learning package commonly consists of a programmed textbook. The learners work through these books, answering the many questions posed, undertaking projects and reviews, and so on. In too many cases, once the pack was received by the learner, that was the end of the contact with the supplying centre, although in organizations that produced their own self-learning packs, usually there was an expect or trainer in the background to whom reference could be made. Few self-learning packages are in this format nowadays, the basic format being enhanced by electronic means of various types.

Computer-Assisted Training

Computer-Assisted Training (CAT) is the 'oldest' form of using real electronic aids in training, and its two basic forms are designed a) to supplement basic self-learning packages, and b) to be stand-alone self-learning instruments.

The earliest uses were to insert into a traditional training programme some form of small computer programme – for example, a demonstration of constructing graphical forms using a programme such as Microsoft Excel; or to include a short animated programme reinforcing a previously presented idea such as a Microsoft PowerPoint slide programme, and so on.

CAT is also used in the case of a number of computers linked in the training room to the trainer's master computer. The trainer enters data or programmes on to his/her master and these are reproduced on the learners' VDUs or slave computers. Of course, the learners and their slave VDUs do not need to be in the training room all the time (or ever, in which case the CAT has progressed to the next logical computer stage). This approach is particularly useful when new computer procedures or programmes have to be introduced into an organization – the learners can have an immediate and supported introduction to the new work and immediate practice at their own workstation, errors being corrected by the controlling trainer.

Early, short training programmes were produced for self-learning on CDs, but these had a number of limitations, not least of which was the absence of interactivity. CD-ROMs and more recently DVDs have the facility for much more capacity and, being computer-based, can include animations and interactivity. The learners are provided with a computer, whether personal or part of the organization's network and, with agreed time slots, work through the programme, referring problems or task results to the trainer.

Computer-based technology or E-learning

These are the techniques that involve interaction of the learner with Internet-provided training programmes, whether the access is directly through the Internet or via the organization's own Intranet (frequently programmes taken from the Internet and broadcast on the Intranet, although they can be internally-produced programmes). The early Internet programmes had a limited appeal, being merely pages of text like a book, but displayed on the small monitor. Few people preferred the VDU to a book that they could carry around with them and the technique showed every sign of dying before it had taken off. However, very soon the E-programme producers realized that interactivity was essential and, in addition to providing (costly) telephone and fax links, introduced into their programmes an immediate form of interactivity in which the learner could 'speak' to the programme, answering questionnaires, following projects and reporting on their achievements, and so on.

A full and acceptable definition of E-learning has not been produced, and in fact some of the so-called techniques in E-learning are not fully for this purpose. The means existing at the present are:

- **Internet learning programmes** purchased from the provider and transmitted to the learner via the Internet and the PC (non-interactive programmes)
- **Internet learning programmes** purchased from the provider and transmitted to the learner via the Internet and the PC (interactive programmes via telephone and fax links and other independent technology)
- **Internet learning programmes** purchased from the provider and transmitted to the learner via the Internet and the PC (fully interactive programmes through the PC and where necessary the other means of contact)
- **Internet learning programmes** purchased from the provider and transmitted to the learner via the organization's own Intranet, problem or task contact being provided by, for example, the training department of the organization.

The Internet and Web sites

If a PC owner has a modem and subscribes to a server, through browsing the Internet a vast amount of knowledge information is made available, on virtually every subject under the sun. If the 'training' you require is simply in the form of information, this approach saves substantial time, rather than searching bulky reference books that may exist in a variety of places. In fact, the amount of information on the Internet can be an embarrassment of riches, as so many sites of varied levels are available.

E-mail

This is the technology that is taking over, to a major extent, the use of ordinary mail and faxes, and has certainly facilitated the support contact mentioned above. E-mailing in itself is not a programme means of learning, but is a valuable support, as well as in some circumstances standing alone. An example of the latter is the contact between two or more people via e-mail, in which information, suggestions, programmes, activities and all the aspects of training/learning as a whole are passed from one to the other. This enables the recipients – and to some extent the sender – to learn from the experience. One project in which I have been involved on several occasions is one of coaching the development of a trainer who is at some distance from me. One trainer is fairly inexperienced and raises problems by e-mail, to which I respond with advice, guidance, suggestions, references, cases, and so on. In this way I obtain a tremendous amount of satisfaction from helping somebody, and they 'benefit' from my experience.

The Intranet

It has been mentioned above that a purchased electronic package can be used through the organization's own system of linked VDUs. This type of facility has been in use for some time in some organizations for widespread communication and operating procedures. More recently it has been used for internal staff training, frequently in the form of material transmitted to staff members who are to attend a training course and need to arrive with the same level of knowledge. In recent years this type of system has been updated and has become a flexible interactive tool in its own right, known as the Intranet – essentially an internal form of the Internet.

Two principal methods are in use: the reproduction over the Internet of the commercial programmes described earlier (Internet, CD-ROM or DVD), and also programmes constructed by the organization's trainers and used over their Intranet. This second method demands much wider-ranging trainer skills with the initial work involving basically all the planning skills required of the trainer in the production of a 'traditional' training programme, but modified to utilize the additional effects available as a result of the electronic means. The extension of this is, of course – particularly where the organization is widespread, even international – for the trainer to extend the Intranet programme to the worldwide Internet.

Attitudes to E-technology and learning

Not everyone is yet convinced that the Internet or on-line routes are going to be all-pervasive and all-answering, the most economic and/or the most effective route for the future that is being suggested, and much has yet to be proven.

Positive statements by all advocates, for and against the Internet, include:

- Training in the more traditional way is proven as the best
- The Internet and electronic approaches are the best for the future
- Anything can be taught via the Internet
- Soft-skills can only be taught in the more traditional way
- The Internet and the like is only suitable for technical and procedural training
- The use of the Internet training programmes is too expensive
- Although initially expensive, the Internet programmes are more economic in the long run
- People are now used to, and like using, the computer
- People hate sitting in front of a computer screen for a long time (and it's not healthy)

and so on.

The 'traditionalists' defend their own corner, arguing against the Internet approach for the majority of forms of training, particularly the so-called soft-skills training (mostly for supervisor and management levels).

There is, however, a growing group of 'Rationalists' who are trying to balance the opposing sides with the strong and increasingly supported argument for a multi-media (in the widest sense) use in learning programmes. There will be many occasions when the best practice of any, or every, approach can, and should be, combined to produce the optimum training/learning medium – that is an integrated training programme.

Let us take a very typical soft-skills area – an interpersonal or interactive skills programme. The scenario for this programme might be:

1. Pre-course reading of background material on behavioural models, using books, CD-ROMS, Internet or Intranet pages, supported by telephone, e-mail, Inter/Intranet contact with a trainer or other subject expert if problems arise.
2. Completion of behavioural assessment questionnaires, the completed instruments being sent to the trainer by electronic means.
3. Pre-training tests sent to the participants by post or electronically for completion and return electronically or otherwise to the trainer. The data received by the trainer could be collated and analysed electronically for subsequent discussion with the learners.
4. Start of programme. Discussion of pre-course results using electronic apparatus (computer-generated data and large image projector), or more traditional training methods (OHP, flipchart, whiteboard).
5. Testing of initial skills and knowledge by means of experiential activities, discussion and feedback.
6. Initial traditional inputs using a full and appropriate range of media aids.
7. During course. Continuing validation of the learners' skills and their learning from the full range of techniques available – traditional and electronic. Use of Internet programmes or parts of them, CD-ROM programmes, videos, interactive videos etc. Behavioural observation could be undertaken manually, but the results stored electronically and, at relevant intervals, summarized and fed back to the learners in display projection plus individual hard copy. The basis of this part of the programme is the full and varied use of many of the approaches and aids available, of whatever nature, the specific approach and aid being selected according to its effective relevancy.
8. At the end of the programme, in addition to the learners completing validation questionnaires (which are collated and summarized by the trainer using the most effective electronic means) and Action Plans, a final feedback of new behavioural skills can be given and compared with earlier observations. Again these would be collated and prepared for issue by electronic means.

Similar mixtures of the available media approaches, instruments and techniques can be introduced for every type of programme, the means being adjusted to suit the purpose of the programme and the approach adjudged the most effective for that type of programme and subject.

Assessment of E-technology

This new type of learning medium demands its own forms of assessment:

*   Knowledge of the availability of various types of electronic learning programmes

- Knowledge and assessment of the learning suitability of the various programmes
- Assessment of the new skills demanded of the trainer.

The last-named item is considered in detail in a companion book (Rae, 2002).

Selecting and assessing Internet or other multi-media programmes

Assessment, validation and evaluation of the new e-technology approaches are very similar to the methods used for more traditional training and learning, but the particular approaches do require some varied methods.

SELECTING

The instrument shown in Figure 10.1 is one that can be used when a decision has to be made about the method of training/learning to be offered in the satisfaction of identified training needs. The instrument suggests a number of questions that should be asked before a decision is made, particularly where Internet or other media-based training methods are being considered. Questions 5a to 5e relate specifically to Open and Distance Learning packages, but these questions can also relate to programmes in the higher levels of e-technology.

ASSESSMENT

Whether open or e-learning programmes are used, the LQ and Action Plan recommended in Chapter 9 should always be used in conjunction with the following assessment instruments, these relating more directly with the different forms of training.

The instrument shown in Figure 10.2 can be used as an assessment tool for all forms of Internet or other media-based learning. It can be modified according to the particular medium used in the training package, but should always be used accompanied by an end-of-programme learning questionnaire (LQ) used to assess the participant's learning.

Selecting and assessing Internet or other multi-media programmes

1. What is the learning medium being considered?
2. Has this package/medium been used previously? With what results?
3. Why is this medium being considered in preference to any others?
4. What is the target population of this programme?
5. Are the programme's objectives stated? What are they and do they cover your needs?
    a) Is the written material in line with the values and culture of the learner's organization?
    b) Is the written material in line with the approaches, techniques, models, etc. acceptable within the learner's organization?
    c) Is the written material taking into account, as far as possible, the different learning styles of the potential learners?
    d) Does the material in the package strike a good balance of different learning approaches – text, exercises, activities, other reading recommendations, case studies, and, where necessary, supporting videos and computer material?
    e) Are all the relevant types of material included in the package?
6. Has the learning environment the necessary technological equipment and back-up services available?
7. If this is not complete, what additional facilities need to be obtained? At what cost? Is this cost budgetable?
8. Is the hardware capable of running the installed package in the most effective manner – from the hard-drive or a CD?
9. Where technological equipment is involved in following the programme, do the learners have the necessary skills for operating the equipment?
10. Is all the information in the site correct, clear, intelligible and comprehensive? Describe any feature that is not.
11. Is the language used in the programme appropriate to the material and the target audience?
12. To what extent is the programme interactive? Do you consider this to be sufficient?
13. To what extent do the graphics or other site additions enhance the site or interfere with the learning?
14. How easy is it to move about the site to areas required?
15. Does the site have a) internal links, b) external links?
16. How effective are these links?
17. Are videos included in the programme? If so, how efficient and effective are they?
18. Does the programme give clear, sufficient/comprehensive, logical instructions on the use of the equipment:
    – as equipment?
    – for the learning programme purposes?
19. What is the minimum operating knowledge necessary?
20. To what extent is a trainer's/supervisor's presence necessary?
21. What is the cost of the programme?
22. Is this within your budget?

Figure 10.1   Questions to ask about programmes being considered

Name   **Date**
Title of learning programme followed
Type of programme

Please circle the scoring rating nearest to the way you feel about the item. Always include comments on why you have given this rating.

1. Was the package easy to install on the computer or did it require technical help?

2. Was the package easy to uninstall (if this was necessary)?

3. As a result of the learning package, were you able to meet
    a) your learning objectives
    Completely   6   5   4   3   2   1   Not at all
    If you have rated 1 to 3, please comment why you have given this score.

    b) the programme's stated objectives?
    Completely   6   5   4   3   2   1   Not at all
    If you have rated 1 to 3, please comment why you have given this score.

4. To what extent did the package include activities and skill checks for you to perform?
    Sufficient   6   5   4   3   2   1   Few

5. Which activities were less helpful? The least helpful? Why?

6. To what extent was the package interactive with the producers/trainers/other?
    To a large extent 6   5   4   3   2   1   Hardly at all
    In what way?

7. Was the interactivity more than you wanted or less than you wanted?
    A lot more   6   5   4   3   2   1   A lot less
    In what way?

8. Did you find any instructions difficult to follow? If so, which ones?

9. Were any of the activities uninteresting? Which ones? Why?

10. Were you given sufficient information to enable you to perform the activities?
    Sufficient   6   5   4   3   2   1   Insufficient
    If rating is 3, 2 or 1, please state in what way.

11. Were there any instances in which you felt you were given too much information? What were they and to what extent too much?

12. Were the instructions and the material always clear and understandable? If not, which parts were not?
    Always   6   5   4   3   2   1   Never

13. How easy was it to move between the different parts of the programme?
    Very easy   6   5   4   3   2   1   Very difficult

14. How much time did you spend on the programme?
        More than 25 hours
        Between 15 and 25 hours
        Between 10 and 15 hours
        Less than 10 hours?

15. Was the time you had available sufficient to enable you to complete the programme as you would have wished?
    Sufficient   6   5   4   3   2   1   Insufficient

16. How accessible was a trainer/tutor/other person to provide help?
    Very   6   5   4   3   2   1   Not at all
    If you have scored 3, 2 or 1, to what extent was help limited?

17. Was the person mentioned in (16) helpful when asked for assistance?
    Very   6   5   4   3   2   1   Not at all
    If you have scored 3, 2, or 1, to what limited extent?

18. How often did you have to ask for assistance?

19. How isolated did you feel completing the package?
    Very   6   5   4   3   2   1   Not at all
    How?

20. How difficult did you find the package as a whole?
    Very   6   5   4   3   2   1   Not at all
    For what reasons?

21. What is your overall rating of the programme?
    Excellent   6   5   4   3   2   1   Poor

22. Any other comments?

Figure 10.2   Evaluation of media-based learning

You will notice in the evaluation of media-based learning that, as with traditional evaluation, reliance is not placed on tick list or scoring alone, but textual comments to justify any ratings given are sought.

11 *After the euphoria*

On too many occasions still, evaluation (or what is frequently and erroneously described as 'evaluation') extends no further than the end of the training course and, at best, the completion of a Learning Questionnaire (LQ). With no further action, all this questionnaire does is to approach validation of the programme,the achievement of its objectives and those of the learners. But if evaluation of training is to show more than this, up to and including the assessment of the ROI on the training, it must be taken much further.

In order to do this, four further stages are necessary:

1. Post-programme debriefing
2. Action Plan implementation
3. Review of implementation action
4. Medium and longer-term evaluation.

Post-programme debriefing

The essential link between the training and the learning achieved occurs immediately after the end of the training programme and when the learner returns to work: this is the post-training debriefing meeting between the learners and their line managers, a meeting that corresponds with the pre-training briefing meeting. The line manager must ensure (and it is without doubt one of their main responsibilities in the evaluation process) that the meeting does take place and is not treated as 'just another meeting', but the start of a process that makes the training worthwhile to both the learner and the organization and ensures that there is an effective ROI.

The line manager must ensure that this meeting not only takes place, but must do so very soon after the learner returns to work, it being made obvious to the learner that this is a real case of support and not just a matter of form.

It may sound easy to say that this event should happen as described above, but on so many occasions learners comment that the only reaction (if at all) they had from their line manager on their return to work from training (remember that substantial money from the organization has gone to this training) was a comment of the nature 'Oh, have you been away! I though I hadn't seen you around', or 'Did you enjoy the course? That's a nice hotel, isn't it?', or 'Oh, by the way, I want you to drop everything and do this report by tomorrow'. And so on.

The learner will be feeling under pressure in any case, particularly if the absence has been for some time – there will probably be a mountain of work waiting in the in-tray, even if delegation arrangements had been made. The atmosphere is far from conducive to practising what has been learned, and many learners report that because of this environment they simply had to forget about the training for a while to catch up with the job. By that time the motivation to practise the learning had gone.

The line manager may also have some pressing reasons why he or she cannot fulfil his or her arrangement with the learner for the debriefing meeting. Some managers use the excuse of work commitments to avoid what some may feel is a threatening situation. Even if the original appointment cannot be kept, another one should be made for as soon as possible after the original date. It is useful not to meet the learner *too* soon after the event, say on the first day of their return from a fortnight's training programme – there will be the inevitable in-tray – but it should not be delayed any longer than later in the week following the end of the event. If the delay becomes longer, the interest and motivation of both manager and learner will diminish, perhaps until they both feel that it would be worthless to hold the meeting.

So the meeting *must* be held and soon after the return of the learner. Both the manager and the learner should consider whether it would be worthwhile to invite the trainers to take part in the meeting. They could be useful in helping the transition from learning to work by suggesting ways in which the learning could be applied in the particular work situation. They could also help in any discussion about further training needs for the learner (and the boss). There must be agreement that this role is a minor one in the discussion: the two principals are the learner and his boss. There is always the danger that the manager will try to transfer responsibilities to the trainer because 'after all, it's all about training'. It isn't about training. It is about putting the lessons learned during training into the context of the real world of the learner's work, and the line manager is the only one with any responsibility in this area.

Action Plan implementation

The possible content of the debriefing meeting has been mentioned in Chapter 6. Many managers avoid these debriefing meetings because they lack confidence in holding them as they say that they don't know what to discuss. The following list contains the most important questions that should be asked and issues raised:

1. How effective was the training as far as you were concerned? How did you rate it? Were these views any different from the others on the course?
2. How effective were the trainers in your view? Were they approachable? Were they logical and clear in their presentations; did they use their aids well; were they too hurried, etc?
3. How appropriate to you was the training material? All of it; some of it; very little of it; none of it?
4. How up to date was the material?
5. Were the stated programme objectives achieved? If not, in what way?
6. Were your personal objectives (that we discussed before you went on the course) achieved? If not, in what way?
7. What did you learn, have confirmed or were you timeously reminded of? (Reference might be made to the end-of-course Learning Questionnaire.)
8. Can we discuss your Action Plan? What have you planned? How is it to be implemented? When and over what period? What resources are required? Do you want any help from me or anyone else?

9. Can you see any benefit in making your views and or information about the training available to anyone else, here or elsewhere? Particularly, is there anything we have discussed I should pass back to the trainers? (Feedback of this nature is valuable to the training organization to help in the continuous development of the training programme.)

10. Is there anything else we should discuss?

This list is not complete, but even if it is all that is discussed there is plenty to keep both participants well occupied for a considerable time!

Before the end of the meeting, a date should be arranged for between three and six months hence, to discuss the implementation results of the action plan. Interim reviews should also be offered and agreement reached for you to keep a natural eye on what the learner is doing and give any immediate feedback that they might feel is necessary.

Action of this nature will satisfy the line manager and the learner. In most cases much information will emerge which would be valuable to the trainer in validating and evaluating the training. Yet rarely does information pass back to the trainer. Perhaps one of the reasons for this is the apparent divide which exists so often between line operation and training – they simply do not talk to each other. If both sides make an effort to produce a continuous dialogue they will both find not only plenty of topics for discussion, but the emergence of much of value. In the case of the trainer there will be an additional form of validation of the training for which he has been responsible, perhaps feedback in a more open way than was presented directly to him. The learners may feel that they can speak more openly to their line managers about the training than to the trainers.

The final benefit of this post-training action to the trainer is in the field of overall evaluation. Methods of evaluation often include the trainer going out from the training ivory castle to the field to interview, talk with learners and have questionnaires completed by both the learner and the line manager. The type of discussion considered above sets the scene for this action which is then seen almost as a continuation of the post-training discussion.

Pre- and post-training discussions rarely just happen, although more and more line managers are realizing their value. Much more could be done and it is obviously in the interests of the trainer to take the initiative in trying to encourage their wider use. It is all part of validation and evaluation.

Review of implementation action: medium and longer-term evaluation

Following the initial post-training, debriefing action the learner should not be left alone to carry on without support – this is an almost certain way of ensuring that the learning is not fully put into action, so reducing the ROI. In most cases, a time between three and six months following the training is the optimum period to initiate longer-term follow-up action, although there are approaches that can be taken before then. There may be occasions when there are reasons why the longer-term, post-training follow-up is not done in this way by the learners' line managers. If the line manager, for whatever reason, is not to undertake the follow-up, the training department *might* take follow-up action. But there must be very strong reasons why this should take place and the action must be a last resort, otherwise the line manager is being allowed/encouraged to avoid his or her responsibilities in the evaluation and training process. The training department may not, in any case, have the resources to free a trainer to take any action, and there is no guarantee that a trainer is capable of observing effectively or is available to do this on a long-term basis, as may often be necessary.

However, there are a number of ways in which post-training action can be taken by the line manager and/or the training department, but it must be remembered that the line manager is the only person who is in the optimum position to make the necessary observations and take action from their managerial/supervisory roles. The approaches can include:

- Line manager observation and assessment
- Trainer observation and assessment
- Trainer interview and telephone interview
- Follow-up questionnaires
- Repertory Grid
- Self-diaries
- Control groups.

Line manager observation and assessment

This should be the major method of assessment of how the learners are implementing their learning. Before the three to six months' review, the manager should be observing, in the normal course of their duties, the learners working and implementing their Action Plans, as would have been agreed at the debriefing interview. This observation is a natural process, rather than an audit or inspection, as it is simply an extension of the managerial responsibility to ensure that their staff are carrying out their work effectively. The observations for the particular review purpose should be made with the Action Plan items in mind and the programme discussed earlier. The manager should not wait for the formal review to comment on the learners' work, whether to correct or commend, but should do so immediately the item comes to notice, although there should be no intention or action of 'looking over the learners' shoulder'.

The interim review meetings are supportive events at which the learners can discuss their implementation to that point and seek help or support in any difficulties they might be having. It is important to emphasize that these observations and reviews should be made with the full agreement of the learners, and the manager again should avoid any suggestion that they are 'looking over the learners' shoulders'. The more open the atmosphere between the two parties, the greater the likelihood of successful implementation, in addition to a probable betterment of the relationship between the manager and the members of staff.

FOLLOW-UP REVIEW MEETINGS

Every attempt should be made by both the learners and the line manager to keep to the programme of interim reviews, but particularly to the follow-up main review meeting. The Action Plan is the key item in this process as it is used as the instrument by which the learning is translated into implementation action. At this review the action taken should be discussed openly and analysed with reference to the plan. This process can be helped by such questions as:

1. Which items of your action plan have you tried to implement so far?
2. How successful were you in these?
3. What factors or reasons do you attribute to your success in implementing these items?
4. With which items did you not have success in your attempts to implement them?
5. What were the reasons for this lack of success?
6. What plans have you to retry your unsuccessful implementations?
7. Which items have you not yet attempted to implement?
8. Why have you not attempted implementation of these items?
9. What plans have you to implement the as yet unattempted items?

It is also important to ask:

10. How did you feel about the extent of the support you received from me?
11. What was the extent of the support you received from your colleagues and others?
12. What were the major problems you found in trying to implement your Action Plan?
13. What more could we have done to make the process easier?
14. To what extent do you feel that the training you received has helped you in achieving your development?

And finally:

15. What further review meetings are necessary?
16. Have you identified any further training you need?

Any further, longer-term review and evaluation can follow the approach just described, until all possible action has been completed.

Trainer observation and assessment

Where there has been no arrangement, or no arrangement is possible for the learners' line managers to undertake a follow-up when the learners return to work and intend to implement their action plans, it can be possible for the trainer to take some action. This must, of course, be with the agreement of the line manager who should be kept in the picture at all stages. The trainer must be aware that this is a very difficult task and it is very expensive in terms of their time and resources if realistic support is given. The trainer could be in an environment that is a foreign one and, however unobtrusive they make themselves, they will always have a presence of which the learners, and others, will be aware. This can introduce a strong element of artificiality, although this can be overcome when all participants are committed to the action and the need for this.

There must be agreement with the learners and the line manager for a programme of observations fitting in with occasions when the learners are attempting to implement parts of the Action Plan within their day-to-day work. This, of course, can cause problems of timing.

Observations of this nature must not look like, or be, appraisals or inspections of the learners, as the objectives include giving learning support to the learners and their intentions of implementing their learning. The trainers must be able to be available at almost any time and, of course, must be skilled in objective methods of observation.

A major disadvantage, which is repeated whenever the trainer has to take on what is really the role of the line manager, is the expenditure of a significant amount of time and resource. This can be substantial even when there is one learner to observe on a number of occasions, but if the course contained 12 participants, all of whom, or even a number of them, are to be observed, this means a minimum of something like 36 visits (12 learners x 3 observational visits). The problem increases if the learners are not in one location, but scattered around the country, requiring the trainer/observer to travel long distances on a number of occasions. The situation is obviously better if there is only a small number of learners to observe who are in one location. But the arguments for this approach must be cogent to justify the considerable expenditure.

As far as the actual observations are concerned, the observer must know exactly what information is being sought, must be aware of the best methods of performing the observation, and be sufficiently skilled in the method or methods. The type of observation will depend to a large extent on the type of implementation being considered.

Probably the most useful aid in this direct observation is the job or task analysis approach performed prior to the training event and described earlier. This is particularly more important when the activities are very practical rather than dealing with more subjective relationships. The example of practical observation described earlier was of the hotel receptionist, an activity in which a considerable amount of the work is practical and observable, although there are more subjective aspects that can still be observed and recorded.

The individual may have attended a training programme for receptionists and returned to work with an Action Plan of both practical and interpersonal tasks to perform. When the work location is visited by the observer, the receptionist can be observed quite easily while the duties are being performed. The performance of the particular tasks can be logged and checked off as they are performed, with comments on the skill of the performance. Interpersonal aspects can be observed and recorded similarly with an instrument such as Behaviour Analysis. What is being observed is whether the learned tasks are being performed in the way in which the receptionist was trained and whether they are being performed correctly. In this way both the training and the effective execution of the learning can be assessed. The activity and behaviour analyses obtained can be compared against the agreed model of effective performance, and any variations discussed after the period of observation.

Such an observation is both time-consuming and difficult: other occupations will be even more extensive and complicated and in these, particularly if the observations are made some time after the training, the possibilities of contamination of the results by factors not attributable to the training can increase.

Other problems that an observer has to face include the length of time that an observation or series of observations may take. This is particularly so with a long or complicated task being implemented since the observer must remain with the worker long enough, or on enough occasions, to observe at least one full cycle of the task, a specific problem if the task does not have a regular and/or continuous sequence of activities.

One method of reducing the long period of observation is the SISCO method used by the London School of Economics surveys. SISCO stands for Standard Internal Sampling with Continuous Observation. In this method the observer is recording every two minutes during a period of two hours, the periods being spread over the working day and the week. This method will obviously be a useful research tool but there is some doubt whether it is a feasible approach in the environment described earlier.

Trainer direct interview, telephone interview and tele-conferencing

These methods of approach, although fairly common, unless linked to direct observation of the learner at work by either the trainer or line manager, afford the least value of the range of assessments. They can also occupy a period of time that is not commensurate with any objective information obtained. There is no implication that the learners will make false statements but, unless there is other 'evidence', what is learned will be based solely on what the learners see fit to tell the trainer.

DIRECT INTERVIEW

There is little doubt that a direct interview with the learners is superior to the more indirect approach of the questionnaire sent to them. In the interview 'confrontation' the interviewer can probe for fuller and exact details of any reported incidents, and, if relevant, elicit emotional as well as factual information. At such an interview a follow-up Action Plan can be formulated which commits the learners to action from any plans which have not been implemented, although this will require additional work. There can also be the advantage that the learners' boss can be involved at the construction of the second Action Plan.

The interview general format for this purpose is very similar to other interviews held for many other reasons; particular emphasis can be placed on probing questions designed to produce answers deeper than the superficial.

The interview has two main aims: to identify what learning has taken place, and thus how effective the training has been, and how much of the learning has been put into active practice. The approach, therefore, must be a logical one with the intention of obtaining the maximum amount of information possible. The questions will normally follow the format and guidelines described earlier for the line manager's debriefing and review meetings, although some variations may be necessary depending on the circumstances. Where a number of learners are being interviewed, the same questions should be used within a similar format, although the interview should not be so strictly structured as to inhibit follow-up of useful subjects that might arise during the interview.

As with most interviews, the form of questions posed can be useful with the most favourable ones being:

- open questions
- probing questions
- testing understanding
- reflecting
- closed questions (when brevity is required).

Ones to avoid include:

- too many closed questions
- leading questions
- multiple questions
- ambiguous questions
- rhetorical questions.

But, apart from questioning, the role of the interviewer is to listen carefully to the learner so that any signals or covert messages are not missed and consequently not taken up.

In addition to the questions described earlier, the trainer interviewer should include as part of the process:

1. At the start of the interview, describe the objectives and reasons for the interview and any link with the learner's line manager
2. The questions described earlier relating to the implementation of the action plan, including in particular any plans for future action
3. Seeking comments about the learner's linkages with the line manager, such as comments about the briefing and debriefing meetings and the outcome of the latter, and details about the support received from the line manager and colleagues
4. If time is available, and the principal purposes of the interviews have been achieved, some questions can be asked about the learner's views, after the period of time that has elapsed, on the training programme and the learning achieved.

TELEPHONE INTERVIEW

If it is necessary that a follow-up interview takes place with the learner, but the trainer is unable to physically visit the work location – for example, it might be at the other end of the country or even in another country – then a telephone interview might be appropriate. This can also have the possibility of reducing costs, and saving on expensive travel and possibly accommodation, particularly when, as referred to above, the interviewees might be in separate locations.

The interview success will suffer, to some extent, depending on the verbal skills only of the interviewee. There is an obvious absence of face-to-face interaction which enhances most people-communication, with a consequent loss of rapport and the absence of most non-verbal clues. There is also the chance that the interviewee might not give the same depth of attention to a telephone interview as to one held face-to-face with the interviewer.

A telephone interview would follow the same pattern as the structured, face-to-face one, the interviewer being prepared with a series of appropriate questions. The responses can be probed for clarification or to seek a further depth to the answer. The interviewer must be very alert for clues that might be given in the manner and tone of voice when the learner responds, suggesting there has been something left unsaid.

Arrangements must be made prior to the telephone interview in the same way as for the face-to-face one and will include:

- A telephone appointment must be made beforehand to ensure availability of the interviewee and to give them time to prepare. This appointment should be looked on in the same way as a face-to-face appointment, being entered in the diaries and kept

- The interviewee should make arrangements to ensure that they are free and that there will be no interruptions
- The interviewee should be alone so that there are no inhibitions about what might be said
- The interviewer must put the questions in a clear voice and ensure that the interviewee has heard and understood them
- Unless there are strong financial reasons, the pace or length of the interview should not be dictated by the possible cost
- The interviewer must be aware of the possible problems some people have when trying to take part in an in-depth discussion on the phone
- With the permission of the interviewee, the interview should be recorded so that reference back can be made to points of the interview without having to return to the interviewee. A guarantee must be given about any particular parts of the recorded interview that the interviewee requires to be kept confidential.

TELECONFERENCING

This is a telephone-type method that can be used when it is feasible or desirable to 'interview' a group of learners as a group at the same time. Before the learners leave the training programme, having completed Action Plans, an agreement is reached between them and the trainer for a tele-conference to be held at some time – perhaps up to three months – following their return to work. This may take some organization of detail as anyone who has tried to obtain such agreement among a number of people will know, realizing all the difficulties and problems that could arise!

When the conference day and time arrives, the individuals of the group are linked by the tele-conference system and each then reports back to the trainer and the group what has happened to them since the end of the programme and what they have done about the implementation of their Action Plans – methods, successes, failures, those yet to be implemented, help or hindrance encountered, and so on. This, again, is a reasonably cost-effective approach, albeit not as good as a direct face-to-face situation, and is a useful way of helping to achieve commitment from the members of the group. Nobody will want to admit in the group situation, even though it is in a slightly impersonal way over the phone, that they have done nothing and/or learned nothing.

An alternative to the tele-conferencing, perhaps a little more costly depending on the organization's facilities, is the similar approach of video-conferencing. In this way, the members of the group are able to see, as well as hear, each other.

In both cases, the trainer can be the facilitator of the process, guiding the learners to disclose the type of information that will be helpful to the trainer, the other members and themselves.

Follow-up questionnaires

WITH THE LEARNER

Follow-up questionnaires that are sent to the learners by the training department that was responsible for the attended training programme can be used when the previously described approaches are not feasible or desirable. But again, as with any follow-up run by the trainer rather than the line manager, the caveats described earlier relate, plus one or two that are relevant to this remote type of contact.

In most cases, following agreement with the learners (and if necessary the line manager) that this approach is acceptable, a questionnaire sent to the learners will start the action, at a time agreed between the trainer and the learners. The agreed first contact will normally be at the three-month follow-up stage when the learners have returned to work and have had time to try to implement the action plan. The receipt of the follow-up questionnaire should also be helpful to the learners in acting as a reminder (sometimes a spur) to the proposed implementation of the action items, and also a reminder and reinforcement of the learning achieved.

Again depending on circumstances, the questionnaire will either be sent directly to the learners at work, or via their line managers. A suggested form of questionnaire is shown in Figure 11.1.

Apart from the caveats mentioned earlier, the originating trainer must be aware of at least two further pitfalls to a questionnaire sent by mail or e-mail – there may be difficulty in obtaining return of the form by the agreed date (or even obtaining a return at all), and the learners may be hesitant in committing to paper comments, some of which may reflect unfavourably on their boss and/or colleagues. On this latter point, there can be a reverse effect with the learner commenting profusely on these people, so demonstrating the highly subjective nature of this follow-up. As in other cases, a guarantee of confidentiality must be given. It can also help if there is a local contact who can encourage the return of the questionnaire. This is particularly the case if the line managers, although they may not be directly involved in the follow-up, are involved by sending the questionnaire via them to pass on to the learners. This accepts the natural line of command as well as helping to involve the line manager to a greater extent. The learners are aware that the line manager knows of the enquiry and may chase up its return. Return should not, however, be via the line manager as this may inhibit some of the responses.

WITH THE LINE MANAGER

An alternative to questioning the learners about their own actions, successes and failures, on some of which they may not be able to comment objectively, is to send a follow-up questionnaire to their line managers. This will ask what they have observed since the learners returned from the training programme.

At the end of the training period, when the learners have completed their action plans, the agreement of the learners to this posting should be obtained, and arrangements made with the line managers that they should receive the follow-up questionnaire some three months hence. This action can have the benefits of encouraging the learners to start implementing their action plans, reminding the line managers of their responsibilities in evaluation as part of the Evaluation Quintet and encouraging them to talk to and have contact with the learners.

Course attended ....   **Dates** ....

PART ONE: When you completed the training programme, you contracted to implement an Action Plan which detailed the following items:

1.
2.
3.   etc.

Would you please answer the following questions as completely as you can:

1.   Which items of your action plan have you implemented so far?
2.   What degree of success have you achieved in respect of these items?
3.   To what factors or reasons do you attribute your success in implementing these items?
4.   Which items of your action plan have you not yet implemented?
5.   Which of these items have you tried but failed to implement?
6.   Why did this occur?
7.   Which items have you not yet attempted to implement?
8.   Why have you not yet attempted these?
9.   What plans do you have to:
     – attempt to rectify your unsuccessful items
     – implement the as yet unattempted items?
10. Have you any additional plans? Please comment.

PART TWO: It will help our organization of training and the involvement of different people if you could answer the following questions, the responses to which will be kept confidential.

1.   Did you have a debriefing meeting with your manager on your return to work?
2.   If so, how quickly after the course did this take place?
3.   What was the nature of the debriefing meeting and its outcomes?
4.   What was the extent of the support promised by your manager?
5.   What was the extent of the support received from your manager?
6.   What was the extent of any support arranged with colleagues?
7.   What was the extent of any support received from colleagues?
8.   How valuable do you feel was the post-programme support?
9.   Any other comments you wish to make?

Figure 11.1   Follow-up action plan questionnaire to the learner

Figure 11.2 suggests a format for this questionnaire, which, as with the questionnaire to the learners, should include a 'reply-by date'.

WITH BOTH THE LEARNER AND THE LINE MANAGER

Ideally both the learner and the line manager should receive questionnaires, if this is to be the approach, although if the line manager is brought in to this extent, it should be only a

Course reviewed ....   **Dates** ....

PART ONE: When .... completed the training programme, they contracted to implement an Action Plan which detailed the following items:

1.
2.
3.   etc.

Would you please answer the following questions as completely as you can from your own knowledge or observation:

1.   Which items of the action plan do you know that they have implemented so far?
2.   What degree of success have they achieved in respect of these items?
3.   To what factors or reasons do you attribute their success in implementing these items?
4.   Which items of the action plan have not yet been implemented?
5.   Which of these items have they tried but failed to implement?
6.   Why did this occur?
7.   Which items have they not yet attempted to implement?
8.   Why have they not been attempted?
9.   What plans have you discussed with the learner to:
       – attempt to rectify the unsuccessful items
       – implement the as yet unattempted items?
10.   Have you any other comments?

PART TWO: It will help our organization of training and the involvement of different people if you could answer the following questions.

1.   Did you have a debriefing meeting with the learner on their return to work?
2.   If so, how quickly after the course did this take place?
3.   What was the nature of the debriefing meeting and its outcomes?
4.   What was the extent of the support you promised?
5.   What has been the extent of the support you have given?
6.   What was the extent of any support arranged with colleagues?
7.   What was the extent of any support received from colleagues?
8.   How valuable do you feel the post-programme interactions were?
9.   Any other comments you wish to make?

Figure 11.2   Follow-up action plan questionnaire to the line manager

short step to complete integration of the two in the post-training period. However, there are cases where this does not happen and the trainer has to take the initiative – in this instance, the double approach is much better than a single one to either of the parties.

   This approach can be extended to include other people who can comment – for example, colleagues – where some form of 360 degree appraisal or similar is operated in the organization. Figure 11.2 can be modified for this further reference, questions about the line manager's involvement, for example, being omitted.

   When the questionnaires have been returned, they can be analysed and compared for similarities and differences, so that a) a complete picture of the learner's development is obtained, and b) problems that need further action can be identified.

It is often difficult to correlate the two responses. In fact, on the occasions when I have been able to follow the approach, the surprising result has been the question raised about whether the two responses related to the same learner. It is natural that there should be some differences in response owing to different points of view, but on many occasions this made correlation impossible. The differences related to the actual implementation of action plan items, the extent to which they had been successful, and failure to implement certain items when the other party reported that they had gone ahead successfully! The conclusion as to why these differences occurred and were so extreme was that either there was a communication failure between the learner and manager, or that the manager needed training because of a lack of skill, or both!

Eventually I included further questions. The learner was asked:

• How often do you meet your boss to discuss your work and your development?
• How often does your boss have or take the opportunity to observe you at work or examine your work?

Similar questions were posed to the manager. The most disappointing, and sometimes startling, responses, even when other factors were taken into account, were the statements which occurred very frequently:

• Once a week (rare)
• Once a month (common)
• Infrequently and irregularly (very common)
• Rarely (common).

If this direct observation or examination does not take place, it is not surprising – and worrying too – that the manager is unable to comment realistically on the worker's performance – a worker who is one of the prime responsibilities of the manager. It is not surprising that realistic evaluation is difficult under these conditions.

There were also a number of cases in which the responses showed interaction and support at a much more effective level. These cases were usually quickly identified by the close correlation between the two responses and supporting comments of frequent interaction. In these cases both the learner and the manager identified the helping relationship, whereas in other instances the manager alone saw a helping relationship on his part.

Whether correlation is good or not, a useful supplement to the questionnaire is a follow-up by face-to-face interviews with the learner and the manager.

If there are variations in the responses, or if the Action Plan has not progressed as it should have done, the interviews will help to clarify these variations. The interviews are not only to ensure that real information emerges, but also to help both learner and manager to appreciate better each other's point of view and development needs.

The second reason is highly altruistic and supportive and should form part of the trainer's objectives. The action must remain evaluative, however, to determine whether the learner has achieved real learning, has put it into practice and has developed as a result, and that consequently the business has improved accordingly – bottom line evaluation. If all this is so, the training will have achieved the prime objective.

Even when there appear to be no problems of correlation between the responses or successful application of the learning it is often still valuable for the trainer to take part in face-to-face discussion meetings with the two parties. There will always be some points for clarification and the trainer can develop an effective helping relationship with the manager and the worker for future development.

Repertory Grid

The Repertory Grid can be considered as a particular form of depth interview in which, for the second or third time the interviewee produces his or her constructs from the same set of elements used on the previous occasions. The constructs of each grid can then be compared and analysed and from this comparison it may be possible to detect any further changes of attitude. As an alternative, so that direct comparison can be made even easier, the grid can be used with the same elements and constructs, but on this occasion the interviewee is asked to reconsider his or her scoring scales.

Self-diaries

One method of deciding an individual's training needs is the completion of a diary before the training event. For a specific period the potential learner keeps an activity diary which details everything the learner does and how long is spent on each event. From an analysis of the diary entries it can be determined whether the learner is operating efficiently: is too much time being spent on tasks which could be delegated; are interruptions allowed; are meetings not planned sufficiently or are they planned too much; and so on.

At the follow-up stage the learner is required to repeat the diary completion for a comparable period. The second diary is then analysed to see if it reveals a more appropriate pattern of behaviour or skills.

The disadvantage of the diary method is that it depends on the honesty and integrity of the individual completing the diary. It is so easy to enter in the diary the items which *should* be entered rather than those which actually occur so that the completer is presented in the best possible light. This of course negates completely the value of the diary from the point of view of both the trainer and the learner. It does, however, reveal that the learners know what should be entered in an effective diary; entries of this nature just *may* encourage them to actually behave in this way!

CONTROL GROUPS

The value of involving a control group which has not been subjected to the training has been described earlier. This requirement is an absolute necessity when we are trying to evaluate learning over a period of time, as so many factors can contaminate the apparent learning. Both the control group and the trained group can change over the period, with many of the changes not being attributable to the training, even in the case of the training group. Such non-attributable factors can include the issue of improved guidance or instructions for the job, a natural progression of development as a result of exposure to the work, enforced development due to pressures of various kinds, and so on. Many of these factors could fall equally on the trained and control groups. Consequently, although the absence of a control group could materially affect the objectivity of an evaluation, the presence does not necessarily guarantee complete objectivity.

Long-term evaluation

If, as has been suggested earlier in this chapter, evaluation after the relatively short period of three to four months is very difficult if not impossible, then this view must be consolidated when evaluation is considered after an even longer interval. Warr, Bird and Rackham have in fact stated that at such levels the evaluation of training is usually impossible. However, others have suggested that it might be possible provided that the whole process has been subject to strict controls from the earliest stages. An approach is possiblé if a full task analysis has been obtained, specific training needs identified and tight training objectives set, end-of-course validation obtained and subsequent evaluation undertaken, with control activities at all stages.

In theory it makes little difference whether subsequent evaluation occurs after 12 months or longer, but obviously the longer the interval, the greater the likelihood of contamination through non-attributable factors.

TECHNIQUES

All the techniques employed at the mid-term evaluation can be repeated at this stage and there is considerable value in consistency. Perhaps the ideal is to use the same evaluation instrument throughout the complete process from pre-course, through post-course and mid-term to long-term. This enables a relatively simple and direct comparison of results and an approach can be made to some degree of objective measurement of change. It may not always be possible, of course, to be as consistent as this.

By the long-term stage, the emphasis has moved almost completely away from the validation of the training *per se* and is concentrating on the effect of the training on the effectiveness of the individual and hence the organization. In the same way that the individual might be observed at the mid-term stage, so this process can be repeated at the long-term stage to show whether the skills have been maintained or improved, or whether they have regressed. We must not take too purist an attitude about these observations, particularly in view of the increased likelihood of contamination by non-attributable factors. If the skills have been maintained since the training, this shows that the training is still of value in the current performance of the job. If, on the other hand, they have improved, does it really matter why? In this instance the organization is receiving a bonus since the individual is required only to *maintain* the trained level. At the other end of the scale, if the performance level has dropped since the mid-term evaluation, this can suggest that either the training has no long-term effects, or something has happened to the individual in the job to reduce motivation to perform to the level to which he has been trained.

If the performed level has fallen, the emphasis of the evaluation must be to discover the answer to this problem. However, in terms of realistic evaluation the question 'Has the training benefited the organization in economic or output terms?' must be answered. Most authorities on evaluation feel that in most instances, certainly above the simple practical level, it is impossible to answer this question. This will certainly be so in most cases of management training and many cases of social skills training.

This disappointing answer will be the only one possible at the completely objective level. But there is good reason to accept a subjective assessment, provided we remember that it is subjective: it may be the only one we are able to obtain! The individual's line manager is in a unique position to make the day-to-day assessment, and in many organizations is forced to do so by the annual appraisal system. At the very least, if at an appraisal subsequent to the training the individual's level of performance has not gone down, but has improved, some of this improvement may be due to the training. Skilled questioning may help to elicit, albeit subjectively, the degree of this effect.

What is the alternative to the approaches discussed in this book? It is surely to conclude that validation and evaluation are too expensive in time, resources and money, and will not necessarily produce an objective assessment – so they are not attempted, and no objective measures at all are available to help the training which occurs at considerable cost. This decision can be taken by the organization in the same way that it could decide to contribute to *any* form of training. Obviously some attempt at assessment must be made.

WHO DOES THE EVALUATION?

There is little controversy over who performs the training and who manages an individual, but it is certainly far from clear who should be involved in the different stages of the validation and evaluation. A complete system is costly in terms of staff time and resources. If only the trainer is involved, more time may have to be spent on evaluation than training; if only the manager is involved there will be little time for them to manage. An external assessor can be introduced who can follow the system with complete neutrality and bring expertise to the evaluation, but such individuals are rare and can be unacceptably costly if they have to get to know the organization as well as follow an evaluation approach from start to finish. It will be less costly if such an expert is already employed within the organization, say a psychologist, but even then there is a substantial notional and actual cost.

The most realistic approach will be to have an amalgamation of at least the trainer and the line manager, with, preferably, some support from the neutral assessor. There are many permutations of this combination and one realistic approach could be:

Pre-course. Analysis and identification of needs: trainer and manager.
During course and at the end of course. Trainer.
Control group. Throughout: external assessor.
Mid-term. Trainer to some extent, but more particularly the line manager.
Long-term. External assessor and line manager.

Whatever permutation might be used and how much subjectivity might be acceptable, the important aspects of validation and evaluation are that:

1. Some form of validation and evaluation should be attempted
2. There must be as much co-operation between the trainer and line manager as possible, for, after all, the manager is the first line client and the trainer the provider.

12 *Evaluation and the business ROI*

The final, major part of the evaluation process is probably the most important and also the most difficult, namely assessing the cost- and value-effectiveness which leads to assessing the return to the organization in business, people and financial terms of the investment made in the training. This is the Return on Investment or ROI. In the same way as prior to the training it is essential to know the levels at which the learners are starting so that the achieved learning is recognized and can be measured to some extent, so it is with the ROI. It is necessary to know before the start of any programme what the value of the employees' contributions are and to consider what changes following the training are anticipated. Also, after the training, in the same way that the training is validated at the end of the programme, so it is then necessary, once the learners have implemented their learning, to assess the change in their value to and the work they do for the organization.

It is easier to write this than actually go through the process of the ROI as, in most cases, so much of the assessment, before and after, is subjective and difficult to express in quantitative terms. In some cases, however, the assessment is easier, although there are very few cases where it is straightforward and completely objective.

One of the simplest examples of looking at the ROI in business is in the case of a straightforward financial investment, say £10 million in a company that is linked to the investing company as one that supplies essential parts and looks as if it is going to expand physically and financially over the next five years. The main organization invests the £10 million, the anticipated progress occurs, and, at the end of the five years the £10 million has increased to £20 million, a 'ROI' of £10 million. But there are always other factors, both positive and negative, to consider. The £10 million ROI is not quite that amount as, since the investment was from existing money, if it had been left in a normal banking investment, it would probably have increased in any case. So the £10 million ROI is reduced by the interest that would have accrued in any case and, of course, also any taxes that might be imposed.

But, because the company invested in is one of the suppliers to the investing company, and it has increased performance, efficiency and perhaps reduced costs and prices, the investing company will have gained some extra benefits. It may not be so simple to calculate the firm values of these, but they are there in the same way as the positive financial ROI.

Even these considerations may not be the end of other costs or benefits, so, even in the apparently straightforward cases, the calculations turn out to be more complex than first imagined.

A training example is when the training agreed is for a group of new representatives who will be responsible for a new block of work. Here the basic cost value will only involve the new product development costs, marketing costs and the administration costs related to setting up the training and arranging for the learners to attend (this is a gross over-simplification as will be seen later but, for the purposes of this example, the cost description is sufficient). Following the training, which of course will have costs to add to that side of the equation, when the reps start effective work, the new business (i.e. extra business) they bring in and its nett value can be weighed against the original costs, plus the new ones connected with the training, sales travelling and accommodation, new admin costs, and so on. The value may in the early stages show a loss, but as time progresses and extra costs become less, the value additions should increase.

People who are involved in such an operation will realize the over-simplification of the example, but it does at least indicate a way of producing a value assessment. However, there are other hidden factors that may get in the way! Such aspects as changing market factors, emerging prior experience or innate ability among the reps, various and varying levels of motivation, and so on all may modify what is apparently a straightforward approach and cast doubt on whether the training was the only factor involved – these additional factors being given the title 'contaminatory factors'.

Even the apparently very straightforward example of the new meter reader has problems, for although the 'then' and 'now' situations are a) unable to read meters, therefore not earning, to b) having learned can now read meters and is therefore producing business, many questions of costing and assessing the value of reading the meters are produced.

The increase in interest (? use) of the ROI related to people going on training programmes has unfortunately increased the relationship of effectiveness to money *in extremis*. For example, one writer (Kearns, 2001) advocates unequivocally that if £s and $s cannot be measured as a major part of the benefits of any training, then that training itself has little or no value and was not worth performing! Such an attitude obviously ignores the almost-impossibility of assessing the monetary worth of many forms of training other than by a 'finger in the wind' approach (this itself may have little value) and ignores the important value of the learning itself and its implementation in the workplace by the individuals or groups of people concerned. People and their attributes hold an important position in business effectiveness and cannot be ignored, even if their contribution or changed contribution cannot be quantified fully in monetary terms.

The universal application of ROI in financial terms is one that is currently a controversial issue. There can be no doubt that to produce a fully accurate and comprehensive ROI assessment is a very difficult task. There are so many aspects to be taken into account and so many of these where it is very difficult if not impossible to define in financial terms. At best, so many of the assessments quoted are 'best guesses'. One saving factor is that, although a complete assessment may not be possible, if the same measures are used from occasion to occasion, at least a comparison of like with like can be made. Sometimes that is all that can be hoped for, even in what appear to be the simplest events – it may not be simply a matter of, for example, after the training of sales representatives as suggested above, the number (and value) of new sales made; the drop in absenteeism following motivation training; and so on.

The problems are enhanced when public and non-profit-making organizations are considered – government departments, charities, voluntary bodies, and so on. These problems are so difficult, and in some cases insurmountable, that the organization remains satisfied with general approximations and perhaps comparisons, or accepts wider forms of justification for the training without invoking detailed costing.

I have experienced an even more extreme, non-financial evaluation situation. During a game of golf, my golf partner, a superb golfer, suggested that he give me some hints that might improve my game (i.e. a coaching or training situation). He did so and I implemented my learning with improved results. Hence the change as a result of the training/coaching was validated and the evaluation was that my game had improved. But, although the event satisfied all the aspects of change, training/coaching, learning implementation and continued review, the training had no cost at all – we are both fully paid-up members of the golf club which would be the same without the training, it occurred during the normal course of a game, and I certainly did not pay anything for the event. In this way an ROI could be expressed as 0, 100 per cent, 500 percent, 1000 per cent, or any other figure you like to float. BUT the event demonstrated benefit effectiveness and satisfaction to us both.

None of this is to say that cost- and value-effectiveness assessment should not be attempted. At the very least, direct costs must be restrained within the agreed budget, and if it is possible, attempts at more detailed returns should be made.

In basic terms, training must generally result in a profit or loss to the organization in £ or $ terms; after all that is why the organization is 'in business', whether or not it is a profit- or non-profit-making organization. People must enter the equation in various ways. As a result of their attending the training programme, hopefully their skills and knowledge have improved to the extent that they are more effective people in every way; in its turn this benefits the organization by their having a more effective workforce. If the organization is more effective (i.e. has a better opportunity of maintaining or increasing its business) it will become a more likely employer for its employees, not just the ones for whom the training costs were expended, but all the employees.

Calculating the ROI

A simple cost- and value-effectiveness, the ROI, consists of identifying the costs and the benefits and calculating the difference between them. There are several ways in which a ROI can be calculated – unfortunately none of them are absolutely comprehensive and accurate. The ROI can be expressed as the monetary return an organization has made over a specified period as the result of investing some of its resources, for example money, into a range of projects, including training. The calculation of the amount is frequently expressed as what seems to be a simple and straightforward equation:

% ROI = gross benefits of the training minus costs of the training
                                    costs   x 100.

However, another commonly quoted equation is the apparently simpler:

%ROI = benefits
             costs   x100.

Using the first equation, a benefit assessed at £100 000 at a cost of £20 000, would result in 100 000 – 20 000 = 80 000 / 20 000 = 4 x 100 = 400% ROI. The second equation would show £100 000 / £20 000 = 5 x 100% = 500% ROI. Quite a difference!

However even more 'problems' arise! I posed the question of the different equations to an on-line trainers' forum (TrainingZone) and received six comments, all of which placed different interpretations on the equations and their results, using such terms as 'capital and revenue costs'; 'technically'; 'accountants use costs, trainers should use investments'; 'the differences are due to "gross" and "net" benefits'; and so on. In addition, a third equation appeared – ROI = net benefit/total cost – an equation 'in which there is no ambiguity in the math calculation'. One very useful comment was that it didn't matter which approach is used as long as you are consistent.

More problems arise when you try to put actual figures to the benefits and the costs, calculation of the latter being considerably easier to achieve, although there are many hidden pitfalls.

The ROI is sometimes expressed as the 'payback period' which relates to the number of months it will require before the benefits of the training match the costs, so financing the training effectively. However, the problems of calculating the benefits also remain in this method.

Of course, consideration of the ROI does not look coldly at only the financial return, so in addition to:

- justifying the expenses incurred in training

it is concerned with:

- ensuring that the individuals are provided with all the best training the organization can provide
- the design of training is continuously consistent and assessed to provide better value and increased benefits to the organization
- the most effective form of training method is selected.

A practical approach to this difficult problem of assessment of the ROI is to consider it at the earliest opportunity, even before an individual goes forward for training, and even preceding the selection of training method stage, perhaps at the 'definitive statement' stage described in Chapter 6. For this purpose, if they are available, any performance indicators can be used. In addition to the evaluation agreement, the existing cost of the untrained person can be assessed compared with the financial position of people who have been trained and are performing the task. This approach has the parallel in the pre- and post-training skills and provides the opportunity for assessment over the 'change' period, rather than trying to do so when there is nothing with which to compare. So the 'definitive statement' can be extended thus:

1. Define the reasons for and objectives of the proposed ROI assessment
2. Select the criteria for and means of measurement/estimation of the resulting costs and benefits
3. Attempt an 'as is now' assessment of the costs and values as they stand without the training
4. Define the measures that will be used following the training to assess the ROI.

Of course, in some cases it may be argued that the financial value of a benefit need not (cannot) have a figure given to it, even in a profit-making business. Take for example the case of a group of employees who attend a training programme to learn about new regulations affecting their industry. On return to work they ensure that the regulations are put into place. It is difficult to imagine a benefit value being applied to such an instance, other than a totally negative benefit if the organization does not apply the statutory regulations – a heavy financial sanction or even closing down!

The costs and benefits of training

If a full analysis of the cost-value-effectiveness of the training is to be attempted in financial terms, the following material offers some suggestions on the basic aspects that must be taken into account in both the cost and value information.

Value for money

Assessment of the value for money given by the training has similar problems to the assessment of the amount of increased business described in the previous section. A simple cost evaluation consists of costs and benefits.

The costs are related to the charges made for the training. The costs involved in a learner attending a training course external to the employing organization could include:

- The fees charged to the organization by the trainer
- The cost of travelling and accommodation involved
- Costs incurred, notionally and actually, by the organization's staff in connection with arrangements for the trainee's attendance
- The trainee's time
- Loss of production as a result of the trainee's absence.

The costs of other forms of training are much more difficult to assess, particularly where some form of on-the-job project work or coaching is involved. In these cases, where real work is involved, it is difficult to separate the work content from an oncost of training content. Even more difficult to cost is the provision of in-house training, by company trainers for company trainees in company time on company premises. However, since exact costs are difficult to obtain, a reasonable estimate may be made.

The benefits to the organization, on the other hand, are as difficult to assess in monetary terms as they are in product benefits.

If observation inventories of the types described in the previous chapter are to be used to assess the training as an event and this assessment shows that it is effective and valid, the employing organization can be reasonably sure that it is receiving value for most of the money it is expending. Virtually any assessment of the monetary worth of training can be as subjective and as difficult as the validation of some of the training events previously mentioned. If the cost or value analysis is extended to include monetary value in an overall evaluation, the difficulties are even more evident.

Cost–value analysis must form part of a training assessment. Otherwise the organization will have no idea, for example:

- How many trainers it must employ to perform the training desired.
- How much is a trainer worth?
- What is the total, net cost of the training to the organization?
- What is the cost of a training day? How many trainers/training days can the organization afford?
- What is the cost of training in relation to production or provision of services costs?

In order to assess these values, the assessor must be able to attribute a cost to everything connected with the training.

THE COSTS OF TRAINING

The costs attributable to the training function can be divided into three main sections:

1. Fixed costs relating principally to the training department
2. Supportive costs in respect of (a) trainers; (b) learners
3. Opportunity costs.

FIXED COSTS

These include the costs which are reasonably permanent and regular and fixed over a period of time, say a year. They can comprise:

1. Salaries, insurance and pensions contributions for all the people involved in the training function including any guest speakers (or at least a proportion of their costs related to their input to the training).
2. Cost of the training accommodation in terms of yearly rates, water rates, capital equipment (e.g. furniture, cabinets, etc.) and cleaning and regular maintenance costs. This accommodation would include any office accommodation allocated to training and, of course, accommodation used for training.
3. Electricity, gas, oil, telephone costs attributable to the training function.

SUPPORTIVE COSTS

These are the expenditure items for which costs are incurred for (a) the trainers and (b) the learners. They are the more occasional items than the fixed costs and can include:

(a) 1. External accommodation costs for the training and the trainers – training room hire, equipment hire, bedroom and meals costs for the trainers in hotels and conference centres
   2. Travelling and out of pocket subsistence costs for the trainers
   3. Equipment, books and aids purchase and other provision and maintenance.
(b) 1. Accommodation costs for the learners
   2. Travelling and other subsistence costs for the learners
   3. The learners' salaries.

OPPORTUNITY COSTS

Although the salaries of the learners have been included in the costing summary, while the learners are away on the training course they are not directly contributing to the company output. The value of this is often described as the 'opportunity' cost – the value of that individual's services if they had been contributing directly in their job to the company output. In many ways this will have to be a subjective amount, although some companies claim that they are able to calculate this lost opportunity value accurately. Others have formulae which are used for different skill and job levels. Although it can appear to be a highly quantitative and objective calculation, in reality its basis is very subjective.

EVALUATION

Even more subjective will be any attempt to prove that the training is responsible for any increase in work output, efficiency, higher earning value, and so on. We have seen earlier that it is very difficult, it not impossible, to attribute a value to the total learning process, unless a wide measure of controls with a number of control groups is used.

Trained people who are involved in direct operation tasks can have their efficiency assessed and, if they were unskilled before the training, this increased skill and the output value resulting can be attributed to the training.

Let us take the example of the meter reader who has been trained to perform his duties. Before his training he needed to be accompanied by another reader to help him in his duties; this entailed two wages, one of which would be saved following the training because both people would be productively employed – an obvious direct-benefit cost. Similarly, if before the training the meter reader required 6 hours to read 36 meters, and after the training he was able to read 72 meters in the same time, a further cost-benefit is obvious.

The meter reader case is a relatively straightforward one: most are much more complex and difficult, if not impossible, to assess in terms of cost-benefits. Physical work activities by an individual can produce identifiable benefits but, even in the case of physical activities, complications arise when the learner is part of a working group. The evaluation becomes even more difficult, and often completely impossible, if the training has been of a human relations nature, or involving mental or social skills, or a mixture of these and physical activities.

In some cases the problem is so great that organizations attempting to assess the cost of training simply ignore this factor. If ignoring it is a consistent feature, then comparisons between one period and another are possible, but it has to be accepted that a valuable part of the training function is being ignored.

COST ANALYSIS

The figures related to the costs summarized above can be used to produce a monetary statement from which a number of conclusions can be drawn: cost of the training function; cost of the training function per individual; cost of the training per learner, and so on. The principal value is often in comparing one period with another. In such a comparative case it does not matter too much if the figures are not completely accurate representations, provided the same calculations and methods of calculation are used on each occasion. Even in this simplistic approach there are many possible variables which can corrupt the estimates.

In the simplest analysis, a unit cost of training per trainer can be obtained by adding together all the known costs – fixed, support and opportunity. If this figure is divided by the number of people who contribute towards this training – the training manager, the training officers, the administration staff and the attributed external speakers – the resulting figure is one form of cost. For example, if the sum of all the costs if £750 000 per annum with a training function staff of eight, the unit cost per trainer is about £94 000. This calculation masks a number of factors – cost of external training and open learning (which would increase the cost per trainer), high course numbers (which should decrease the cost per trainer) and a value based on the evaluation of the training and transfer to work (which would further reduce the unit cost). Without these other factors it at least gives a baseline measure which can be used as a comparative costing from one year to another, using the same sets of factors. If in the following year the total cost of the same factors has risen to £900 000, the cost per trainer will have increased to about £112 000. If the general cost of living index had risen by 8 per cent, a simple increase to £972 000 would have occurred. However, the actual rise represents an increase of 17 per cent. There may in fact be a good explanation for this rise, but the additional 9 per cent increase requires some form of enquiry to be made.

The costing can be approached in another way. If the total training cost is £750 000 in one year and 9000 learners pass through 600 courses in that time, the cost per learner is £83 and the cost per course is £1250. If, using the increase in the example above, in the following year when the cost is £900 000, the number of learners is increased to 12 600 and the courses to 900, but with the same training input, the relevant costing will decrease to £71 per learner and £1000 per course in spite of the previously demonstrated increase of 17 per cent!

It is also possible to cost the training in terms of the number of learners who have attended the events. One method by which course 'costs' can be reduced is to increase the number of participants on each course – the trainer salaries and training accommodation, and so on, costs remain the same, there is a small increase in the learner salary attribution, but the net result is a lower cost per learner. This effect is particularly noticeable when external providers are brought in to tutor courses. If, for a five-day course, the consultant's fee is £2500, all other factors remain more or less the same, but the learner unit cost reduces considerably with the increase in course participants. If the course population is normally eight, the unit learner cost is £312. If the number is increased to 15 with only a relatively small increase in learner salary costs, the unit learner cost reduces to only £167.

When cost reductions are considered for internally resourced or externally provided training by means of increased course participant numbers, care must be taken that in increasing these numbers the quality of the learning does not suffer.

Value- or business-orientated results

The examples quoted above are all approaches to costing which fail to take into account the many plus and minus factors. This may also happen if an attempt is made to use as a balancing figure the *value* of the training to the organization in terms of increased business and hence profits. Apart from the difficulty of using evaluation to try to produce a figure of this nature, it is almost impossible, except in the simplest of cases, to be absolutely sure that any improvement in performance has in fact been due to the training.

In an attempt to assess the business or real-value results of any training programme, these results can be viewed as categories of change. Some are *easier* to assess and the areas in which change might be observed following training and development programmes include factors back at work such as:

- Time usage – meetings are kept to time and are time-effective; appointments are kept efficiently; reports etc. are submitted at the due time, and so on. These, and many others, could of course be the result of putting into practice the learning achieved on a time management programme.
- Work practices – these can be suggested by a stricter adherence to health and safety practices; following effective operating procedures (perhaps modified following a programme that looked at the existing procedures) – these changes might be observed at the operative, supervisory or management levels. In the two latter cases, assessment might be made from observation of an improvement in checks made that were not made previously; a closer support of subordinates in their work practices; and, linking with the next category, an increase in output and reduction in waste.
- Output of products or services – an increase in the amount of work produced, sales or other visits made etc. Positive results of this nature may be achieved following programmes aimed at effective supervisory or management practices; project management; team development; problem-solving, etc.
- Costs – many industrial and commercial costs are attributable to people – their efficiency, interpersonal relationships, discipline, attendance, leaving and recruitment and other personnel matters. Any changes may be the results of programmes concerned with people skills, interviewing techniques, interpersonal skills, effective working, etc.
- People – team development, interpersonal skills and people relationship programmes might result in improvements of these aspects of the people undertaking tasks – how well they get on with each other, how much support they give each other, how well they listen to each other, and to what extent they work as a team rather than a collection of individuals.
- Individual development – a number of programmes aim to increase the creative ability of people; help them to present themselves in more favourable lights; demonstrate their promotability, and in general, be more effective and 'wider' people. Observation of these aspects is probably the most difficult of all the assessments, but, over an extended period, a supervisor or manager who is in fairly constant contact with the individuals can note examples of these improvements.
- Quality of products and services – this can be assessed from a reduction in the number of rejects of products and customer complaints; reduced operating costs; increased levels of evaluation; increased business etc. Customer service and quality control programmes might have been responsible for changes in these aspects; skill development programmes; audit and inspection methods, etc.
- Improvements in the organizational climate and culture – without doubt the most difficult to assess. Reduced resignations and discharges, fewer sick absences, increased production and a reduction in customer complaints – these and other indicators may give the opportunity to assess a change, but all are highly subjective, particularly when confirmation of a direct link with a training/ learning programme is attempted. If there is a good line of communication from every part of the organization to the personnel or human resource development department, this may be the most valuable part of the organization to assess the global picture.

Specific assessments will depend on the susceptibility to objective measurement of the areas being observed. The comparison must always be with the pre-training situation, otherwise you are not measuring anything – the pre-training position might of course be zero in the case of a completely new event. Otherwise, an example might be:

Area of change	Pre-training performance	Post-training objective	Actual post-training results
Number of widgets rejected at quality control point	10% of production	1% or less of production	0.5% of production

A successful result such as this, if it is measured immediately after the training, can be assumed to relate directly to the training although there will still be some other aspects involved – motivation, fear of dismissal, change of staff, and so on.

The 'softer' type of changes – for example, team development and interpersonal relationships – which have no quantitative measures, are more difficult to assess for success, but if some form of model exists against which the learners were assessed before the training programme, the model observation can be used again for post-training, work-environment practice.

As always there is no absolute guarantee that any improvement or change, such as those suggested above, that is observed or assessed is completely, or even minimally, due to the training programme, but any changes may be an indication of success along these lines. These problems do not suggest that no attempt should be made at assessing a costing or other value analysis of training. Quite the reverse, but the problems and difficulties must be recognized and care taken in attributing success or failure and a change in cost/value. It may be necessary to accept the subjective views and estimates suggested earlier because the area being considered is too subjective to be *measured*.

Assessments at this stage are principally concerned with evaluation (the total benefits) rather than the simple validation of the training programme itself. A significant number of people might be involved in the evaluation and it may be necessary to involve people from multi-disciplines. The person responsible – senior management, line manager, training manager or trainer – must decide to what extent resources are to be provided for this, often extensive and expensive, exercise; whether the time involved (time that may be disproportionate to the time taken on the training itself) should be expended; and to what extent the degrees of subjectivity and objectivity should be accepted.

Guidelines for value-effective analysis

A number of organizations have developed their own formulae (based on the ROI equation quoted earlier) for calculating the costs and the benefits of training investment. These quote for most of the difficult areas of measurement, for example on the costs side, the opportunity costs (that is the value of profit, and so on, lost while the person is away from their job) and on the benefits side, the changed value of the trained person. The quotes are frequently stated as 'scientific' measurements, although many assessors agree that they are simply intelligent guesses. If a lot of training is being undertaken over a substantial period, these 'intelligent guesses' (the best measures available) can be used in a comparative manner, even though the absolute accuracy is not there. Measures are guessed intelligently on the first occasion and a ROI figure arrived at. In similar successive circumstances, the figures are used again and the calculations will show, compared with the first occasion, whether the ROI has increased or decreased – frequently there will be some increase as some of the initial costs may not be repeated.

Garry Platt, Senior Consultant at Woodland Grange Training and Conference Centre (www.wgrange.com) has developed a model over the last few years that seeks to measure the Recoupment on Salary Expenditure (ROS), similar to ROI. He uses a spreadsheet for recording these measures, a format that can be added to or amended as necessary. His model requires six major data entries, resulting in four sets of output data.

Input data entries required:

1   The annual salary of the person being trained
2.   The combined overhead costs of the person being trained. These can be extensive and will include the costs described earlier in this chapter – some will be at the 'guesstimate' level, such as opportunity costs, but many are fixed costs, for example pension payments, work benefits, reimbursed car expenses, etc., etc. This figure may result in, say 55%, 75% etc.
3.   The course length in days or fractions of a day
4.   The course fee
5.   Costs allied to the training, e.g. travel costs, allowed expenses
6.   The assessed productivity increase. This can only be guessed or estimated, but it forms the basis for later calculations. The increase is entered as a percentage, e.g. 5%, 50%, etc.

Output data provided:

1.   The organization's total investment
2.   The return made for each day the learner returns to work
3.   The ROI over the first year as an investment as a percentage of the initial investment
4.   The payback period.

A worked example of this method is shown in Figure 12.1

SUMMARY OF GUIDELINES

The following summarizes the guidelines that should help in the analysis in this difficult area.

1.   Don't be put off by the apparent, or real, difficulties and subjective nature of the areas to be assessed – try something. The method and results may not be fully quantitative but, if you have to assess the value of repeated events, using the same method gives at least a standard for comparison between events.
2.   Particularly in subjective assessment try for comparisons with similar events under similar conditions.
3.   Seek the views – albeit subjective ones – of others. For example, ask for the critical views

Recoupment on salary expenditure

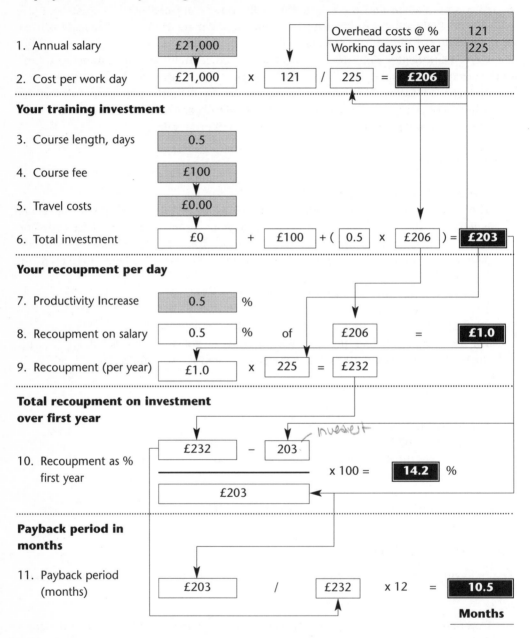

Figure 12.1   Recoupment on salary expenditure

(Reproduced with the permission of Garry Platt, Woodland Grange Training and Conference Centre)

of customers, internal and external, about whether any changes have been noted in the period and area of work you are keeping under review.

4. Compare results against models or even concepts when the areas are completely subjective in nature – e.g., behaviour change can be assessed against such models as the ones that are applied to Behaviour Analysis.

5. Only gather information or data that you will be able to use, however interesting or easy to obtain other 'data' might be.

6. Try to determine the value baseline by asking the line manager of the learners before the events for their estimate of how much it will be worth to them and their operation to have an effective person. This approach will probably be resisted, but if it is not achieved, it then becomes impossible to assess value after the event. After the training evaluate the success and ask the line manager whether their initial estimates have been achieved.

7. Seek, but do not necessarily take as positive proof, organizational effects linked to the training areas – increased productivity, decreased absences, discipline incidents, grievances, etc. Link these to other evaluation processes to ensure that contamination has not occurred.

8. An obvious message results from the foregoing discussion in that the crux of ROI assessments must be an effective form of performance measurement. Without this any 'calculations' at the final ROI stage become difficult, if not impossible. One side effect I have encountered is the case of one organization that, realizing this need, introduced a process of performance measurement linked with training needs and found that some of the training they were considering could be more effectively achieved by other means – an immediate positive ROI!

13 *Customizing your evaluation programmes*

The requirements of and for evaluation vary as widely as the methods that can be used; the potential evaluator must be able to assess the value of these methods as effectively as possible. If this is done, not only is a successful evaluation achieved, but it is achieved without any waste of resources – time, money, people and paper. But the ideal is not always (if ever) achievable.

A decision on an evaluation approach requires two initial steps:

1. Awareness and knowledge of the various evaluation tools available;
2. The resources available to perform the evaluation.

From (1) and (2), an approach that satisfies, as far as possible, the optimum requirements of both can be produced.

Unfortunately, because of the compromises forced on to the evaluator, the selected approach may fall short of what, in the best of all possible worlds, would be a fully effective method. This is a fact of life in evaluation, based on the advice that you can only do the best you can. These compromises mean that the evaluation approach achieved may:

- not be as complete as you would want
- be more subjective than objective
- leave gaps in the information provided.

But some form of evaluation, even incomplete and subjective to an extent, if applied consistently is better than no evaluation at all provided the limitations are recognized and taken into account in any analysis for which the evaluation might be used.

The Evaluation Quintet

Some comments were made in Chapter 1 on the interests of different people roles and levels in the organization in validation and evaluation. Some time ago I coined the expressions 'The Training Quintet' and 'The Evaluation Quintet' to describe the people who should have interests and responsibilities in the wider aspects of training and development and in particular in the evaluation (leading to the ROI) of this training and development. The training aspect has been described elsewhere, so the evaluation features are concentrated on here, namely the roles and responsibilities of the Evaluation Quintet. This Quintet consists of the same members as the Training Quintet, namely – Senior Management, Line

Management, Training Management, the Trainer and the Learner. The various responsibilities of these roles can be summarized as follows, and for an effective evaluation approach, all members must play their parts in full at all times. The format of the Quintet is shown graphically in Figure 13.1.

SENIOR MANAGEMENT

Although senior management is not directly involved in the day-to-day performance of evaluation itself, they have a role and responsibility in:

- authorizing resources and responsibilities to enable it to be performed
- taking an active part in requiring it to be done
- taking an obvious, real and active interest
- accepting and demonstrating their ultimate responsibility for the ROI of training to the business.

There is little value if senior management, training's major clients and sponsors, offer only a superficial interest. This can be enhanced by organization-wide statements that it supports the evaluation aspect of training and development and demonstrating this support in as practical a manner as possible. The support can be shown by:

- requiring evaluation to be performed in the organization
- showing a continuing interest in progress
- examining and discussing evaluation results.

THE TRAINING MANAGER

The training manager must be a moving force in the progress of evaluation of training *for which he or she has a responsibility*. This manager acts as the link between the senior manager

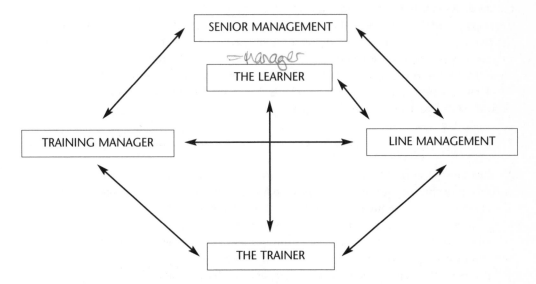

Figure 13.1   The evaluation quintet

clients and the trainers, and also has to be the person who reminds the trainers that evaluation of their area is an essential element. Trainers can only too easily forget this when they become involved in the complexities and difficulties of the training itself. The training manager may have a network of a number of trainers from whom sets of evaluation instruments arrive as the training year progresses. These *must* be analysed and collated so that meaningful analytical reports can be prepared for senior management. The trainers should be encouraged to take an active interest in the progressive collation of the evaluation sets and the training manager will want to hold discussions with the trainer group about what these collations show.

The trainers may need to be motivated to make a commitment to evaluation, to regard it as an essential part of the training cycle and not simply an enforced chore; the training manager is an important part of this encouragement.

The training manager role in evaluation can be summarized as:

- linking with the senior management or other top level groups to ensure that training is included at an early stage of new projects and evaluation is included in arrangements
- enabling the practice of evaluation policy
- examining validation and evaluation results
- completing evaluation reports for senior management
- organizing training and education programmes on evaluation for line management.

THE LINE MANAGER

In most organizations the line manager is underused in the training and development area, certainly so in the evaluation process and particularly in the assessment of the immediate ROI as it relates to the training provided for their staff, how it affects their area of work and hence the business. Certainly, many line managers will claim that they are already overloaded with work without adding further activities that many of them will also claim is the province of the trainer. The simple response in every case to these claims is that they cannot afford *not* to be involved. Whether or not they are making direct financial contributions to the training and development of their staff, training is costing them money – loss of productive resource during the training period – and hence a devaluation of their department's production. Trained staff should provide effective production and training them costs money: does the line manager know how much this cost is and whether value for money is being provided?

There are eight basic activities in which line managers should be involved with their learning staff and also the training department:

1. Involvement in the design of the evaluation process for training in which their staff are likely to be involved and which will affect them
2. Effective selection of the appropriate training programme for their staff
3. Ensuring that any pre-course training requirements are enabled and completed
4. Holding pre-course briefing meetings with the learners
5. Holding post-course debriefing meetings with the learners
6. Giving the learners implementation support and holding review meetings
7. Holding longer-term and/or final review meetings
8. Assessing the ROI on the training results and implementation.

But the value of the line manager's intervention should not stop here and, if commitment is encouraged, they can be invaluable to the trainer, not only in supporting the training but also by becoming directly involved in the long-term evaluation.

Trainers often complain about the apparent lack of interest from line managers in the training programmes. If this is so, surely it would be valuable to involve the line manager in the training plans at the earliest opportunity – certainly at the planning stage and also at the content design stage. This involvement will ensure that the manager feels some ownership of, and hence commitment to, the training. Similarly, when the evaluation approach is being planned, the line manager should be invited to contribute and in so doing, with the accompanying commitment, can be encouraged to take a more active part thus enabling more extensive evaluation to be possible than otherwise. A specific instance of this latter involvement is long-term evaluation when the learner's implementation of planned action is being assessed. Such evaluation leads to the line manager's assessment of the cost-effective value of the training which the members of staff have attended or otherwise taken part in.

Many line managers have to be convinced of the value of any contribution they might make to the evaluation process in what, traditionally, they consider to be what trainers do. The benefits of mutual involvement are so great that a trainer's or training department's plans must include a programme of activities to encourage line managers to accept their Evaluation Quintet responsibilities. These activities might include:

- invitations to line managers to become involved in the planning of training programmes
- invitations to line managers to become involved in the evaluation process planning
- visits to line managers or the normal meetings of groups of line managers to discuss training and evaluation and to try to obtain agreement for involvement in these activities
- invitations to attend training programmes so that they can observe at first hand what happens
- workshops facilitated by the training staff for line managers to discuss and agree actions relating to the evaluation processes in which they should be involved
- offers by trainers to give active support to the line managers at different stages of the post-training evaluation, for example by accompanying the line manager, but not taking the major role in medium- and longer-term review meetings
- workshops facilitated by the training staff for line managers to learn about, discuss and make arrangements for assessing the ROI on the training programmes.

THE TRAINER

The direct and active involvement of the trainers in the evaluation of their programmes is an absolute necessity. They are in the position to:

- support (as agreed) the line manager's pre-course activity with the learner – supplying *full* programme information, support for the pre-course briefing, etc.
- identify the knowledge and skill levels of their learners at the start of the programmes (unless this has taken place before the learner attends)
- monitor the level and extent of learning as the programme continues

- modify the programme as an immediate result of the interim monitoring
- identify the knowledge and skill levels of the learners at the end of the programme
- steer the learners to the production of post-training action planning
- undertake with the learner a validation of the training programme itself (and in some instances, assessment of the trainer's performance)
- support (as agreed) the line manager's post-course debriefing with the learner
- support (as agreed) the line manager's long-term evaluation of the implementation of the learning (this might be an activity performed by the trainers themselves or their representatives so that not only is the learning evaluated, but a longer-term validation of the training can take place).

THE LEARNER

Finally, although the principal role of the learner in the programme is to learn, they must be involved in the evaluation process – essentially so, as without their comments much of the evaluation would not occur. Learners must be committed to completing honestly and totally any assessment instruments for the evaluation, avoiding, as far as possible, contamination of their comments by euphoric feeling (or otherwise!). They must not be allowed to feel that they are completing a paper-chase or number-crunching exercise, and should be made aware of exactly why they are being asked to do certain things and what the assessments will be used for and by whom. This type of knowledge will help to ensure that meaningful and realistic comments are made.

One common omission is a failure to let the learners know the results of their support – evaluation questionnaires appear, are completed by the learners then disappear never to be heard of or seen by them again. If the results are to be used in subsequent evaluation activities, let the learners know this and seek their advice on how the information might be used most effectively.

If this culture atmosphere is induced in an organization among the senior training and line managers, trainers and learners, not only will the evaluation be more effective as a result of commitment, but the training and development will also be more effective and seen as valuable throughout the organization.

The development of this supportive culture will not happen overnight in organizations where it does not already exist, nor will it develop without committed work, usually by the trainers and their training manager. The claim of lack of time by line managers is often well founded and the apparent lack of interest by senior management often exists only because of ignorance of their role, or perhaps relegation of the process because of a non-understanding of the reason for and value of evaluation. A programme of education should be embarked upon preferably on all fronts at the same time, otherwise one element might negate the agreed intents of other sectors.

Customized evaluation approaches

The evaluation model that I use in my own work, and which I recommend for consideration, is not a simple one with its sixteen stages (see Chapter 1, Figure 1.1). This model may in fact represent an ideal situation and, although ideal, may be too expensive in time and resources to be carried out in full on every occasion. Other aspects may also get in the way of its introduction, such as lack of interest on the part of some or all of the members of the Training/Evaluation Quintets. However, at any time, somebody, perhaps senior management, may ask the training department 'Is your training effective?' and receive the response 'Yes it is'. It would not be unusual for this initial approach to be followed up by the supplementary (and perhaps even more important) question 'Can you prove that statement?' This, of course, is where evaluation enters the scenario: if there has been no evaluation attempted, the training department must admit this, with the obvious consequences. However, if an effective evaluation has been performed, the documentation, instruments and analyses can be produced to the satisfaction of the 'bill payers'.

So, it is obvious that, in an organization that is interested in how its money is being spent and is liable to ask the questions quoted above, validation and evaluation are not just 'nice things to have' but essential aspects of the training operation. This leads us back to considering, within the constraints that exist, what can be done?

In terms of what can be done, there will be considerable variation in the extent and quality of the evaluation performed, variations due to a number of factors such as those mentioned above, but particularly problems of resource and time. From the items in Figure 1.1 the evaluators can select the aspects that they feel are most relevant to their situation and for which resources are available. If these decisions indicate only some of these aspects, these decisions may be seen by some people as having less value than a fuller evaluation, even of having no value. But I believe that *any* evaluation approach is of *some* value, particularly if it is applied consistently so that comparisons can be made over time. Obviously the more detailed and in-depth the evaluation, the more effective it should be, but you must be satisfied with what you are able to do. This does not exclude (using evaluation evidence as part of the argument) trying to persuade senior management for sufficient resources to enable a fuller approach to be attempted.

This section of the chapter describes some variations from the simplest (in which nothing is done!), through an increasing complexity of methods, to a full evaluation process. The assumption is made that, whatever else might be done, the early stages of the process, namely identification of needs and design of the training programme, have been performed, and most require the education of line managers to give maximum support to the evaluation. The basic criterion is that evaluation is not for the trainer alone to carry out, but it is the province of the various members of the Evaluation Quintet.

APPROACH ONE – NO ACTION

At the most elementary end of the evaluation spectrum is the situation where no validation or evaluation is attempted. As suggested earlier, this may be due to a lack of interest on the part of the training practitioners or their clients or stakeholders, or specifically the latter, as a result of which no resources are available. It may be, of course, that the senior levels are totally uninterested. The training practitioners then have alternatives, in this case:

- to accept the constraints and reflect the lack of interest in the non-evaluation, concentrating on the training and hoping that learning has been achieved
- to accept the higher level attitudes, but to try to do some evaluation in spite of this, if only for their own peace of mind.

APPROACH TWO – AT LEAST OBTAIN A REACTION

This is probably the simplest approach that will offer some element of apparent validation with the minimum use of resources. The approach concentrates principally on the reactions of the learners to the learning event, and, because feelings and opinions only are being sought, there is little real validation. However, some useful information that will be helpful to consideration of the future of the programme can be obtained by this method.

Although the instrument used is a reactionnaire it should be as far removed as possible from the 'happy sheet' and it should be given an important place in the programme. A suitable instrument for this approach is described in Chapter 8 and shown, for example, in Figure 8.2.

What should be a common aspect of *all* training programmes is the completion of and commitment to an Action Plan by the learners. Although not directly an evaluation instrument, the Action Plan can reflect the learners' attitudes to the programme and its content and value as a learning event. The request for the learners to complete an Action Plan will reinforce the value of the learning and help towards the commitment of the learners to implementing their learning.

APPROACH THREE – THE MINIMUM EFFECTIVE APPROACH

In the 16-stage ideal process, the use of the minimum effective approach Steps 1, 2, 6, 8 and 11 is absolutely essential for use with any and every training programme. Steps 1 and 2 should be automatic processes. Steps 6 and 8 must be conducted by the trainers during the training programme – if not, they will be, apart from totally subjective assessments, unable to state definitively that learning appears to have been achieved. Step 11, the Action Plan, *must* be completed by the learners at the end of the training programme, otherwise they can go back to work with no future intentions based on the learning – so, however good the training has been, if it is not implemented by learners back at work, it has been a waste of time and money.

In summary, Approach Three consists of:

- Step 1 – Training needs analysis
- Step 2 – Design of the evaluation process
- Step 6 – Start of course testing or assessment of knowledge, skills and attitudes
- Step 8 – End of programme testing or assessment of learners
- Step 11 – Learner action planning at end of programme.

This approach assumes that there will be no support action by the learners' line managers and that the trainers will not remedy this failure by their interventions.

APPROACH FOUR – ONE UP FROM THE MINIMUM

This is the next stage up and introduces a reasonably realistic attempt to include an assessment of the learning achieved, supplementing the assessment made from an inspection of the Action Plans. There is little extra resource involvement than that needed in Approach Three, since the only difference is that the full Learning Questionnaire (LQ) is used (Chapter 9, Figure 9.1).

This extension, however, continues the concentration on *learning* rather than reaction to the training, although this is not ignored. If the learning stated is minimal or varies significantly from the objectives of the training programme, there is something wrong with the programme and some form of more in-depth investigation is called for.

Time *must* be built into the training programme to allow this document to be completed effectively, rather than the all too frequent last-minute handing out of a questionnaire, almost as the learners are leaving the training. The trainer should stress the value and importance of the approach so that there is a maximum chance that the questionnaires will be completed fully and honestly. The responses also give good indications for the effectiveness of the training programme: if the scoring and comments relate to the lower end of the range, this indicates, as suggested earlier, that there is something wrong with either the construction of the programme or of the learning population. If the good learning comments suggest aspects which were not intended from the objectives of the programme, again there are validation indications – it may be that emphasis is being placed during the programme on subjects other than those intended in the initial design of the programme, right or wrong. The trainer will need to investigate these indications whatever they may be.

The summary of Approach Four actions is the same as for Approach Three plus:

- Step 9 – End of programme validation of objectives – both of the training and the learners, by Learning Questionnaire.

APPROACH FIVE – THE PART OF ASSESSMENT DURING THE PROGRAMME

Chapter 7 describes the various approaches and techniques that might be used during the course of a training programme to assess how the programme is progressing and the participants are learning a) the types of material they should be learning, and b) the types of material they want and/or need to learn.

This approach introduces the simple addition of such interim measures in order to include, as part of a more extended approach, Step 7 – interim assessment and validation.

APPROACH SIX – ENTER THE LINE MANAGER

With this approach and its additional activities we are approaching the ideal situation of a full and comprehensive evaluation process. This situation is brought about by the introduction of the line manager into the evaluation process, although the additional problems and difficulties must not be ignored or minimized. In many organizations it may be, as suggested earlier when the Evaluation Quintet was being discussed, that an educative process might need to be introduced to encourage the line managers to accept their responsibilities and commit themselves to supporting fully both the training of their staff and the evaluation process. Without the commitment of line managers to even the minimal involvement suggested in this approach there is little hope for anything more extensive.

The approach takes Approach Five several stages further with pre-programme and post-programme meetings between the line managers and the learners, and other activities external to the training course itself. Steps that can be added in this approach, depending on the extent to which the line managers have agreed to take their responsibilities in hand, will be:

1. Step 3 – Establishing the business base level for post-training implementation to determine the ROI
2. Step 5 – Line-manager pre-course briefing
3. Step 12 – Line-manager post-course debriefing and support for implementation of learning
4. Step 13 – Medium-term follow-up and review of implementation of learning – learner and line manager
5. Step 14 – Long-term follow-up and review of implementation of learning – learner and line manager
6. Step 15 – Cost and value effectiveness analysis by line manager (ROI – Return on Investment on the training)
7. Step 16 – Assessment and report on achievement of the programme.

Although not performed by the line manager, Step 4 – Pre-course testing or assessment of knowledge, skills and attitudes – is taken outside the training programme itself. This is when the training programme requires some form of pre-training activity and, unless there are unusual circumstances, if there is to be any form of supervision of the learners performing these tasks, the line manager will be the person to undertake this supervision, and so on.

The approach descriptions above demonstrate the requirements for evaluation processes within the evaluation model described in Chapter 1, ranging from the situation when, for some reason, no form of validation or evaluation is undertaken, through progressively time- and resource-consuming stages to Approach Six, in which a number of activities for the line manager to perform are introduced. This approach as a result includes all the 16 steps of the model and is the nearest to an objective assessment of the training/learning that may be possible. If any of the additional steps included in this approach can be identified as more important than others, these would be the pre- and post-programme interviews between the learner and the line manager, leading to the supported implementation of the learners' learning.

Within these approaches most evaluators will find a menu of Steps depending on the time and resources available to them.

Other customized evaluation approaches

There are a number of other approaches to evaluation outlined under this heading, each customized according to the type of learning, the resources available and so on.

EVALUATION USING COMPETENCE STANDARDS

Competence standards and their associated NVQs have been described in Chapter 2 and it was stated that the main application of these standards is the link with the NVQ system. A number of organizations have taken advantage of this, and they offer a range of competence guidelines in a number of other areas. One of these areas is in the field of evaluation. The competence standards lead us to list not only what should be performed in an occupation, but also the level required and the range of functions, all of which are assessable with a minimum of subjectivity. These facilities direct the standards, whether or not an NVQ is sought, to a restricted but usable task and job description and level specification. They also identify the person specification in the same terms, terms concerning whether a particular person satisfies the relevant criteria of being able to perform the function as required.

With a little more imagination the value of the competence standards in the evaluation of training and development and learning offers an almost ready-made instrument for assessing this learning. I use the word 'almost' because the competence standards consider the function holder only in terms of being able to, or not being able to, perform at the competency level determined and not taking into account varying levels of skill. 'Almost' is also a caveat because many people find difficulty with the format of the standards and the language used to describe them. The Training and Development Lead Body (TDLB) NVQs were reviewed in 1994 with the language factor as one of the review objectives. The descriptions were simplified, made more logical and understandable. The EmpNTO, currently responsible for the standards and the detail of the training and development N/SVQs have now completed a project which has revised, and hopefully simplified, the numbering and wording of the training and development N/SVQs. This was referred to in Chapter 2.

USING THE COMPETENCE STANDARDS IN AN EVALUATION APPROACH

One of my recent personal encounters with the problems of using the standards in this way was in my development of an evaluation strategy for one of my Associateship clients. Previous experience with NVQs had made me language-conscious with their content and also as an interpreter for NVQ candidates who found difficulties. The client was developing an extended, supervisory management development programme, the content of which was to be linked with the MCI/NVQ at Level 3. Initially the participants were also to be given the opportunity to be candidates for the NVQ itself and subsequently, after some hiccups, this was built into the programme.

A strategic approach was required for the evaluation of the programme and the ensuing learning by the participants. Approach Six (described earlier in this chapter), modified because of the particular programme format, was used. Part of this evaluation approach was the use of a pre- and post-programme assessment questionnaire for completion by the learners, their line managers and also their subordinates. Because the programme was linked with the NVQ, the natural approach was to think in terms of using the relevant competence standards, with questions applied to them so that current levels, pre- and post-course could be assessed. The questions were listed in Unit and Element order, with the actual questions constructed from the performance criteria and the range indicators. It quickly became evident, from discussion with the potential target population, that the NVQ competence standards language could not be transferred simply to a questionnaire. In addition, the use of the full NVQ would have produced too long a questionnaire and many areas, although correctly so in the NVQ, would be over-repetitive in an awareness questionnaire.

Therefore a pre-/post-assessment questionnaire was developed based on the standards, but tailored to the needs of the particular situation. The line manager version of the questionnaire replicated that of the learners with words such as 'you' and 'your' being replaced by 'she/he' and 'her/his'. The questionnaire for the participants' subordinates was shortened and simplified from that of the learners/line managers, seeking comments on areas that would be observable by the subordinates.

Even though the revised questionnaire reduced the length of the linked NVQ format, it included 101 main questions and more than 300 subordinate questions. Some concern was felt initially about this length, but in practice the learners and their line managers were quite happy to complete the questionnaire on the two occasions when it was used. Because of the time period for the programme – 12 months – it was considered that the 3-test approach was not appropriate.

The questionnaire used with the learners' subordinates was much simpler and shorter, and was directed at observable elements of the standards. Even with the simplification a total of 100 main and subordinate questions were posed, although this was later reduced, accepting incomplete information made available as a result. The main problem with this approach, although there was some easement because of the length of the programme, was in the recording and analysis of the data produced but this was not over-demanding once a computer spreadsheet programme was formatted and the results were kept up to date with frequent inputting of the data.

Figures 13.2 and 13.3 demonstrate parts of each of the learner and subordinates questionnaires to show how they were constructed, with some of the text used to precede and explain how to complete the questionnaire. The questionnaire for the line managers is similar to that for the learners with the substitution of identification words only. The format can be read against the MCI/NVQ Level 3 for supervisory management.

Evaluation of practical or technical training

The evaluation of practical or technical training, as opposed to more general or people-type skills, can frequently require a rather different approach. A typical example of this might be in the installation into an organization of a completely new procedure which has just been introduced. In this case the training required is the introduction of the procedure to learners who have no previous knowledge or experience of the subject. Alternatively, training might be directed to an additional procedure. The approach to validation and evaluation of this form of training might be as follows, although consideration must be given to factors that might modify it or require reversion to previously described approaches:

1. Whatever the possible modifications, it is essential that the pre-training briefing meeting between learner and line manager should take place so that the learners and their managers are completely clear about how and why the training is being undertaken, and that the learners have the full support of their line managers.
2. Two options are possible here depending on the unique innovation or not of the training subject:
    a) If the subject is completely new and the responsible trainers are convinced beyond any doubt that the learners will have no previous knowledge of the subject or any relevant material, an initial test of knowledge or skill is unnecessary. Any such test would result in zero scoring for all the learners, with a possible reduction in their confidence or commitment.
    b) If the training is an extension of previous practical skills, a test should be constructed to determine the extent of the knowledge of the learners. This test should be given if possible before the learners attend for the training event – this will give the programme trainers advance warning of the learners' existing knowledge levels and enable them to modify the programme as necessary, in addition to providing pre-training levels information.

LEARNERS' QUESTIONNAIRE

About this booklet 1 (this page is used in the pre-programme self-assessment booklet)

- You are about to commence the Supervisory Management Development Programme which is based on the competences required of individuals to perform their job. The programme concentrates on your work activities and responsibilities and aims to build on the competences you already possess. If at any time you decide to seek the MCI/NVQ Supervisory Management award, you will have covered in this programme all the aspects included in that award.
- This programme is the pilot one and as such your honest views and feelings about the programme are very important in ensuring that it satisfies the needs of the learners.
- You will be asked to complete this questionnaire twice during the programme: once at the start of the programme in an attempt to identify your current or recent work experience, and the second time at the end of the programme to assess any changes that might have taken place.
- The responses you make will be used for programme evaluation only and will be confidential to the training department. If at the end of the programme the questionnaire suggests that any problems remain, discussion will take place with you to determine how these problems might be approached and your needs satisfied.

About this booklet 2 (this page is used in the post-programme self-assessment booklet)

- You have now completed the Supervisory Management Development Programme which was based on the competences required of individuals to perform their job. The programme concentrated on your work activities and responsibilities, and aimed to build on the competences you already possessed. If at any time you decide to seek the MCI/NVQ Supervisory Management award, you have covered in this programme all the aspects included in that award.
- This programme was the pilot one and as such your honest views and feelings about the programme are very important in ensuring that it satisfied the needs of the learners.
- You were asked to complete this questionnaire before the programme started in an attempt to identify your current or recent work experience to that time. You are asked to complete the questionnaire a second time to assess any changes that might have taken place.
- The responses you make will be used for programme evaluation only and will be confidential to the training department. If analysis of the questionnaire suggests that any problems remain, discussion will take place with you to determine how these problems might be approached and your needs satisfied.

How to use the booklet

- Scan through the booklet to see what is involved.
- You will see that each section of the booklet relates to an area of supervisory management.
- In each section, against each activity/responsibility or aspect of skill or knowledge, circle what you feel is the appropriate skill level number – please note that the final column should be circled if you do not have the opportunity to practise that particular function.

- Please answer the question as it really is, not as you would like it to be or how you think you should answer.
- If there is any part of the booklet that you do not understand, please do not hesitate in contacting the training department for further information or clarification. The contact is:
  Name of contact:
  Telephone:

1 SERVICES AND OPERATIONS

1.1 Maintaining services and work activities

	Very well				Poorly		No opportunity
How well do you ensure that work activities comply with:							
• current employment legislation?	6	5	4	3	2	1	0
• customer requirements?	6	5	4	3	2	1	0
How well do you pass information affecting customers, work activities and services to:							
• your staff?	6	5	4	3	2	1	0
• your line manager?	6	5	4	3	2	1	0
• your customers?	6	5	4	3	2	1	0
How well do you communicate with others:							
• in writing?	6	5	4	3	2	1	0
• orally?	6	5	4	3	2	1	0
How well do you monitor and control:							
• the operations for which you are responsible?	6	5	4	3	2	1	0
• your resources?	6	5	4	3	2	1	0
How well do you keep relevant records?	6	5	4	3	2	1	0

	Very often				Rarely		
How often do you recommend improvements in work activities and services?	6	5	4	3	2	1	0

1 SERVICES AND OPERATIONS

1.2 Maintaining an effective and safe working environment

	Very well				Poorly		No opportunity
How well do you ensure that the working conditions for which you are responsible comply with:							
• current health, hygiene and safety legislation?	6	5	4	3	2	1	0
• organization policies and procedures?	6	5	4	3	2	1	0
• special needs requirements (e.g. disabled colleagues)?	6	5	4	3	2	1	0
How well do you ensure that your staff comply with:							
• current health, hygiene and safety legislation?	6	5	4	3	2	1	0
• organization policies and procedures?	6	5	4	3	2	1	0
How well do you communicate health and safety information to:							
• relevant colleagues?	6	5	4	3	2	1	0
• customers?	6	5	4	3	2	1	0
How well do you:							
• maintain security systems and procedures for which you are responsible?	6	5	4	3	2	1	0
• deal with potential and actual breaches of security requirements?	6	5	4	3	2	1	0
How well do you deal with:							
• accidents and incidents?	6	5	4	3	2	1	0
• potential and actual breaches of health and safety requirements?	6	5	4	3	2	1	0

	Very often				Rarely		
How often do you recommend improvements relating to:							
• health, hygiene and safety?	6	5	4	3	2	1	0
• organization policies and procedures?	6	5	4	3	2	1	0
• special needs (e.g. disabled colleagues)?							

Figure 13.2   Learners' questionnaire

SUBORDINATES' QUESTIONNAIRE

About this booklet 1

- Your manager is about to commence the Supervisory Management Development Programme which is based on the competences required of individuals to perform their job. The programme concentrates on their work activities and responsibilities and aims to build on the competences they already possess.
- This programme is the pilot one and as such your honest views and feelings are very important in ensuring that it satisfies the needs of the learners. Please do not feel that you are reporting on your manager and we would ask you to contain your comments to how your manager's skills and knowledge are seen from *your point of view and how they have an effect on you as a member of their staff.*
- You will be asked to complete this questionnaire twice during the programme: once before the programme starts in an attempt to identify your current views on your manager's skills and knowledge as seen from your viewpoint, and the second time at the end of the programme to assess any changes that might have taken place.
- The responses you make will be used for programme evaluation only and will be confidential to the training department.

About this booklet 2

- Your manager has now completed the Supervisory Management Development Programme which was based on the competences required of individuals to perform their job. The programme concentrated on their work activities and responsibilities, and aimed to build on the competences they already possessed.
- This programme is the pilot one and as such your honest views and feelings are very important in ensuring that it satisfied the needs of the learners. Please do not feel that you are reporting on your manager and we would ask you to contain your comments to how your manager's skills and knowledge are seen *from your point of view and how they have an effect on you as a member of their staff.*
- You were asked to complete this questionnaire before the programme started in an attempt to identify their work skills and knowledge at that time. You are asked to complete the questionnaire a second time to assess any changes that might have taken place.
- The responses you make will be used for programme evaluation only and will be confidential to the training department.

How to use the booklet

- Scan through the booklet to see what is involved.
- You will see that each section of the booklet relates to an area of supervisory management.
- In each section, against each activity/responsibility or aspect of skill or knowledge, circle what you feel is the appropriate skill level number – please note that the final column should be circled if they do not have the opportunity to practise that particular function.
- Please answer the question as it really is, not as you would like it to be or how you think you should answer.
- If there is any part of the booklet that you do not understand, please do not hesitate in contacting the training department for further information or clarification. The contact is:
  Name of contact:
  Telephone:

1 SERVICES AND OPERATIONS

1.1 Maintaining services and work activities

	Very well				Poorly		No opportunity
How well do they ensure that work activities comply with:							
• customer requirements?	6	5	4	3	2	1	0
How well do they pass information affecting customers, work activities and services to:							
• you?	6	5	4	3	2	1	0
• the customers?	6	5	4	3	2	1	0
How well do they communicate with you:							
• in writing?	6	5	4	3	2	1	0
• orally?	6	5	4	3	2	1	0
How well do they monitor and control:							
• the operations for which you are responsible?	6	5	4	3	2	1	0

	Very often				Rarely		
How often do they recommend good improvements in the work activities and services?	6	5	4	3	2	1	0

1 SERVICES AND OPERATIONS

1.2 Maintaining an effective and safe working environment

	Very well				Poorly		No opportunity
How well do they ensure that the working conditions for which they are responsible comply with:							
• current employment legislation of which you are aware?	6	5	4	3	2	1	0
• syndicate policies and procedures?	6	5	4	3	2	1	0
• special needs requirements (e.g. disabled colleagues)?	6	5	4	3	2	1	0
How well do they ensure that you comply with these requirements?	6	5	4	3	2	1	0

	Very well				Poorly		No opportunity
How well do they communicate health and safety information and requirements to you?	6	5	4	3	2	1	0
How well do they deal with:							
• accidents and incidents?	6	5	4	3	2	1	0
• potential and actual breaches of health and safety requirements?	6	5	4	3	2	1	0

Figure 13.3   Subordinates' questionnaire

3.   At the end of the training programme, whether or not a pre-training test has been used, an end-of-programme assessment test must take place. In the case of no initial test because it was known that the learners had no knowledge or skills, the change from no knowledge/skill to end-of-programme level is demonstrated by the success in the test of the learners. The pre- and post-tests will show this change by means of the two documents.

Many trainers are concerned by this testing of adults as they feel there may be an adverse reaction produced by a 'back to school' feeling. In many circumstances a test can be introduced without the need to refer to it as a test or even give the learners the impression that they are under test. If a procedure, computer program, and so on is being introduced, at the end of the training programme an activity, case study, or problem can be introduced for the learners to complete. This activity should contain all the main aspects introduced during the programme and the success of the training and learning can be measured by the success or otherwise of the learners in the significant stages of the activity.

An actual example of this was at the end of a programme during which the learners had been introduced to a new version of a computer software program. They had been operating the earlier version and needed to be updated for immediate operation of the new version. At the end of the training event they were each given a set of instructions to produce a document using the new program. As this document would include all the significant changes from the earlier program, their execution of the instructions would determine whether they had fulfilled the necessary learning. A scoring sheet was used by the trainer and each individual was rated against this scoring.

The results, which were passed on to the learners, gave the learners an assessment of how they had performed, i.e. learned the relevant material, and in which areas they would need to extend their learning, and also informed the trainers how successful they and the programme had been in achieving their objectives. In fact, at the end of the first event of this programme, the 'test' showed that every learner was unsuccessful in performing one part of the new program. This told the trainers that some further support for this first learner group was necessary and that a change in the next event was necessary if this factor was to be successfully overcome.

4.   A 'learning' questionnaire such as that used in the approaches described earlier in this chapter is not necessary in most cases as the assessment activity described above will

take its place. Similarly, although the trainers responsible for the event and its evaluation will need to consider this question, an Action Plan may not be relevant. Non-use of an Action Plan assumes that learners have been 100 per cent successful in their learning and will be implementing this learning in total. If learning has not been successful to this full extent, an Action Plan would be useful in committing the learner to developing those skills in which they were not effective.
5. Post-programme debriefing between the line manager and the learner will again be necessary as will longer-term evaluation to ensure the effective transfer to work of the learning achieved on the programme and subsequently developed.

Evaluating outdoor training

Not all training and learning is performed and achieved in the environment of the training room, in front of a computer or VDU, or using some other technology. In recent years the development of training in an outdoor environment has occurred, particularly when applied to team building and development. The full outdoor treatment was presaged by an original form of integrated training (now developed to include traditional training and computer-assisted/based programmes as described earlier) of a traditional, indoor training programme that also included at least one activity that could only take place out doors.

The full outdoor treatment appeared to assume, in the early days of its introduction, that if a group or team was brought together to achieve physical tasks, from the support the individuals gave to each other a team spirit and skill would emerge. This spirit and skill would then continue when the participants returned to their workplaces, whether they were together at work or in different places. Unfortunately a number of factors mitigated against this, the principal one being, with the physical activities being presented in the way they were, that many found it impossible to relate the team support of climbing a mountain or delving into a pothole to team support back at work (particulary with the people who came from diverse locations).

One of the major negative features of these early days that did not encourage the translation of what happened to them on the course to the back-at-work situation was the lack of any attempt to enable the learners to recognize this. The early outdoor courses were merely a series of physical events – climbing mountains, climbing down potholes, abseiling, crossing rivers with natural materials, and so on – during the day, and the participants simply crashed out in the evenings. On occasion there was some discussion following the activities, but this concentrated on *what* happened, rarely *why* it happened, and *what use* could be made of the learning points in the work environment. If full discussion facilities along the *why* and *what use* lines are not provided, the training course obviously had little value, other than as a physical testing exercise.

SELECTION

Consequently, before selecting an outdoor form of training, it is essential to pose a number of questions. The same questions, modified for a post-event occasion, can be used as a specific form of evaluation following the learners' attendance. These will include:

About the course

- What does the training sponsor or client (e.g. the line manager) want the learner to achieve through outdoor training that cannot be achieved by other forms of training?
- How will outdoor activities achieve these aims?
- What are the stated objectives of the outdoor training programme? Do these objectives correlate with those of the sponsor and the learner?
- How will the outdoor activities be related to the normal working environment?
- How credible is this implied relationship?
- How will the learners be enabled and encouraged to translate any learning achieved through the physical activities when back at work and be able to reinforce these aspects?
- Is the outdoor event more than just a series of physical activities, outdoor games or 'fun'?
- To what extent is the course designed to address management, supervisory, team or individual issues?
- How much physical exertion is required?
- Will my nominees be able to cope with the physical demands made?
- To what extent do the physical activities take account of gender, age, fitness, disability or medical conditions?

About the course environment

- What are the background qualifications and skills of the trainers?
- What are their qualifications specifically related to outdoor training? For example, are they qualified in the relevant SPRITO national occupational standards of competence?
- What other qualifications and/or experience (other than outdoor training) have they?
- What training background and skills have they?
- What health and safety and medical training have they received? What experience have they of these? What qualifications do they have?
- Are there both qualified and experienced trainers and instructors (in physical activities) involved in the course?
- What is the ratio of trainers to instructors during the physical activities?
- Have all staff had first-aid training (and life-saving where appropriate)?
- Is there a published statement relating to safety regulations and restrictions, etc?
- What are the insurance requirements for and position of people attending the course?
- What are the hygiene facilities (washing, drying clothes, changing, etc)?

Specific evaluation following the course

In addition to using the selection of questions listed above, these same questions, perhaps modified, can be used in evaluation of the course. All the follow-up actions and Action Plans described earlier in the book for indoor types of training events, particularly the Learning Questionnaire and Action Plan, apply equally in outdoor training.

As the outdoor course will be, in the majority of cases, offered by an external provider, unless prior arrangements are made with them either as an integral part of the course or as a special contractual arrangement, there may be no validation/evaluation/learning measures taken in an effective format or process. In such cases, evaluation action becomes even more important and the line manager, on the return of the learners, must, possibly in conjunction with a post-programme debriefing, have Learning Questionnaires and Action Plans completed by the learners. If this will have been the first or second time that your staff will have attended this course, again, modifying the traditional reactionnaire described earlier, this can be completed more than once until you are sure that this programme is what you and your learners require.

If the training has been with an integral team, the follow-up, evaluation issues can be used as the first team development meeting following the programme. The value and effectiveness of the course/provider can be the first discussion subject at this team development meeting. A relevant action report based on the learning and actions considered can be prepared by the team and copied to the 'sponsoring' manager.

Using and assessing external training providers

More and more, in these days when, for economic reasons, various functions are managed by outworkers where formerly these would have been performed internally, learners are being sent on programmes provided by external consultants. This, of course, is not a new event, except perhaps in scale, but in many cases evaluation did not enter the equation. The employing organization or sponsor has been loath to raise the subject, particularly if the provider came from outside the organization. In this case, the additional resource and time by the external consultant would have meant a higher fee. Consequently the consultant, being aware of the likely result, would not raise the subject.

Some course validation has always been performed by some providers, at their own cost, but this was usually for their own interest and confirmation that they were providing training to their own standards and to the needs of the participating learners. But this information was rarely passed on, usually through the lack of interest shown by the organization, and it was often by accident that they learned of any 'back at work' progress.

With the increasing use of this type of training provision, and the financial reasons for doing so in many cases, it would seem to me important that as much evaluation as possible as described in this book is carried out. Otherwise, how does the sponsoring organization(s) know whether their money is being well spent?

THE EXTERNAL CONSULTANT

The external consultant is usually a training and development advisor and practitioner, not connected with the organization, who, having ben informed of the client's training needs, submits proposals and, following acceptance, provides the relevant training either on the client's premises or at an external location. It is at the proposal stage that the client must seek information from the consultant on what action would be taken to evaluate the training and enable action planning, and so on. If there are no included plans, the client must either:

a)   arrange with the provider a Learning Questionnaire and Action Plan process as an absolute minimum. The client then performs the follow-up processes described in this book, when the learners have returned to work or

b)   have the learners complete an LQ and Action Plan when they return to work, in conjunction with the debriefing action as if they were doing so at the end of the training.

A third option, which will depend on the money that the sponsor has available for the training contract and is prepared to spend on evaluation and implementation support, is to contract with the consultant to take on all validation and evaluation activities, and also take on the supervision of the learning implementation and other follow-up. This has been done in some cases of which I am aware, but, with the exclusion of the line manager's direct involvement and action, I do not see it as an ideal approach (other than, perhaps, from the consultant's financial point of view).

ROI AND THE EXTERNAL PROVIDER

When external training provision is purchased, the assessment of the ROI becomes even more relevant and important, and the maximum possible evaluation process must be followed to ensure that this assessment is enabled. In the past, in so many cases, the client paid the provider of the training only, and if they did any evaluation themselves no discussion with the provider took place. Consequently part of the evaluation 'process' took place in a vacuum and, without the other supporting activities, had little meaning. Rather than approach the subject in a meaningful way as described above, the client, in a simple and unformed way, sought feedback from the learners on their return to work in the form of 'OK, was it?, 'Was it worth the money?', 'Did you enjoy it?' and similar *en passant* attempts at 'follow-up'.

The use of external providers can often cost significantly more in the long run than the use of an internal training organization and, when economics are important, it is essential that the client knows whether value for money, ROI, is being obtained. In terms of the ROI calculations, the cost side of the equation can become simpler as many of these costs are included in the fees charged by the consultant. But the difficulties of assessing the value benefits remain as difficult as with any other form of training – more so if there is no evaluation included in the process.

14 *Analysing evaluation data*

Once a training and development or other learning activity has been evaluated, unless all the work involved in these activities is to be wasted, something must be done with all the data generated. In some cases, for example when extensive evaluation instruments are used with a large number of learners and over a large number of programmes, the amount of data can be frightening.

A variety of analysis methods must be used to cope with these data variations and this variety will range from the simplest possible to a complex approach involving the manipulation of hundreds, if not thousands, of bits of data. The approaches will correlate in their complexity with the type of evaluation approach used, which will include:

- simple examination
- test marking
- text comparison
- data and text comparison
- extended data comparison.

All the above approaches assume that both pre- and post-programme evaluation methods have been used to some extent: if not, analysis means little and only highly subjective views can be formed. For example, if an end-of-course 'happiness sheet' only is used, all that can be done is to look at the sheets and say 'it looks as if *they* are saying that *they* have enjoyed the course and that something of value has been learned' – not a very valid consideration if your boss has asked you to prove that your training programme is worth continuing in cost and resource terms!

The scoring analysis approach

The simplest analytical approach can be used with the simplest validation approach. For example, if all that has been included, apart from pre- and post-briefing of the learner with the line manager, is an end-of-course validation questionnaire which asks for a learning score and/or other session or opinion scores, this document (multiplied by the number of learners on the programme) can be 'examined'. The 'examination' can take the form of the trainer who conducted the programme looking at the questionnaires and forming an impression of the responses made. The impression will be gained from a mental comparison of the range of scores given for the level of learning – 'most of the scores seem to be in the 4 to 5 range, with one or two 6s, so that seems OK' and 'the learning statements seem to cover the main objectives I had constructed for the programme'. This type of 'validation' is obviously highly subjective, and not very satisfactory, but how many trainers take this approach, often because they have little time to do anything more demanding?

Although requiring further time, a simple extension of this subjective examination can at least produce permanent results which can be used for comparison purposes over an extended programme or number of programmes. A table can be produced in which the learning scores can be entered. A typical example would appear as Figure 14.1.

An analysis of the scores shown in Figure 14.1 suggests that the 'average' score for the programme is 5.2. This score can be compared with the average scores for other similar programmes and the result will indicate whether achievement of the programme objectives is remaining constant or changing. If a number of scoring questions are included in this validation questionnaire or reactionnaire, the relevant number of tables will be necessary.

An indication of a significant change of the scoring signals that an investigation is required. A simple analysis of this nature must be considered with care, on the basis that 'one swallow does not make a summer'. During a run of events which produces a common scoring of about 5, if one event shows an average score of 3 with each learner distributing their scores at about this level, the immediate assumption must not be made that the programme has gone wrong. The reasons for the change are almost endless including:

- a course comprising learners who should not have been attending
- a catastrophic environmental fault
- a new trainer involved who had been ineffectively prepared,

and so on.

If the reasons are not as obvious as these and a deeper enquiry is either not possible or delivers little further information, other approaches should be used or the validations of successive events should be considered closely, preferably with a more investigative type of instrument.

The scoring and text analysis approach

My recommendations for evaluation questionnaires throughout are that scoring tables are not sufficient for effective evaluation, and have obvious dangers. These dangers can be reduced and the value of the questionnaire increased if, in addition to any scoring

Name of learner	Learning score	Name of learner	Learning score
a	6	g	5
b	5	h	4
c	5	j	6
d	4	k	5
e	6	l	5
f	5	m	6

Figure 14.1   Scoring analysis table

requested, the learners are also *required* to make comments about their scoring. One main example of this type of questionnaire is demonstrated in Figure 9.1. Analysis of this approach starts with the construction of a table as in Figure 14.1 from, say as in the Figure 9.1 instrument, the level of learning reported.

This numerical analysis is then supported with a review of the textual comments made giving the learners' views about what learning has been achieved and what is to be done about it, or why learning has not been achieved to a rated degree. There must be some statement with which the learners' comments can be compared – every training programme, not only for evaluation purposes, should have a list of the significant learning points or objectives which are included in the programme. These show what the learning programme is meant to provide to the participants.

In general terms, if the learners demonstrate that, apart from the knowledge and skills they already possessed at the start of the programme, they have learned the 'learning points' listed, there is an indication that the programme has been successful in helping the learners to learn. This demonstration will be in the form of comments following a higher score, stating what they have learned and what they are going to do to implement the learning. Comparison in such cases is relatively simple. Figure 14.2 demonstrates a hypothetical

Effective communication course learning objectives	Learner statements
Interacting effectively with others	'I now know that I have difficulties in relating to others' 'I can now relate to others more effectively by seeking their views rather than always giving mine'
Knowledge of the different types of assertiveness	'I realize now that my approach to people has always been aggressive whereas it should be assertive'
Skill in demonstrating the different types of assertiveness	'During the course I tried not being aggressive with others and found that it worked. I shall try this out with my colleagues at work when I return'
Giving effective praise to others	'I still have problems in telling others that they have done a good job, but I tried it out fairly successfully on the course and shall continue trying to do so'
Accepting criticism from others	'I have always fought against being criticized, but I shall now look for real messages in any criticism I receive in future'

etc.

Note: The above comments were made at the end of courses of this nature that I have facilitated.

Figure 14.2   Positive text recording

comparison table of this nature based on part of the learning objectives of an effective communication programme.

Not every learner who makes positive comments will cover the same objectives and in the same terms: some will omit what you see as very significant objectives and others will include comments about some aspects of learning that were not included in your list of learning points! In the former case, if you have the opportunity you can question the learner about the omission – the responses might include statements such as:

- 'I already knew how to do that'
- 'I felt that there were other more important things I had learned'
- 'I didn't really understand that part of the course'
- 'I can't remember that on the course'.

These responses will certainly give you good feedback about the event, particularly the last two statements!

A listing of the negative comments can also be made for post-event consideration. If the Figure 9.1 questionnaire is used and the learning scoring is in the range 3 to 1, the learners are asked to comment why they have given that scoring. The responses given will obviously range widely, although there may be a number of common comments found in the questionnaires. These might relate to the learning environment, to the level of the training material, to the attitude of the trainers, and so on. The simplest analysis is to list the (summarized) comments with a frequency annotation, such as that shown in Figure 14.3.

The frequency of the comments will demonstrate their significance – if with a course of 12 members, eight or more make a similar comment, take particular notice of this comment. Comments that perhaps only one or two participants have made have to be considered in a different way. It may be that the trainer must make a value judgement on the importance or significance of the nature of the comment, or in some cases, because one learner has commented in a particular way, this means for that learner there were problems – this may be significant as a reminder that a particular factor can cause problems for some learners.

Graphical representation

If one event only, with a small number of participants, is being considered, tables constructed as above are sufficient for consideration. But when much larger numbers of participants and their scores are involved over a large number of events, the numbers in

Comments	Frequency
The pace of the course was too fast to take in the material	III
I couldn't understand the differences between the forms of assertiveness and it wasn't explained clearly	HHf
The training room was too warm for comfort	III
and so on	

Figure 14.3   Negative text recording

tables such as these become too large to make immediate sense. Fortunately analysis of this type of data has become easier. Instead of a manually constructed table which is complicated enough for those purposes already considered, a computer spreadsheet can be used to produce a basic chart which can be updated and manipulated. The chart produced on the spreadsheet is almost the same as the one produced manually, but, instead of the evaluator having to amend the table on each new occasion or, at worst, construct a new table on every occasion, a few computer keystrokes will suffice. New figures can be added to the spreadsheet, automatically replacing and updating the original ones. Formulae for mathematical calculations can be built into the spreadsheet: for example in a chart of scores with rows of learners and columns of separate events, a formula can be included at the end of a row to sum the numbers in that row and produce an average. Similarly, an averaged summation can be produced for each learner in each activity or session scored. A typical table would appear as Figure 14.4.

If a table such as the one in Figure 14.4 contained all the scores for the 26 participants, and all the sessions and activities, it would be confusing. But most people are able to interpret more easily a graphical representation of the scores. Again the production of such information is straightforward using a computer spreadsheet. The abbreviated scores shown in Figure 14.4 would appear in graphical format as in Figure 14.5.

Change analysis

The analyses so far discussed have related to the end-of-programme questionnaires only. If any form of pre- and post-programme analysis is necessary, the data produced for analysis becomes even more extensive and, viewed as a numerical chart, if the numbers are large, produce difficulties for the evaluator. Therefore, a numerical chart of this nature should be accompanied by a graphical representation similar to, but more extensive than, that in Figure 14.5.

In the case of a pre- and post-programme assessment, the two questionnaires used probably each include about 15 questions – i.e. 15 questions x 2 questionnaires x say, 12 participants = 360 items of data for each course or event for analysis. If the 3-test approach

LEARNER	SESSION 1	SESSION 2	SESSION 3	SESSION 4	Sum sessions 1–4/4
a	5	6	6	5	5.5
b	4	5	5	4	4.5
c	6	5	6	6	5.75
...					
x	5	6	6	4	5.25
y	6	6	6	5	5.75
z	5	5	6	4	5
26 learners	Sum of all rows/26	Sum of all rows/26	Sum of all rows/26	Sum of all rows/26	Sum of all rows/26

Figure 14.4   Spreadsheet chart

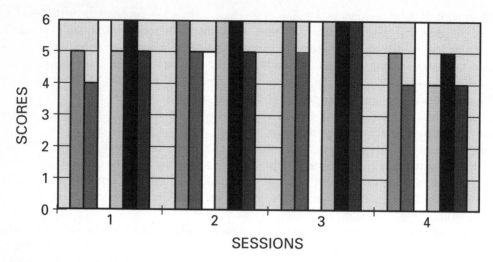

Figure 14.5   Graphical representation

is used, a third questionnaire is introduced producing another 180 items of data. If we include the line manager in the pre- and post-event assessment, a further 360 items need to be included, a total of 900 items of data.

The method of producing an analytical report from data of this nature would normally require the evaluator to compare the pre-event score for each item on the questionnaire with the same item on the post-event questionnaire and note the difference, i.e. the change in knowledge, skill or attitude over the duration of the programme. The basic data could again be plotted on the spreadsheet with the use of formulae to calculate the changes – this use also makes the introduction of the third questionnaire in the 3-test relatively simple. The results could then be exhibited in table or graphical chart form.

Test results in change analysis

The results of paper or computer-based tests can be analysed in a similar way to that described above, except that, instead of self-assessed data for analysis, the marked results of the tests would be tabled and charted. Weighting could be given to the answers and a numerical total of success produced.

Rather more difficult is the analysis of testing when objects or procedures are used, but scoring can be given to sections of the test and final scores allocated for analysis when the participant has completed the test – perhaps with a score ranging from 0 to 100 per cent depending on the accuracy of the progressive parts of the test. Nil would be awarded for complete failure (which might occur at the start of the training) with scores ranging to 100 per cent for complete success. Again the test results could be tabled and/or charted.

Analysis reporting

Considerable emphasis has been placed on reporting the results of analyses, either in textual, tabular or graphic chart form. If evaluation is performed, a permanent record should be made, at the very least so that successive courses, events or programmes can be compared. But if the trainers' senior managers, training managers and the learners' line managers are sincerely interested in the results of training they will wish to be kept informed of the progress of the evaluation performed. A report in some form, usually with the tables and charts as previously described, will be required. The simpler and more graphic the report, the more likely it will be accepted.

The statistical analysis of evaluation

I have indicated earlier that there is a significant difference between evaluation using objective tests of learning of knowledge and skills, and the more subjective approaches only possible when assessing people skills, attitudes and behaviours. In the former, objective measures are used; in the latter, the 'measures' are much more subjective, although not necessarily less valid because of this.

Test analysis

A statement in Chapter 1 related to the question to ask about your training (or have it asked by others) – 'Can you prove it?' Objective tests of knowledge and skills in tasks and procedures can be scored objectively, often on a right or wrong basis. As far as tests of this nature – provided they have been constructed in an unbiased manner – can be considered as 'proof', your evaluation has been proven because they are objectively based and in most cases provide numerical evidence which can be used to analyse and validate the measures.

The two most common approaches of this numerical method are location and dispersion.

LOCATION ANALYSIS

Location analysis identifies the middle position of results and provides what is commonly referred to as the 'average'. There are, however, three types of 'average':

* the average or mean – calculated by summing all the individual data items and dividing by the number of items. The mean can then be expressed in the raw numbers or as a percentage of the summation. For example, if for a set of test questions the resulting data was 6, 6, 5, 4, 6, 5, 5, 6, 6, 6, 5, 4, 6, 5, 6, 5, 6, 6, 3, 5, the mean would be: 5.3, i.e. 106 (total of scores)/20 (number of scores)
* the median – the scores are arranged in numerical order and the median is the middle value of the set of scores
* the mode – the score value that occurs most frequently in the set of data.

On occasions it is necessary to examine the average in greater depth, and in such cases the median numerical sequence is used. From the data arranged in numerical order, the lower and upper quartiles are calculated. The lower quartile is obtained from the score data below which 25 per cent of the score items fall and above which 75 per cent occur; the upper quartile is obtained similarly from the value above which 25 per cent of the score items occur and below which 75 per cent fall.

In most cases, a simple mean is all that is necessary to indicate the level of test success, the other approaches being used more by researchers and external experts considering evaluation.

In statistical analysis, validation has a particular meaning and has a link with another measure of reliability. Practical analysis will probably involve little more than comparing the mean results of a number of event tests. Wild variations will suggest investigation as described earlier and will relate to either an invalid and unreliable testing approach, or problems relating to the training itself.

DISPERSION ANALYSIS

The problems raised by location analysis can often be further refined by the use of an examination of the data dispersal – this will identify cases where there are obviously problems related either to the testing or the training, and will lead to the need to investigate further.

Although there are a number of dispersion measures, of the three most common – range, inter-quartile range and standard deviation – range is the most commonly used in practical evaluation. This measure, at its simplest, shows the lowest and highest values in the scoring data set. A wide range suggests investigation of either the testing and scoring procedure, or of the training itself.

To a statistician the approaches described above are simple in the extreme and have only limited validity, but statistical analysis is a complex technique and, unless the trainer is also a statistician and there is a need for such an investigation, simple measures will not only be acceptable, but may be all that is possible in a limited timeframe.

Other analysis

Evaluation can be analysed statistically to whatever depth is possible or desirable by methods such as those described above, and the many other approaches possible when the evaluation has been by means of an objective testing procedure from which numerical data has been obtained. But a large amount of training and development is in the subjective area of people skills and attitudes. As we have seen, evaluation of these types of events is highly subjective and, therefore, does not offer itself for statistical analysis on as definitive a level as we found for test approaches.

Scoring questionnaires for this form of training is risky, if not dangerous, and, depending on a number of factors, may be worthless, but at times the trainer is required to provide 'numerical evidence' of achievement, which may involve 'number-crunching'. Material for this type of analysis is obtained from end-of-programme questionnaires, and self-assessment questionnaires of the pre- and post-event nature, including the 3-test. The more valuable material in these questionnaires comes from the textual comments made by the learners. But a numerical analysis of any scoring tables included in the questionnaires and the numerical results so obtained, manipulated in the ways of the test statistical analyses, can be performed.

Although this 'analysis' is highly subjective and cannot be compared in validity with test analysis, it can be useful in giving *indications* of achievement and change. If we assume that the questionnaires are completed by learners on a number of courses to the same level of honesty and self-awareness, a range of events can be compared and variations questioned and investigated.

It must be accepted, however, that the subjective results obtained in this way cannot be viewed in the same way as objective analyses. But in the same way that I recommended the use of subjective evaluation rather than doing nothing, subjective analysis should not be ignored because of its inherent nature. If you are going to evaluate, all your work will be wasted or worthless if nothing is done with the results – subjective or objective.

Appendix One
The evaluation process as part of the training process

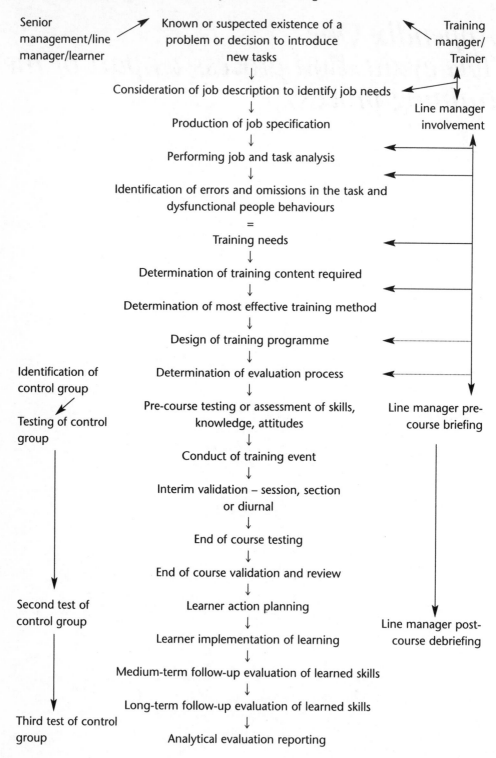

Senior management/line manager/learner

Known or suspected existence of a problem or decision to introduce new tasks

Training manager/ Trainer

↓

Consideration of job description to identify job needs

Line manager involvement

↓

Production of job specification

↓

Performing job and task analysis

↓

Identification of errors and omissions in the task and dysfunctional people behaviours

=

Training needs

↓

Determination of training content required

↓

Determination of most effective training method

↓

Design of training programme

↓

Determination of evaluation process

Identification of control group

Pre-course testing or assessment of skills, knowledge, attitudes

Line manager pre-course briefing

Testing of control group

↓

Conduct of training event

↓

Interim validation – session, section or diurnal

↓

End of course testing

↓

End of course validation and review

↓

Second test of control group

Learner action planning

↓

Learner implementation of learning

Line manager post-course debriefing

↓

Medium-term follow-up evaluation of learned skills

↓

Long-term follow-up evaluation of learned skills

↓

Third test of control group

Analytical evaluation reporting

Appendix Two
Summary of validation and evaluation use

1. **During course approaches**
   a. *Verbal critiques or surveys*
      - Can upset participants
      - Can become slanging matches
      - True views or feelings not expressed
      - Can take a long time to resolve

      + Are up-to-the-minute opportunities for statements
      + Give trainer some immediate feedback
      + Give trainer and participants opportunity to learn how to handle feelings and conflict.

   b. *Tests*
      - Require a lot of work in construction
      - Trainer has to ensure there is no bias
      - Some are difficult to mark in a comparative fashion
      - Open answers require full examination-type marking and scoring
      - If too frequent, can become boring
      - Textbook answers possible without real learning

      + Can be simple and straightforward
      + Require little of trainer's time to implement the tests themselves
      + If Closed answer type can be quick and easy to score
      + 'Right' answers available for marking
      + Score comparison simple on Closed question type.

   c. *Session questionnaires*
      - Can be treated as mini-happiness sheets
      - Over-frequent use can make them boring and answers can become 'standardized'
      - Require effective construction by the trainer
      - Effective questions or statement must be constructed
      - Single sessions may be taken out of context

      + Are quick and simple to administer
      + Once constructed take little maintenance
      + Scores can be analysed and compared.

    d.   *Progressive Interim Validation method*
- Takes a considerable time to
  - i)   enable the progressive discussions
  - ii) take action on the final feedback statements

- +   Enables discussion to clarify views and firm up opinions
- +   Gives influencing and negotiating skills an opportunity for real practice
- +   Gives the trainer considered and argued feedback of views
- +   Is almost completely learner led.

2. **End-of-course validation**

    a.   *End-of-course critique session*
- Can develop into a slanging match between participants or between participants and trainer
- Vocal participants can repress the views of the quieter members
- True views and feelings may not emerge
- On a long event, earlier sessions, etc., may be forgotten
- Views not expressed because people want to get away
- Measure is often of enjoyment rather than learning
- Too late to remedy any problems

- +   A final opportunity for participants to have their say if they so wish
- +   Views expressed are open for rest of group to disagree or consolidate
- +   Trainer demonstrates he is willing to take the group's views publicly.

    b.   *Critique session preceded by group discussion*
- May be problems of division of participants into relevant groups
- Vocal members might still dominate groups
- Longer time necessary so each group can give report
- Other problems as 2(a)

- +   Although problem might still exist, quieter members more likely to speak up in small group
- +   Anonymous feedback report
- +   Groups can each be given a different aspect to discuss.

    c.   *Tests*

The problems and advantages are similar to those quoted for interim testing.

    d.   *Interviews*
- Very time-consuming particularly with large course
- Trainer must ensure consistency of questioning
- Analysis difficult because of varying ways of expression
- Some participants may be difficult interviewees

- +   Trainer can ensure all required information obtained
- +   Doubtful answers can be probed for clarity
- +   Much more personal than group approaches.

e. *Tests of knowledge*
   i) Open question test
      • Difficult to score
      • Cannot be scored objectively
      • Time-consuming to score
      • May measure writing or communication ability rather than learning

      + Questions relatively easy to formulate.

   ii) Binary choice
      • Percentage correct answers by chance
      • Time to construct can be lengthy
      • Construction of questions can be difficult

      + Ease of marking and scoring.

   iii) True/false test
       Problems and advantages as for Binary choice test.

   iv) Multiple choice
       Problems as for other tests plus

      • Considerable time and difficulty in producing non-correct choices for each question.

f. *Tests of skill*
   i) Practical application
      • Feasible objectively only with practical skills

      + Total validation of whether learner can operate the practical event as trained.

   ii) Observation
      • In 'non-practical' situations, subjective
      • Presence of observer(s) may alter performance
      • More than one observer may view skill approach in a different way
      • Difficult to produce a really effective observation system for untrained observers
      • Feedback can take considerable time

      + The only method available in the testing of some skills
      + Different views can accumulate to produce comprehensive view
      + Enables a number of people to 'participate' in an event
      + Observers can learn from the actions of the direct participants
      + The observers may see more than the participants.

g. *End-of-course questionnaires*
    - Can be treated as happiness sheets
    - Need to be revised and maintained
    - Decision needed on scoring numbers
    - Need to use appropriate questions
    - Questions can be loaded to produce good reviews
    - Need to be analysed
    - Immediate rectification of problems impossible

    + If effectively produced and time given for completion, can give a lot of information
    + If numbers used, a numerical comparison analysis is possible
    + Justified answers give lead to action follow-up.

3. **External evaluation**
    a. *Appraisal by line manager*
        - Highly subjective
        - Manager may not have knowledge/skills himself
        - Manager may not have time or may use this as an excuse for not appraising

        + Manager is usually the only observer available
        + If obligatory, the manager may learn something from the observation
        + Observation and assessment can be aided by validated instruments.

    b. *Achievement of plans and objectives*
        - Who decides whether the action has really been achieved?
        - There may be subjective reasoning
        - Avoidable barriers may have been reason for failure to complete actions – loss of enthusiasm, loss of motivation
        - Action may have taken place without training intervention

        + Unavoidable barriers may have been reason for failed actions – boss, colleagues, additional work, domestic problems
        + Action demonstrates learning.

    c. *Improvement in work skills and organizational benefit*
        It is necessary to ensure that the improvements in both the individual and in the organization bottom line are due to the training. Many other factors can be involved – changes in the economy, in the market, in working practices, and so on.

Appendix Three
Practical applications

Techniques and methods of validation and evaluation have been applied to training and development in this book. However, it takes very little modification to transfer the application to other activities.

A practical example of this can be the personal evaluation of this book by the reader! Obviously we can do nothing about the identification of needs; these must be assumed by the fact that you have read the book. Nor can we do anything now about mid-term and long-term evaluation; the reader should be able to do this for herself. However, we can do something positive in terms of the immediate outcome level, both as internal and external validation.

As an example, limited use can be made of a control group. Take one aspect from the book which was new to you and about which you have learned. Then ask some people who have not read the book – people who can be directly compared with you in a range of aspects, such as age, training, experience, and so on – what they know about the aspect selected. This is your control group.

Another possible approach is to assess one's immediate personal reaction to the book (training). This can be attempted by completing the type of questionnaire discussed in the book. Reproduced here is a limited questionnaire of this nature. It is purely for your own self-assessment and interest, but if you care to send a copy to me via the publisher, I would be very interested to receive it.

Place a ✓ in what you feel is the most appropriate space for each scale. For example | | ✓ | | | | |

1. I found the reading of this book

Easy | | | | | | | Difficult

Why have you given this rating?

2. I found understanding the material in the book

Easy | | | | | | | Difficult

Why have you given this rating?

3. Before reading the book my knowledge of the subject was

A lot | | | | | | | Nothing

Why have you given this rating?

4.   Having read the book I now rate my knowledge of the subject as

A lot |___|____|____|____|____| Nothing

Why have you given this rating?

5.   The range of material in the book was

Too wide |___|____|____|____|____| Too narrow

Why have you given this rating?

6.   What interested me in the book overall was

Everything |___|____|____|____|____| Nothing

Why have you given this rating?

7.   The presentation of the material in the book was

Very
interesting |___|____|____|____|____| Boring

Why have you given this rating?

8.   The presentation of the material in the book was

Too
academic |___|____|____|____|____| Too
                                                     practical

Why have you given this rating?

9.   The book satisfied the objectives of the author, as set out below

Fully |___|____|____|____|____| Not at all

Why have you given this rating?

10.   My overall assessment of the book is

Very good |___|____|____|____|____| Very poor

Why have you given this rating?

Please add any other assessments you wish to make. Thank you.

Objectives (refer to Appendix Two)

1. To survey the range of validation and evaluation approaches available to the training assessor from the identification of training needs to long-term evaluation.
2. To demonstrate the range of validation and evaluation instruments available.
3. To provide a practical guide for practising training assessors.
4. To introduce some validation and evaluation methods not in common use but which can be used with value.
5. To encourage the inclusion of thinking about and practising the assessment of ROI in the evaluation process.

References and recommended reading

Annett, Duncan, Stammers and Gray, *Task Analysis*, Training Information Paper 6, HMSO, 1971.

Bartram, S. and Gibson, B., *Training Needs Analysis, 2nd edition*, Gower, 1997.

A practical book containing, in addition to guidance on the TNA process, 22 instruments for performing the process – developing the organization, organization climate, managing resources and job skills. A wide range of methods is described – existing and new.

Bartram, S. and Gibson, B., *Evaluating Training*, Gower, 1999.

This book is basically a collection of validation and evaluation instruments, 24 in total, preceded by a short introduction to the evaluation 'audit' giving guidance in looking at your organization in various terms. The instruments range from training needs assessment to an impact questionnaire.

Bee, Frances and Roland, *Training Needs Analysis and Evaluation*, Institute of Personnel and Development, 1994.

A comprehensive book covering a wide range of both these subjects, although there is a tendency in the evaluation half of the book to concentrate on reactions and 'happiness' level approaches. The training needs part of the book cannot be faulted and leads the reader logically through a wide variety of approaches and applications.

Boydell, T. H., *A Guide to the Identification of Training Needs*, BACIE, 1976.

This booklet considers the important aspect that the identification of training needs must be resolved before training can be undertaken. Models for the consideration of present and future training needs are presented in a practical way and a variety of processes and approaches are described.

Boydell, T. H., *A Guide to Job Analysis*, BACIE, 1970.

A companion booklet to *A Guide to the Identification of Training Needs*. It describes a process for job analysis which, although specifically applicable to operative, craft, clerical and technician occupations, when used in conjunction with other approaches in management development, is relevant also to supervisory and management activities.

Bramley, Peter, *Evaluating Training Effectiveness*, McGraw-Hill, 1990.

A practical approach showing how well-established theories can be applied to the evaluation of the effectiveness of training. The process of evaluation; methods of measuring changes at individual, group and organizational levels and the broader issues of evaluation strategies are considered in a practical manner. The emphasis is on linking the value of training to organizational effectiveness.

Buckley, Roger and Caple, Jim, *The Theory and Practice of Training*, Kogan Page, 1990.

This book contains two chapters (8 and 9) concerned with assessing the effectiveness of training, and, in the latter, auditing the training system. Both chapters offer practical advice on validation approaches; tests and other instruments in Chapter 8, and the wider aspects of auditing the total training function in Chapter 9. The two chapters are useful introductions to these complex subjects.

Craig, Malcolm, *Analysing Learning Needs*, Gower, 1994.

A rather academically-biased book which considers the hypothesis that as the way we work is changing dramatically, how we analyse training needs should also be changed. The author offers a range of 'investigative' methods with many examples, case studies and self-diagnoses.

Davies, I. K., *The Management of Learning*, McGraw-Hill, 1971. (Chapters 14 and 15.)

Chapter 14 of this book is concerned with the evaluation of a learning course, discusses criterion tests and tests of educational achievement, and looks at the nature, importance and techniques of evaluation. Chapter 15 looks at the measurement of learning in terms of nominal, ordinal, intervals and ratio scales and criterion power tests. Formulae are given for the various test types and the different types of scoring are compared.

Easterby-Smith, M., Braiden, E. M. and Ashton, D., *Auditing Management Development*, Gower, 1980.

The 'audit' approach to the effectiveness of training and development is described with the use and analysis of special questionnaires or audit instruments. Descriptions of actual audits undertaken are also given.

Easterby-Smith, M., 'How to Use Repertory Grids in HRD', *Journal of European Industrial Training*, Vol 4, No 2, 1980.

Easterby-Smith, M., *Evaluating Management Development, Training and Education, 2nd edition*, Gower, 1994.

Fletcher, Shirley, *NVQs Standards and Competence, 2nd edition*, Kogan Page, 1994.

One of the most helpful books so far published on this subject, covering NVQs from history to application in a very readable form.

Hamblin, A. C., *The Evaluation and Control of Training*, McGraw-Hill, 1974.

One of the few published books at this period specifically devoted to evaluation, it is intended to be a link between how-to-do-it approaches and theoretical dissertations. Hamblin aims the book at training specialists and bases his discussions on a cycle of evaluation of objectives and effects. A range of techniques at each level is discussed.

Honey, P., 'The Repertory Grid in Action', *Industrial and Commercial Training*, Vol II, Nos 9, 10 and 11, 1979.

ITOL, *A Glossary of UK Training and Occupational Learning Terms*, ed. J. Brooks, ITOL, 2000.

Kelly, G.A., *The Psychology of Personal Constructs*, Norton, 1953.

The original work by Kelly in which he introduces the concepts of personal constructs and domains from which the repertory grid techniques were developed.

Kirkpatrick, D. L., 'Evaluation of Training', in *Training and Development Handbook*, edited by R. L. Craig, McGraw-Hill, 1976.

Kirkpatrick, D.L., *Evaluating Training Programs: The four levels*, Berrett-Koehler, 1996.

A comprehensive guide to Kirkpatrick's model for evaluating training programmes, describing in detail the four levels he proposes. A description of a widely used, albeit frequently criticised, model based on his original writing about these steps in 1959. Very useful book for evaluators who wish to understand this model.

Laird, D., *Approaches to Training and Development*, Addison-Wesley, 1978. (Chapters 15 and 16.)

A book which covers the spectrum of training and development approaches and contains one chapter (Chapter 15) on instruments for measuring training and development and one (Chapter 16) on a discussion on the wider aspects of evaluation.

Mager, R. F., *Preparing Objectives for Programmed Instruction*, Fearon, 1962. (Later re-titled: *Preparing Instructional Objectives*, Fearon, 1975.)

Manpower Services Commission, 'A Glossary of Training Terms', HMSO, 1981.

Newby, Tony, *Validating Your Training*, Kogan Page Practical Trainer Series, 1992.

One of a series of practical booklets aimed at trainers. Its principal strength is in the area of the testing of practical training, although the remainder has limited value owing to a biased approach.

Odiorne, G. S., *Training by Objectives*, Macmillan, 1970.

The specific setting of objectives and the need to achieve these objectives are discussed as the positive indicators of training effectiveness and success.

Parker, T. C., 'Statistical Methods for Measuring Training Results', in *Training and Development Handbook*, edited by R. L. Craig, McGraw-Hill, 1976.

Peterson, Robyn, *Training Needs Analysis in the Workplace*, Kogan Page Practical Trainer Series, 1992.

A very useful, practical guide to a wide range of training needs approaches in a handy form for the trainer, written in a user-friendly language with a multitude of trainer tips, checklists, charts and advice sections.

Prior, John (ed.), *Handbook of Training and Development, 2nd edition*, Gower, 1994.

Contains chapters on competences, organizational and job training needs and using evaluation techniques – and on 36 other subjects.

Rackham, N. and Morgan, T., *Behaviour Analysis in Training*, McGraw-Hill, 1977.

This book, by two of the initiators of Behaviour Analysis, describes the BA approach to interactive skills training and discusses the use of BA in the testing, immediate reaction and validation approaches to this training. A chapter (Chapter 5) is devoted to the subject of evaluation and many examples of interactive skills training evaluation in practice are cited.

Rackham, N. et al., *Developing Interactive Skills*, Wellens, 1971.

This book was in many ways the predecessor of *Behaviour Analysis in Training* as it introduced the concept of BA and its use in training. Some mention is made of the use of BA in evaluation.

Rae, L., 'Towards a More Valid End-of-Course Validation', *The Training Officer*, October 1983.

Rae, L., *The Skills of Human Relations Training*, Gower, 1985.

A companion book to *Techniques of Training*, it contains a chapter describing the possible evaluation and validation approaches to subjective subjects such as those contained in the book.

Rae, L., 'How Valid is Validation?', *Industrial and Commercial Training*, Jan.–Feb., 1985.

Rae, L., *Using Evaluation in Training and Development*, Kogan Page, 1999.

This book is a practical approach to the validation and evaluation of training and development from pre-course training and management action, through the training programme to the post-training implementation of learning and management support and assessment. Guidelines are suggested, methods described, and practical, tried and tested resources detailed.

Rae, L., *Effective Planning in Training and Development*, Kogan Page, 2000.

This book demonstrates a planning process which will vastly improve the chances that the training will achieve the right results. All the stages in the training planning and design process are described, the coverage including setting objectives, planning and designing both on and off the job training, and preparing the evaluation.

Rae, L., *Training Evaluation Toolkit*, Echelon Learning, 2001.

This is a toolkit of instruments contained in an A4 ringbinder and also containing a CD which reproduces the diagnostic parts of most of the hard copy instruments. The instruments are mainly questionnaires and reactionnaires ranging from training needs through validation of training programmes, to the full evaluation process including assessment of the implementation of learning. The questionnaires, etc. can all be photocopied and customized from the hard copy or printed and customized from the CD.

Rae, L., *Trainer Assessment*, Gower, 2002.

This book was conceived as a companion volume to the present book, but it deals with the trainer's skills rather than with train*ing*. Methods and assessment plans, both tactical and strategic, are suggested, and the necessary instrumentation is provided. As in the present book, the approach is extremely practical and the methods described have been tested in many organizations and events. The objective is to enable the statement to be made 'My trainers are highly effective. I can prove this because … '.

Rae, L., *Techniques of Training, 3rd edition*, Gower, 1995. (Chapter 10.)

This book, which is an introduction to training approaches, methods and techniques summarizes in Chapter 10 the trainer's approach to validation and evaluation, and introduces some of the approaches.

Robinson, K. R., *A Handbook of Training Management*, Kogan Page, 1981. (Chapter 7.)

A substantial chapter (Chapter 7) is included in the book on the measurement and follow-up of the results of the training process. It also considers the 'biggest headache a training manager has', namely the measurement and assessment of the training for which the manager is responsible.

Schmalenbach, Martin, 'The Death of ROI and the Rise of a New Management Paradigm?', *Journal of the Institute of Training and Occupational Learning*, Vol. 3, No.1, 2002.

This article discusses some of the drivers behind the constant demand for ROI calculations and demonstrates why in all but the more trivial or less involved situations, ROI calculations have little validity. A new management paradigm is suggested in its place.

Sheal, P. R., *How to Develop and Present Staff Training Courses*, Kogan Page, 1989.

This is a practical book on the skills and techniques of training and Chapter 6 outlines the approaches and techniques of validation and evaluation at the various levels. The principal methods are summarized and a useful approach of describing comprehensively the benefits and limitations of each is welcome. A very useful basic introduction to the subject.

Smith, M. and Ashton, D., 'Using Repertory Grid Techniques to Evaluate Management Training', *Personnel Review*, Vol 4, No 4, 1975.

Stewart, V. and Stewart A., *Managing the Manager's Growth*, Gower, 1978. (Chapter 13.)

Another book of the general management training and development nature which includes a chapter (Chapter 13) on evaluation, presented in the very readable style of the Stewarts. A broad approach is taken although a number of specific methods are also discussed.

Thurley, K. E., and Wirdenius, H., *Supervision: a Re-appraisal*, Heinemann, 1973.

Warr, P. B., Bird, M. and Rackham, N., *The Evaluation of Management Training*, Gower, 1970.

This book offers a strongly practical approach to validation and evaluation, identifying the needs in a framework called CIRO which emphasizes context, input, reaction and outcome evaluation, the latter having three levels of immediate, intermediate and ultimate outcomes.

Whitelaw, M., *The Evaluation of Management Training: a Review*, Institute of Personnel Management, 1972.

The contents of this book are only marginally of an original nature as the publication sets out to be a review of the subject. Some methods of evaluation are described, principally at the three outcome levels and some useful summaries of some classical studies are given. A very extensive bibliography over the period 1939 to 1971 is included, listing publications ranging from *Personnel Psychology, Journal of Applied Psychology* and *Journal of Abnormal and Social Psychology*, through *Journal of the Academy of Management* and the *Harvard Business Review*, to the *Industrial and Commercial Training Journal* and the *Journal of the Institute of Training and Development*.

Wills, Mike, *Managing the Training Process*, McGraw-Hill, 1993.

A book which is about the complete process of training in addition to its management. Contains chapters on training needs identification and evaluation; certifying trainers; validation; learning transfer and evaluation among others. A practical book, user-friendly with numerous checklists, figures, examples and above all, algorithms and flowcharts.

Index